Spiritual
Classics

———

Other RENOVARÉ Resources for Spiritual Renewal

Devotional Classics
co-edited by Richard J. Foster and James Bryan Smith

Embracing the Love of God
by James Bryan Smith

Songs for Renewal
by Janet Lindeblad Janzen with Richard J. Foster

A Spiritual Formation Journal
created by Jana Rea with Richard J. Foster

A Spiritual Formation Workbook
by James Bryan Smith with Lynda L. Graybeal

Streams of Living Water
by Richard J. Foster

Wilderness Time
by Emilie Griffin

Other Books by Richard J. Foster

Celebration of Discipline
Freedom of Simplicity
The Challenge of the Disciplined Life
Prayer: Finding the Heart's True Home
Prayers from the Heart

Spiritual Classics

Selected Readings on the
Twelve Spiritual Disciplines

Edited by

RICHARD J. FOSTER & EMILIE GRIFFIN

A RENOVARÉ Resource for Spiritual Renewal

HarperOne
A Division of HarperCollinsPublishers

HarperOne

Credits are listed on page 369 and are considered a continuation of this copyright page.

HarperCollins books may be purchased for educational, business, or sales promotional use. For information please write: Special Markets Department, HarperCollins Publishers, 10 East 53rd Street, New York, NY 10022.

HarperCollins Web site: http://www.harpercollins.com

HarperCollins®, h®, and HarperOne™ are trademarks of HarperCollins Publishers.

Library of Congress Cataloging-in-Publication Data

Spiritual classics: selected readings on the twelve spiritual disciplines / edited by Richard J. Foster &
Emilie Griffin.
    p. cm.
    Includes bibliographical references.
    ISBN: 978-0-06-062872-7
    1. Spiritual life—Christianity.   2. Devotional calendars.
  I. Foster, Richard J.   II. Griffin, Emilie

BV4501.2.S71357   2000
248.4—dc21   99–056027

07 08 09 10 11 RRD(H) 10 9 8 7 6 5 4 3 2 1

Contents

———

Inward Disciplines

Meditation

Prayer

Fasting

Corporate Disciplines

Readings for the Fifth Week

Introduction

———

Many Christians throughout the world are looking for ways to grow closer to God and to act according to God's will. This book is meant for them. It provides a year's worth of weekly readings keyed to twelve important spiritual disciplines for the Christian life. These twelve disciplines are not new. In fact, they have been part of Christian life from the earliest times. Yet, in our generation, we are rediscovering those disciplines with some surprise. Have they been with us all along? Why didn't we know more about them? How can we best practice them?

Many people were introduced to these twelve spiritual disciplines through Richard J. Foster's *Celebration of Discipline*. That book made clear that there is no exhaustive list of the spiritual disciplines. Many more than twelve have been practiced by Christians over time. Yet the twelve spiritual disciplines identified in this volume, for which readings have been carefully chosen, offer major help toward spiritual maturity.

We have planned this book to be used over fifty-two weeks, by individuals or groups. Do bear in mind that your year of reading can begin with any week. You can start with the first week of January or the last week of March or the third week of November. Each of the twelve disciplines has four readings from major figures over the history of Christian spirituality, ranging from early centuries to our own. At the end of the book, because some months will have a fifth week, we have provided four additional readings for those weeks, wherever they may fall.

HOW EACH READING WORKS

With each selection you will find an introduction to the author and a carefully chosen selection excerpted from a longer work of the author's. Sometimes the wording may have been slightly modernized for easier reading. Each week's reading also includes an appropriate Bible selection, followed by discussion questions and suggested exercises.

A reflection by Richard Foster, which is included in each week's reading, is meant to become an example of what reading with the heart might look like. As Richard's own way of commenting will show you, there's an inward way we can respond to the sense of a text, under the leading of divine grace. It is spontaneous, easygoing, sometimes lighthearted, sometimes more thoughtful, but always a matter of openness to God's ways, spoken to the heart.

READING WITH THE HEART

Probably one of the most important things we could ask of you as you work with these readings is to slow down, breathe deeply, and read with the heart. Much of our life today is lived at breakneck speed. Often our tight schedules are well motivated. We want to give our families and ourselves the best of everything: sports practice, music lessons, visits to the zoo, good schooling, stimulating after-school events, family gatherings, church life, and social life. All this has great merit. But if our schedules are so overcrowded that we begin to miss the real meaning of things, we are paying too high a price.

Often in our work and study we are reading to absorb information. Again, we need to remember that these readings are not chosen to stuff our heads with interesting facts. We will not be given an exam or asked to recite the crucial points from these selections in the usual educational way. Yes, reading with the heart does involve learning, but a certain kind of learning. The learning needs to have depth, to work at the level of heart and spirit. How do we allow this to happen? In a sense, it is by yielding to the text, by letting the message flow into us, rather than by attempting to master the lesson at hand. Our hope is that you will listen and hear and absorb and be taught by these spiritual teachers throughout the centuries.

Still another important way of relating to these people is to let the differences of time and place be washed away. Identify with these people who lived, in some cases, many centuries ago. Put yourself into their context: enter into their fears, their concerns, their hopes. As you do so, you will come to recognize that they confronted the same human dilemmas and were driven by the same questions and doubts as we are. Delight in the depth of faith that they brought to bear on difficult circumstances. Be encouraged by their lively faith and intimacy with Jesus Christ.

A WORD ABOUT THE RENOVARÉ APPROACH

RENOVARÉ (the Latin word meaning "to renew") is an infrachurch movement committed to the renewal of the Church of Jesus Christ in all her multifaceted expressions. Founded by Richard J. Foster, RENOVARÉ is Christian in commitment, international in scope, and ecumenical in breadth.

Emphasizing the best aspects of six Christian traditions—contemplative, holiness, charismatic, social justice, evangelical, and incarnational—RENOVARÉ offers a balanced vision of spiritual life. But RENOVARÉ does not stop with abstract theories. It promotes a practical strategy for people seeking renewal through small spiritual formation groups; national, regional, and local conferences; one-day seminars; personal and group retreats; and readings from spiritual and devotional classics that can sustain a long-term commitment to renewal.

Written and edited by people committed to the renewal of the Church, RENOVARÉ Resources for Spiritual Renewal seek to integrate historical, scholarly, and inspirational materials into practical, readable formats. The Resources can be used in a variety of settings: small groups, private and organizational retreats, individual devotions, church-school classes, and more. All of the materials present a balanced vision of Christian life and faith coupled with a practical strategy for spiritual growth and enrichment.

ABOUT SPIRITUAL FORMATION

It is important, too, when we begin a reading program, to reflect just a bit on our expectations. The spiritual disciplines are pointed toward spiritual formation—and transformation. Spiritual formation involves a fundamental choice. Choosing to live for Jesus Christ may mean adopting a certain style of life, or perhaps more properly, a rule of life. We take on a series of spiritual practices that will open us to God's work in our lives.

At the same time we need to remember that spiritual transformation is a work of grace. It is what God does in us. What we do counts, because we must choose to enter into, and pursue, our friendship with Jesus Christ. This choice, which we hope will become more and more pure and single-hearted, may have to be made over and over again. Readings from the spiritual classics, then, are pointed toward a warming of our heart, a deepening of our friendship with Jesus Christ. Yet we always want to remember that the power of God undergirds our efforts and leads us along the way.

Perhaps we could think of spiritual formation as a pattern, a series of concrete actions that will gently move us toward transformation in Christ. The disciplines themselves, however, are not transformative. The transformation in us is God's work. It is a work of grace. That deeply transformative grace comes to us not through our own doing but as pure gift.

And yet something is demanded from us: the free gift of ourselves, our submission, our willingness to change, our assent to God's grace. In the end our yes is what's required. In our own words and in our own way, we need to say, "Speak, Lord, your servant is listening." We need to say, "Be it done to me according to your will."

One more thing to remember: spiritual formation is <u>ongoing</u>. We need not be impatient; we need take no measurements. As we build a history with God, others may notice from time to time the good ways that God is working with us. The effects of such spiritual formation will be observed, not in terms of abrupt changes, but as a continuous flow.

A FEW ACKNOWLEDGMENTS

We especially want to thank Lynda Graybeal and William Griffin for their help in the completion of this work. Combing through many texts, reading through many drafts, contributing from many sources, they have helped us immeasurably. Also, we need to thank Carolynn Foster for her patience and encouragement during the intensive time of composition.

Members of the RENOVARÉ staff have also been very supportive: Lyle SmithGraybeal, Marian Euler, and Joan Skulley. Throughout this process, we have also had great encouragement from all the members of the RENOVARÉ Board and Ministry Team.

OUR OWN COLLABORATION

Doing this book has also provided us with a way of pursuing Christian friendship! Over some years, we have worked together as speakers at RENOVARÉ gatherings and conferences. Often, we have talked about the spiritual classics that have moved us. Now, for this book, we have pooled our knowledge and enthusiasm for particular Christian writers of the centuries and the recent past. We have delighted in the many different nations, cultures, and Christian traditions represented. We have been amused sometimes, and sobered sometimes, by the many different stories told and insights gained. We have come to appreciate once again the enduring power of the written word and the reasons why these writings deserve to be called spiritual classics. We ourselves have learned in the doing, from spiritual classics read with the heart. We wish that same happy experience for you.

Richard J. Foster   *Emilie Griffin*

FOR MORE INFORMATION

For more information about RENOVARÉ and its mission, please write to:

RENOVARÉ
8 Inverness Drive East, Suite 102
Englewood, CO 80112-5624
USA

Spiritual
Classics

———

Inward
Disciplines

MEDITATION

PRAYER

FASTING

STUDY

Meditation

Thomas More

(1478–1535)

Thomas More is a remarkable figure. The son of an accomplished lawyer, he attended Oxford University but left, probably under pressure from his father, to take up legal studies in London. His legal and governmental accomplishments were considerable. He was also one of the English humanists, a friend of Erasmus, and a prominent literary figure. He was a prolific writer. His most famous work, *Utopia*, is widely read today.

More was also well known for his religious devotion and his commitment to spiritual life. Even at the height of his career, More faithfully set aside one day a week for meditation and prayer.

From 1518, when he was appointed a royal counselor, he was active in the government of Henry VIII. He received many high honors: under-treasurer, knighthood, high steward of both Oxford and Cambridge Universities, chancellor of the Duchy of Lancaster.

When Henry VIII wanted to divorce Catherine of Aragon, More told him, after careful study, that he could not support his case. Later, he refused to support Henry when the king took on the title of Head of the Church. This led to his imprisonment, trial, and execution. He went to his death with great composure, even joking with his executioner.

One of More's personal traits was playfulness. He enjoyed life, often taking part in celebrations, improvising roles for himself when plays were being performed at court. But More did not assign any cosmic importance to such diversions. His heart was all for God.

Notice how More's meditation focuses on God and asks to be free of worldly constraints and attitudes. His meditation has added meaning when we understand how much he was involved in secular activities over his whole life span. Pay attention also to the words of comfort in this reading: "Gladly to be thinking of God" is only one of these, but there are many others.

A GODLY MEDITATION

Give me thy grace, good Lord,
To set the world at nought,
To set my mind fast upon thee.
And not to hang upon the blast of men's mouths.
To be content to be solitary,
Not to long for worldly company,
Little and little utterly to cast off the world,
And rid my mind of all the business thereof.
Not to long to hear of any worldly things,
But that the hearing of worldly phantasies may be to me displeasant.
Gladly to be thinking of God,
Piteously to call for his help,
To lean unto the comfort of God,
Busily to labour to love him.
To know mine own vilety [vileness] and wretchedness,
To humble and meeken myself under the mighty hand of God,
To bewail my sins passed [past],
For the purging of them, patiently to suffer adversity.
Gladly to bear my purgatory here,
To be joyful of tribulations,
To walk the narrow way that leadeth to life.
To bear the cross with Christ,
To have the last thing in remembrance,
To have ever afore mine eye my death that is ever at hand,
To make death no stranger to me,
To foresee and consider the everlasting fire of hell,
To pray for pardon before the judge come.
To have continually in mind the passion that
Christ suffered for me,
For his benefits uncessantly to give him thanks.
To buy the time again that I before have lost.
To abstain from vain confabulations,
To eschew light foolish mirth and gladness,
Recreations not necessary to cut off.
Of worldly substance, friends, liberty, life and all, to set the loss at right nought,
    for the winning of Christ.

To think my most enemies my best friends,
For the brethren of Joseph could never have done him so much good with their
    love and favour as they did him with their malice and hatred.
These minds are more to be desired of every man, than all the treasure
    of all the princes and kings, Christian and heathen, were it gathered and laid
    together all upon one heap.

BIBLE SELECTION
Jeremiah 17:5–10

Thus says the LORD:
Cursed are those who trust in mere mortals
    and make mere flesh their strength,
    whose hearts turn away from the LORD.
They shall be like a shrub in the desert,
    and shall not see when relief comes.
They shall live in the parched places of the wilderness,
    in an uninhabited salt land.

Blessed are those who trust in the LORD,
    whose trust is the LORD.
They shall be like a tree planted by water,
    sending out its roots by the stream.
It shall not fear when heat comes,
    and its leaves shall stay green;
in the year of drought, it is not anxious,
    and it does not cease to bear fruit.

The heart is devious above all else;
    it is perverse—
    who can understand it?
I the LORD test the mind
    and search the heart,
to give to all according to their ways,
    according to the fruit of their doings.

DISCUSSION QUESTIONS

The following can be used for discussion within a small group, or used for journal reflections by individuals:

1. How can I be more single-hearted in my attachment to God?
2. What lessons can I learn from Thomas More's attitude and his meditation?
3. What are some obstacles to meditation for people in secular careers?

SUGGESTED EXERCISES

The following exercises can be done by individuals, shared between spiritual friends, or used in the context of a small group. Choose one or more of the following:

1. Identify another figure whose story is well known to you who is reminiscent of Thomas More. Joan of Arc, John Hus, and Dietrich Bonhoeffer might be good examples. Reflect on the ways that good people are often rejected and persecuted. Hold the mystery of this in your heart and pray through it, without attempting to understand or explain.
2. Try setting aside an entire day for meditation and prayer.

REFLECTIONS

This selection by Thomas More simply does me in. The breadth of it exhausts me. One line maybe I can enter into a little, but even then some single sentences contain a lifetime: "To think my most enemies my best friends." However, the prayer is not just one sentence, but sentence piled upon sentence, covering, as it seems, all thought, word, and deed. It is too much to take in, too much to expect, too much to hope for—in myself or in anyone else.

But then I realize that More is not telling me many things but only one thing. And what is that one thing? <u>Simply to love God</u>. When I see this it all becomes clear. Then I can read each line as another aspect of the call to love. And so, once again, I am struck by the unity of all these writers on contemplative prayer. They all keep calling us back to our first love. Their message, it seems, keeps tune to the beat of our heart . . . love God . . . love God . . . love God . . . love God.

RICHARD J. FOSTER

GOING DEEPER

ROBERT BOLT, *A Man for All Seasons* (New York: Random House, 1962). Bolt's play is well worth reading. It captures More's wit and civility as well as his staunch moral character.

GORDON RUPP, *Thomas More: The King's Good Servant* (Glasgow: Collins, 1978). This is a brief history, heavy with full-color illustrations.

THOMAS MARIUS, *Thomas More: A Biography* (New York: Alfred A. Knopf, 1984). This account treats all aspects of More's life with scholarship and wit.

Joyce Huggett

(1937–)

Joyce Huggett is an internationally known writer, speaker, and broadcaster who was based in Cyprus for many years and now lives in Britain. Her books on the spiritual life include *The Joy of Listening to God*, *Listening to Others*, and *Learning the Language of Prayer*.

For many years she has worked as a teacher for the deaf. She was shaped in this vocation by her early childhood friendships with children (living in a residence near her home) who could not communicate freely because of a profound hearing loss. This life experience has made Huggett acutely conscious of the vital importance of communication and language.

When she moved to Cyprus and began to learn Greek, she was again confronted with the vital importance of language and communication.

In the following selections, notice how Huggett continually applies these motifs of listening, learning, and language to her teaching on prayer. Her instructions on prayer start unabashedly at the beginning, with Jesus' teachings on prayer and our simplest ways of putting those into practice.

LEARNING THE LANGUAGE OF PRAYER

Meditation

"Meditation" is another word . . . people often use about prayer. But Christian meditation must not be confused with yoga, Eastern meditation or transcendental meditation. For, unlike these disciplines, Christian meditation has nothing to do with emptying our minds. Christian meditation engages every part of us—our mind, our emotions, our imagination, our creativity and, supremely, our will.

As Archbishop Anthony Bloom puts it, "Meditation is a piece of straight thinking under God's guidance." Yet it is not the same as an academic study of the Scriptures. This becomes clear when we listen to the Psalmist describing his practice of meditation.

> On my bed I think of you,
> I meditate on you all night long. . . . (Ps. 63:6; JB [Jerusalem Bible])

The word for "meditate" which is used here means to "mutter" or to "murmur persistently," repeating the same words over and over again. In Psalm 119, the Psalmist uses a different word when he refers to meditation.

> *I mean to meditate on your precepts*
> *and to concentrate on your paths.* (Ps. 119:15; JB)

> *Though princes put me on trial,*
> *your servant will meditate on your statutes.* (Ps. 119:23; JB)

> *I stretch out my hands to your beloved commandments,*
> *I meditate on your statutes.* (Ps. 119:48; JB)

The word he uses in these verses means "to muse," "to ponder," "to reflect," "to consider." In other words, Christian meditation involves, not emptiness, but fullness. It means being attentive to God. The purpose of this attentiveness, this reflecting and this pondering is, among other things, to see ourselves in the light of God's revealed word—just as Jesus weighed each of Satan's subtle temptations against the teaching of the Old Testament.

We meditate to give God's words the opportunity to penetrate, not just our minds, but our emotions—the places where we hurt—and our will—the place where we make choices and decisions. We meditate to encounter the Living Word, Jesus himself. We meditate so that every part of our being, our thoughts and our affections and our ambitions, are turned to face and honour and glorify him. Yet another reason for learning to meditate is so that we may become conversant with the will of God. . . .

How to Meditate

We have seen that the English word "meditation" may be variously translated by words like muttering and murmuring, reflecting and recollecting, musing and pondering. With these hidden meanings in mind, it becomes apparent that Jesus meditated on the Scriptures. He knew the Old Testament so well that he easily made the connection between biblical truth and what was happening to him at various stages of his life. In Luke 4, three times Satan tries to deflect him from doing God's work in God's way; three times he combats Satan's suggestions by quoting Scripture:

> *The devil led him up to a high place and showed him in an instant all the king-*
> *doms of the world. And he said to him, "I will give you all their authority and*
> *splendour, for it has been given to me, and I can give it to anyone I want to. So if*
> *you worship me, it will all be yours."*

Jesus answered, "It is written: 'Worship the Lord your God and serve him only.'" (Luke 4:5–8; NIV)

Here Jesus is revealing that Deuteronomy 6:13 has become so much a part of his thinking and behaving that it automatically springs to mind and affects his attitude when faced with Satan's subtle ploys.

Scripture can similarly become a part of our make-up if we meditate on it. And the best way to prepare to meditate is to respond to the invitation God gives us through the Psalmist: "Be still, and know that I am God" (Ps. 46:10).

In the stillness we can shed some of the pressures which would prevent us receiving God's Word into the innermost core of our being. We can focus away from the mundane and the everyday and onto God. Such stillness is to Bible reading what preparing the soil is to good farming. Essential for fruitfulness.

When we have become still, if we read a passage of Scripture which we have previously studied or some verses which refer to something which is troubling us, we may well find that a verse or a phrase or a sentence or a pen picture will draw us to itself. If it does, there is no need to read on. Instead, we should stop to reflect and to treasure the words, to turn them over and over in our minds, repeating them until the truth which they contain trickles from our head into our hearts.

All our faculties can be enlisted to help us meditate. The mind enables us to understand what the words mean as we read them in context. The memory helps us recall what we have learned and experienced of God's character and faithfulness in the past. The imagination is a God-given gift which the prophets used to picture the insights God entrusted them with and which Jesus used to describe his kingdom. (So he likens his Father to a faithful shepherd, a Middle Eastern housewife and a loving, Middle Eastern father, Luke 15.) And the emotions enable us to identify with the characters in the passage we are reading.

Contemplation: The Prayer of Loving Attention

"Meditation" and "contemplation" are often used interchangeably. This is understandable because certain similarities suggest that the two forms of prayer are synonymous. Like meditation, contemplation involves putting ourselves into the hands of God so that he can change and transform our attitudes, perceptions and behaviour. Like meditation, contemplation involves listening intently to the Word of God. And like meditation, contemplation requires stillness in order that we may open ourselves to God and his penetrating, powerful Word.

But meditation and contemplation are also marked by certain differences so they should not be confused with each other. Thomas Merton summed it up when he said: "Contemplation is nothing else but the perfection of love." Or, as others have defined it, contemplation is the prayer of loving regard, the prayer of loving attentiveness, the art of paying rapt and loving attention to God and his world. *Contemplation is about growing in love. If we take the work of contemplation seriously, we cannot escape the theme of love—of God's inexhaustible love for us, for people everywhere, for the whole creation . . . Contemplation is to know and love God perfectly in the depths of your being.* (Quotation from Jim Borst's book *Coming to God* [Guildford, UK: Eagle, 1992].)

Contemplation goes further and deeper than meditation. While the person meditating mutters and muses on God's word, the contemplative pays silent attention to Jesus, the living Word—the one who is central to their prayer. Indeed, contemplation goes one step further. Contemplation goes beyond words and symbols and concepts to the reality words and concepts describe. . . .

How to Contemplate

Contrary to much current thinking, contemplation has nothing to do with making our minds blank or having honey-sweet thoughts. As we have observed, its chief aim is to encounter Christ so that our love for him is rekindled.

If this is to happen, we need to set aside uninterrupted time for contemplative prayer. Such prayer begins, to borrow the imagery of John Donne, by "tuning the instrument at the gate"—that is, by preparing our hearts to pray even before we enter our place of prayer. We can do this while we tidy our room or drive home from work because it is an attitude of mind and heart rather than an activity.

When we enter our prayer place, we need to give ourselves time to relax in God's presence. One of the best ways of doing this is to recognize some of the reasons why we are tense: worry, pressure of things to be done, the quarrel we just had with our spouse or a colleague. It will be impossible to contemplate until these pressures have been handed over to God. When we transfer them to him, we find ourselves gloriously free with an uncluttered expanse of time in which to be met afresh by him. Perhaps that is one reason why Peter invites us to "Cast all your anxiety on him because he cares for you" (1 Pet. 5:7).

Having transferred our burdens and having allowed the tensions to slide from us as snow slides from the roof-tops in the thaw, the next phase of prayer involves becoming aware of the presence of God. Jesus has promised that he will never leave us or forsake us. We take time to tune into his presence . . .

In the quietness, aware of his presence, we open our hearts to receive his love. The prayer is usually wordless and fed by a deep desire for him. This leads us on to a place where instead of seeking God, we are found by him. We discover that, long before we came to our place of prayer, he was seeking us. So he responds to our longing. We bask in the warmth of his love. We feel his gaze on us. He fills us afresh with his Spirit. We receive a new perspective on life—his perspective. We draw so close to his heart that we sense his concern for the world, and from our contemplation flows intercession as we catch his compassion for a hurting world.

BIBLE SELECTION
Psalm 119:12–16, 23–24, 33–34, 58

Blessed are you, O LORD;
   teach me your statutes.
With my lips I declare
   all the ordinances of your mouth.
I delight in the way of your decrees
   as much as in all riches.
I will meditate on your precepts,
   and fix my eyes on your ways.
I will delight in your statutes;
   I will not forget your word.

Even though princes sit plotting against me,
   your servant will meditate on your statutes.
Your decrees are my delight,
   they are my counselors.

Teach me, O LORD, the way of your statutes,
   and I will observe it to the end.
Give me understanding, that I may keep your law
   and observe it with my whole heart.

I implore your favor with all my heart;
   be gracious to me according to your promise.

DISCUSSION QUESTIONS

The following can be used for discussion within a small group, or used for journal reflections by individuals:

1. What is attractive about taking biblical texts as a starting point for "extended thinking about God's guidance"? What benefits might this provide?
2. How can I restate, or explain, Huggett's way of defining meditation and contemplation? What differences do I see between the two approaches to prayer?

SUGGESTED EXERCISES

The following exercises can be done by individuals, shared between spiritual friends, or used in the context of a small group. Choose one or more of the following:

1. Try a creative form of meditation based on scriptural storytelling. Choose a familiar scriptural story in which there are a number of characters, such as one of the healings Jesus did. You may want to look at Mark's Gospel for such stories of healing. When you meditate, play one or more of the roles in order to experience the grace of meditation more fully. A group may do this exercise by assigning the roles beforehand, then praying privately, and returning to reflect on the experience.
2. Consider writing as a form of meditation, or an extension of the prayer experience of meditation. After choosing a subject or a text, devote yourself to a time of prayerful meditation. After this, capture the content of the meditation in written form. Another way to go about this is simply to write a meditation on a given theme, without actually beginning in prayer. As you write the meditation, you discover your own interior state during the writing process. This is an excellent spiritual discipline.

REFLECTIONS

I like what Joyce Huggett writes about meditation and contemplation. She so unpretentiously takes all of the nebulousness out of those words. When we have listened to her down-to-earth counsel for a while we find ourselves saying, "Yes, of course, I can do that." This is all to the good for too often we have shelved these ways of prayer into the category of the supersaint—perhaps they are for a St. Teresa or a St. Francis but certainly not for me. This is the very attitude that Joyce Huggett teases out of us. These ways of prayer are for us; for you and me in all our ordinariness.

Did you notice how the writing never allows us to keep meditation and contemplation in the realm of the theoretical? Each time we are called into practice. The reason for this is fundamental. These simply are not the kinds of things that we can understand in a detached, abstract way. <u>The only way we know, truly know, meditation and contemplation is by experience.</u> There is no other way. So, my dear friend, "Taste and see that the Lord is good" (Ps. 34:8).

RICHARD J. FOSTER

GOING DEEPER

Joyce Huggett has written a number of books to instruct and encourage us in prayer in a readable style. Among these are *The Joy of Listening to God* (Downers Grove, IL: InterVarsity, 1986) and *Listening to God* (Downers Grove, IL: InterVarsity, 1987). *Learning the Language of Prayer* (New York: Crossroad, 1997) draws out the figure of prayer as a kind of language.

ANTHONY BLOOM, *Beginning to Pray* (New York: Paulist, 1970) and *Living Prayer* (Springfield, IL: Templegate, 1966) are modern classics on prayer by a Russian Orthodox monk and bishop; his works have enjoyed wide popularity among English-speaking readers. Huggett has clearly relied on his counsel, which we may do as well.

Thomas Merton

(1915–1968)

Thomas Merton has perhaps done more than any other twentieth-century figure to make the life of prayer widely known and understood. He was born in Europe and attended Cambridge University in England and Columbia University in New York City. During his college years he was deeply attracted to Christian belief and became a Roman Catholic (1938) and later a Cistercian (Trappist) monk (1941). His spiritual autobiography, *The Seven Storey Mountain*, written after he had embraced a life of monastic silence, became a best-seller.

As a monk (and later a priest) in the Abbey of Gethsemani in Kentucky, Merton continued to write extensively on the spiritual life, social justice issues, war and peace. He also wrote poetry and fiction. His interest in contemplation led him to investigate prayer forms in Eastern religion. Zen masters from Asia regarded him as the preeminent authority on their kind of prayer in the United States. Toward the end of his life he suffered some physical and emotional crises; he was hospitalized; he considered leaving the monastery. It was widely rumored that he would not return to the Trappists after his 1968 journey to Asia (during which he died of an accident). All this speculation, however, has not dimmed Merton's reputation as a gifted teacher and practitioner of prayer.

Do not be concerned, as you read the following selection on contemplation, about arriving at precise definitions of "meditation" and "contemplation." Recognize that different teachers and writers define these terms in different ways. Our concern here is not to study prayer, but to practice it. And Merton's main hope is to make the gift of contemplation more accessible to all of us. Notice how he emphasizes the normal, natural quality of contemplative prayer.

WHAT IS CONTEMPLATION?

The Gift of Contemplation

There are so many Christians who do not appreciate the magnificent dignity of their vocation to sanctity, to the knowledge, love and service of God.

There are so many Christians who do not realize what possibilities God has placed in the life of Christian perfection—what possibilities for joy in the knowledge and love of Him.

There are so many Christians who have practically no idea of the immense love of God for them, and of the power of that Love to do them good, to bring them happiness.

Why do we think of the gift of contemplation, infused contemplation, mystical prayer, as something essentially strange and esoteric reserved for a small class of almost unnatural beings and prohibited to everyone else? It is perhaps because we have forgotten that contemplation is the work of the Holy Ghost acting on our souls through His gifts of Wisdom and Understanding with special intensity to increase and perfect our love for Him. These gifts are part of the normal equipment of Christian sanctity. They are given to all in Baptism, and if they are given it is presumably because God wants them to be developed. Their development will always remain the free gift of God and it is true that His wise Providence sees fit to develop them less in some saints than in others. But it is also true that God often measures His gifts by our desire to receive them, and by our cooperation with His grace, and the Holy Spirit will not waste any of His gifts on people who have little or no interest in them.

Contemplation increases our love for God
It would be a great mistake to think that mystical contemplation necessarily brings with it a whole litany of weird phenomena—ecstasies, raptures, stigmata and so on. These belong to quite a different order of things. They are "charismatic" gifts, *gratiae gratis datae,* and they are not directly ordered to the sanctification of the one who receives them. Infused contemplation, on the contrary, is a powerful means of sanctification. It is the work of love and nothing is more effective in increasing our love for God. In fact, infused contemplation is intimately connected with the pure and perfect love of God which is God's greatest gift to the soul. It is deep and intimate knowledge of God by a union of love—a union in which we learn things about Him that those who have not received such a gift will never discover until they enter heaven.

Therefore, if anyone should ask, "Who may desire this gift and pray for it?" the answer is obvious: *everybody.*

One condition
But there is only one condition. If you desire intimate union with God you must be willing to pay the price for it. The price is small enough. In fact, it is not even a price at all: it only seems to be so with us. We find it difficult to give up our desire for things that can never satisfy us in order to purchase the One Good in Whom is all our joy—and in Whom, moreover, we get back everything else that we have renounced besides!

The fact remains that contemplation will not be given to those who wilfully remain at a distance from God, who confine their interior life to a few routine exercises of piety and a few external acts of worship and service performed as a matter of duty. Such people are careful to avoid sin. They respect God as a Master. But their heart does not belong to Him. They are not really interested in Him, except in order to insure themselves against losing heaven and going to hell. In actual practice, their minds and hearts are taken up with their own ambitions and troubles and comforts and pleasures and all their worldly interests and anxieties and fears. God is only invited to enter this charmed circle to smooth out difficulties and to dispense rewards.

BIBLE SELECTION
Psalm 1:1–6

Happy are those
   who do not follow the advice of the wicked,
or take the path that sinners tread,
   or sit in the seat of scoffers;
but their delight is in the law of the LORD,
   and on his law they meditate day and night.
They are like trees
   planted by streams of water,
which yield their fruit in its season,
   and their leaves do not wither.
In all that they do, they prosper.

The wicked are not so,
   but are like chaff that the wind drives away.
Therefore the wicked will not stand in the judgment,
   nor sinners in the congregation of the righteous;
For the LORD watches over the way of the righteous,
   but the way of the wicked will perish.

DISCUSSION QUESTIONS

The following can be used for discussion within a small group, or used for journal reflections by individuals:

1. What obstacles may be standing in my way with regard to contemplative prayer?
2. What stereotypes—about God, myself, or prayer—might I need to work on?

SUGGESTED EXERCISES

The following exercises can be done by individuals, shared between spiritual friends, or used in the context of a small group. Choose one or more of the following:

1. Choose a biblical text with rich content for contemplation. Psalm 23 or Psalm 138 may do well. Read it over peacefully and reflectively until a short phrase invites you deeper into prayer. Once you have "passed in" or "passed over" through the text, relinquish the words and enter into wordless (or nearly wordless) prayer. Be sure you have allowed enough time for this exercise. Often, when we pray in a contemplative manner, we cannot let go of words all at once. They continue to trail behind us as we gradually enter into the peace and silence of contemplation. Be easy with this process. Don't push it, but let it happen, as a gift of grace.
2. Consider using a visual focal point for contemplative prayer. A painting of the face of Jesus may serve in this way. If you choose a painting with many different objects or people depicted (such as a painting of the Last Supper), you may wish to begin with the whole scene and then slowly narrow your concentration to a single detail. An exquisite object, such as a rosebud (being a sign also of God's grandeur) may also serve as an entry point to contemplation.
3. Schedule a series of visits or an extended time in a place you find conducive to contemplation, such as a chapel, a garden, or a park.
4. Consider a group experience of contemplative prayer, in which a number of people go to a place and set aside time for contemplation on a regular basis.

REFLECTIONS

In discussing contemplation Thomas Merton reaches us in the most simple way possible, namely, by calling us to the love of God. He speaks directly to our condition when he says, "so many Christians . . . have practically no idea of the immense love of God for them, and of the power of that Love to do them good, to bring them happiness." In saying this he is teaching us that at its core contemplation is simply and profoundly falling in love with God over and over and over again.

In contemplation we are coming to dearly love and constantly delight in the "heavenly Father" who has been made real to us in Jesus Christ. We "see"—see with the eyes of the heart—that God is out to do us good always. We see, truly see, that there is no limit, no "catch" to God's goodness toward us.

Merton wisely reminds us that this perfecting love is not necessarily tied to what he calls "weird phenomena—ecstasies, raptures, stigmata and so on." Rather the transforming vision of divine Love and of our responding love is a gift of the Holy Spirit that comes by means of "Wisdom and Understanding." In saying this he is following the lead of Thomas Aquinas who writes, "Love follows knowledge." In other words, love is the response of our heart, aroused in our will, by means of our mind's enthralling vision of the goodness of God. That is all. That is contemplation.

RICHARD J. FOSTER

GOING DEEPER

THOMAS MERTON, *What Is Contemplation?* (Springfield, IL: Templegate, 1950). This brief book is an excellent introduction to contemplative prayer for everyone.

THOMAS MERTON, *Contemplation in a World of Action* (Notre Dame, IN: University of Notre Dame Press, 1999). Often, when people engage in contemplative prayer, others may say that they have given up on social concerns. In this book, Merton addresses that issue squarely.

THOMAS MERTON, *The Seven Storey Mountain* (New York: Harcourt Brace, 1948). Readers of many generations have been moved by Merton's account of his postcollegiate coming to Christian faith.

Marguerite Porete

(c. 1250–1310)

————

Marguerite Porete was a member of a creative and original group of prayerful European laywomen in the thirteenth and fourteenth centuries who are known as Beguines. A number of them were mystics and were recognized as such both because of their ways of praying and their ways of writing about prayer.

Porete is the author of *A Mirror of Simple Souls*, a brief and intense work that is mostly about experiencing the love of God. She counsels us to beware of the will, even the will to virtue, and wants us to surrender our wills in order to be fully embraced by God's love.

Her book was condemned in 1306 and was publicly burned in the town of Valenciennes, France. She herself was burned at the stake in 1310. Probably the issues had more to do with writing in the vernacular and acting in nonsubmissive ways than with actual matters of doctrine. About a century later, her work came back into circulation, regained status, and has remained one of the favorite spiritual texts of Western Europe.

Notice the intensity of Marguerite's writing. In this selection she uses love language to make the experience of contemplation attractive to us. Contemplative prayer is described in terms of pleasure and delight. The soul, described as feminine (whether it is a man's or a woman's) is vanquished by the onset of bliss.

A MIRROR OF SIMPLE SOULS

The Soul Describes the Seven Stages

I promised earlier to describe the seven stages in the ascent of the mountain from whose summit only God can be seen. This I shall now do and you should understand that each stage has its own time span allotted to it.

The first stage: Keeping the commandments
The first stage is when a soul is touched by God's grace and set apart from sin, so that her will is set on keeping his commandments to the best of her ability. She sees, in fear and trembling, that God has commanded us to love him above all things and our neighbour as ourselves. This seems hard enough for her, enough work to keep her occupied for a thousand years, if she should live that long.

I was in this position once, I remember. Those of you who are still at this stage must not despair of moving on to higher stages. Be of good heart and have courage: faint hearts will not rise to tackle the demands of love. The faint-hearted take the lead in fear, not love, and do not allow God to work in them.

The second stage: Following the counsel of perfection

The second stage is reached when the soul sees what counsels God gives those who would love him in a special way, beyond his commandments. And seeing this as a means of pleasing God, the soul like any good lover naturally wishes to please her Beloved. And so she sets out to follow the counsel of evangelical perfection, by mortifying her earthly desires and despising riches and honours, according to the example set by Jesus. She feels no bitterness in doing this, and no weakness in her body, but is sustained by the knowledge that God is leading her onwards and upwards.

The third stage: The death of the will

The third stage is reached when the soul looks carefully at the love she had developed for the works of perfection which have multiplied in her during the second stage. And what does this careful look tell her? That there is really nothing she can offer her Beloved except what he most loves, since other gifts are not really worthy of pure love. She sees her will attached to all good works and spiritual comforts, and then the truth is borne in on her that she must detach herself from just the perfections that grace has brought about in her, as these are precisely what she has to sacrifice to love. The sacrifice she is called to make is to abstain from all the good works which had in fact become her greatest pleasure.

So she abstains from all these good works that pleased her so much and puts her will which had become attached to the life of perfection to death. She seeks only to do the will of others and refuses all inclination of her own will, in order to destroy her own will. This is a very hard process—far more difficult than the two earlier stages. It is far harder to master the will of the spirit than it is to master the will of the body in order to do the will of the spirit. But this is what she has to do: break her will so as to leave more space where love can come to live in her. At this point she has to burden herself with the wills of others in order to free herself from the burden of herself.

The fourth stage: Labours give way to contemplation

In the fourth stage, the soul is brought by love to delight in meditation alone, and abandons all labours outside her new task of contemplation, including doing the will of others. The soul is now in a highly delicate and even dangerous state, in which all she can bear is the touch of love's sheer delight. This she takes infinite pleasure in, and pride, out of the abundance of her love.

She now reveals the secrets of her heart, all the tenderness and sweetness of her love; she melts into the embrace of union from which she receives all love's delights. She is convinced there can be nothing higher than the life she now enjoys; love has given her such pleasure that she cannot believe God has anything higher to offer the soul than this love which Love has spread throughout her being.

It is indeed a wonderful thing for the soul to be taken up to these dizzy heights of love. She is in a drunken ecstasy of love and can see nothing but love; love sheds such a blinding light on her that she cannot see that there is a love surpassing even this. In this she is mistaken, for there are two stages beyond even this which can be attained in this life, but at this stage the soul is blinded by the onset of love, seizing her up into bliss as soon as she makes an approach, with a strength there is no resisting. So now the soul is taken up out of herself by a Love exceeding even the love she feels.

The fifth stage: The will abandoned to God

Now the soul sees what God is: that he IS, that all things come from him and that she herself is nothing, being not what is. So she feels an amazing humility at the thought of the infinite goodness of God giving her nothingness free will. She sees herself as nothing but wickedness, and yet with this wonderful gift of free will, this giving of being to what had none out of the pure goodness of God. Then such divine goodness is poured into the soul, in a ravishing flash of divine light, that she suddenly sees that she must remove this great gift of free will from anything that is not God, and never again place it where he is not.

Her will now sees by the spreading brightness of divine enlightenment, prompting her to put her will once more in God, which she cannot do without this divine enlightenment. Her will has to be detached from her own will so that it is given entirely to God. She now sees clearly her own nothingness, and indeed the wretchedness of her own nature, and sees, by divine enlightenment, that she has to will what is God's will for her without consciously willing it. This, in fact, is what she was given free will for. So she is separated from her will and her will from her. She gives it back to God, where it came from originally, in order to carry out the divine will, which cannot be carried out without the complete abandonment of all self-love. So there is no conflict of will left in her.

This gift of complete self-giving of her will brings her perfect peace, makes her the very being of love, nourished on the gift of love that gives her the pleasure of complete peace. . . . In the fourth stage, her will took her fine and free to the heights of contemplation, but in this fifth she sees herself clearly, no longer blinded by love. It is now her knowledge of God's goodness that gives her life, and this leads her to renounce herself, and having done this she is free from all slaveries and possesses complete freedom of being, relieved of all pressures.

The sixth stage: Freedom in enlightenment

In the sixth stage the soul no longer sees her own nothingness from the depths of her humility, nor the greatness of God through his great goodness. Instead, God sees himself in her through his own power, enlightens her himself, so that she sees that nothing exists save God alone, the source of all being. What is, is God, and the soul sees nothing but God, because whoever sees this of God, is God. So in this sixth stage the soul is free, purified and enlightened, but not yet glorified, because glory belongs to the seventh stage, which is the glory of heaven of which no one can speak.

Pure and enlightened, it is no longer her seeing God and herself, but God seeing himself in her, through her, showing her that there is nothing but God. . . . She sees that all is in the being of God, who is love and has paid all debts.

The seventh stage

The seventh stage cannot be described. God reserves it to himself, and will give it to us in his everlasting glory. We cannot know it in this life, but only when our soul has left our body.

BIBLE SELECTION
Song of Solomon 5:1–8

I come to my garden, my sister, my bride;
  I gather my myrrh with my spice,
  I eat my honeycomb with my honey,
  I drink my wine with my milk.

Eat, friends, drink,
  and be drunk with love.

I slept, but my heart was awake.
Listen, my beloved is knocking.
"Open to me, my sister, my love,
  my dove, my perfect one;

for my head is wet with dew,
　my locks with the drops of the night."
I had put off my garment;
　how could I put it on again?
I had bathed my feet;
　how could I soil them?
My beloved thrust his hand into the opening,
　and my inmost being yearned for him.
I arose to open to my beloved,
　and my hands dripped with myrrh,
my fingers with liquid myrrh,
　upon the handles of the bolt.
I opened to my beloved,
　but my beloved had turned and was gone.
My soul failed me when he spoke.
I sought him, but did not find him;
　I called him, but he gave no answer.
Making their rounds in the city,
　the sentinels found me;
they beat me, they wounded me,
　they took away my mantle,
　those sentinels of the walls.
I adjure you, O daughters of Jerusalem,
　if you find my beloved,
tell him this:
　I am faint with love.

DISCUSSION QUESTIONS

The following can be used for discussion within a small group, or used for journal reflections by individuals:

1. Contemplative prayer may involve a deeper intimacy with God. Am I willing to accept this possibility? Why or why not?
2. Often, when we read dazzling descriptions of ecstatic prayer, we think, "Things like that never happen to me." How do I get in the way of such experiences?

3. Teachers of contemplative prayer counsel us to be detached from the desire for certain kinds of prayer—experiences or special favors from God, in order to be open to what God really wants to send us. What kinds of experience have we set our hearts on? Are we ready for whatever God wants?

SUGGESTED EXERCISES

The following exercises can be done by individuals, shared between spiritual friends, or used in the context of a small group. Choose one or more of the following:

1. Use music as a way of being led into contemplative prayer.
2. Identify the words and phrases in the Marguerite Porete reading that connote intense intimacy with God. Among these might be such words as "bliss" and "tenderness." You will find many others. Reflect on these words. Then choose one as the entry point for a time of contemplative prayer.

REFLECTIONS

If Merton introduced us to the topic of divine Love, Marguerite Porete plunges in headlong. Her passionate language of love shocks us. It is not that we are unaccustomed to such language; it is just that we are not accustomed to such language in the context of Christian devotion. We almost blush at her description of the soul's reaching out to God. We instinctively catch our breath at the very phrases Porete seems to revel in: "love's sheer delight," "the embrace of union," "a drunken ecstasy of love." But then, as we saw from the biblical text, Porete's words only echo those of wise, old Solomon.

Frankly, I have never experienced anything even remotely close to what is described in this reading. You may have much the same feeling. If so, is there anything from these writings that we can apply to ourselves—that we are to be filled with the raptures of divine love we see in this selection from Marguerite Porete? Simply this: God loves to love us far beyond our most extravagant hopes. At the very heart of the universe is God's utter compassion and loving care for all of his creation. No doubt many of us today find this hard to imagine. And, even now, God delights to lead us into the "dizzy heights of love"—to the extent that we welcome it and to the extent that we can stand it.

RICHARD J. FOSTER

GOING DEEPER

MARGUERITE PORETE, *A Mirror for Simple Souls* (New York: Crossroad, 1981). Only the second translation into modern English, this work is very readable and inviting. At the time it was made, however, Porete's authorship had not been established. Delightful woodcut illustrations are included.

SASKIA MURK-JANSEN, *Brides in the Desert: The Spirituality of the Beguines* (New York: Orbis Books, 1998). This historical review of the Beguine movement examines the flowering of a laywoman's spirituality and some key images developed from the Beguines' outpouring of prayer.

Prayer

———

André Louf

(1929–)

—

André Louf is an experienced teacher of prayer. He belongs to the Cistercian religious community, which is known both in Europe and America for a life of joyful simplicity. Cistercians (sometimes called Trappists) live carefully regulated lives, doing mostly agricultural work. They observe silence, times of solitude, carefully balanced with times of work. Many people know them for their farm products: jams and jellies, cheeses, and the like. But most often they are known for the depth of their prayer lives.

In the United States, Cistercians Basil Pennington and Thomas Keating are well known as teachers of centering prayer.

In his small book, *Teach Us to Pray: Learning a Little About God*, Father Louf brings a lifetime of experience to us in a way that makes prayer attractively simple. He teaches us how easy and natural prayer can be when he answers the question, "Is Praying Difficult?"

When he speaks about "The Superabundance of the Heart" he is drawing on a very ancient tradition of heart prayer that is a precious resource to the whole Christian community.

Father Louf is Belgian; he has broad scholarly knowledge of the Desert Fathers, but always (as you will notice in the following selections) his concern is to invite us into the delight of prayer.

TEACH US TO PRAY

Is Praying Difficult?

A fourteenth-century Byzantine monk, who for a short time was Patriarch of Constantinople with the name of Callixtus II, answers this question with the illustration of the lute-player. "The lute-player bends over his instrument and listens attentively to the tune, while his fingers manipulate the plectrum and make the strings vibrate in full-toned harmony. The lute has turned into music; and the man who strums upon it is taken out of himself, for the music is soft and entrancing."

Anyone who prays must set about it in the same way. He has a lute and a plectrum at his disposal. The lute is his heart, the strings of which are the inward senses. To get the strings vibrating and the lute playing he needs a plectrum, in this case: the recollection of God, the Name of Jesus, the Word.

So the lute-player has to listen attentively and vigilantly to his heart and pluck its strings with the Name of Jesus. Until the senses open up and his heart becomes alert. The person who strums incessantly upon his heart with the Name of Jesus sets his heart a' singing, "an ineffable happiness flows into his soul, the recollection of Jesus purifies his spirit and makes it sparkle with divine light."

Is praying difficult?

No one is going to give you the answer to that question. This short book has no answer for you, either. It cannot pretend to be an introduction to prayer, much less a manual of instruction. We have been listening together to the witness of a centuries'-old tradition of prayer in the Church of Jesus. Something may have revealed itself to you on the way. Has the Spirit of Jesus, who never ceases from praying in your heart, suddenly disclosed and avowed Himself? Like the embryo that leapt in the womb of Elizabeth when it encountered Jesus in Mary's womb?

If not, that is no reason to feel discouraged: your Hour is still to come.

If so, then you should give everything you have to the task of catching more clearly the still sound of God within you. For there the field lies, and there the treasure is hidden. The moment you discover the treasure of prayer in the field of your heart, you will go off full of joy and sell all that you possess in order to have that treasure. And the lute is at your disposal, and the plectrum too. These are your heart, and the Word of God. The Word is, after all, very close to you, on your lips and in your heart (Rom. 10:8).

You need only pick up the plectrum and pluck the strings. To persevere in the Word and in your heart, watching and praying. There is no other way of learning how to pray. You must return to yourself and to your true and deepest nature, to the human-being-in-Jesus that you already are, purely and simply by grace. "Nobody can learn how to see. For seeing is something we can do by nature. So too with prayer. _Authentic prayer_ can never be learnt from someone else. It has its own instructor within it. Prayer is God's gift to him who prays."

Superabundance of the Heart

We stand now on the threshold of prayer. Our heart has been awakened. It sees Jesus, it hears His voice, it rejoices in His Word. That Word has been turned over and over in our heart. It has purified us, cleansed us, and we have grown familiar with it. Perhaps we are even beginning to resemble this Word. Now too, it can take root in our heart and bear fruit. Now it may even become the Word of God in our flesh.

So long as we ourselves were still intent on the Word of God in our heart, we had come no further than the prelude. There comes a moment when we yield up God's Word to the Spirit within us. Then it is that our heart gives birth to prayer. And then at last the Word of God has become truly ours. We have then discovered and realized our most profound, our true identity. And then the Name of Jesus has become our name also. And together with Jesus we may with one voice call God: Abba, Father!

Prayer is the superabundance of the heart. It is brim-full and running over with love and praise, as once it was with Mary, when the Word took root in her body. So too, our heart breaks out into a Magnificat. Now the Word has achieved its "glorious course" (2 Thess. 3:1): it has gone out from God and been sown in the good soil of the heart. Having now been *chewed over* and assimilated, it is regenerated in the heart, to the praise of God. It has taken root in us and is now bearing its fruit: we in our turn utter the Word and send it back to God. We have become Word; we are prayer.

Thus prayer is the precious fruit of the Word—Word of God that has become wholly our own and in that way has been inscribed deep in our body and our psyche, and that now can become our response to the Love of the Father. The Spirit stammers it out in our heart, without our doing anything about it. It bubbles up, it flows, it runs like living water. It is no longer we who pray, but the prayer prays itself in us. The divine life of the risen Christ ripples softly in our heart.

The slow work of transfiguring the cosmos has had a beginning in us. The whole creation has been waiting for this moment: the revelation of the glory of the children of God (Rom. 8:19). It is going on in secret and quite unpretentiously; and yet already in Spirit and truth. We are still in the world, and we dwell already with Jesus near the Father. We still live in the flesh, and the Spirit has already made us wholly captive. For the veil has fallen from our heart, and with unveiled faces we reflect like mirrors the glory and brightness of Jesus, as we ourselves are being recreated in His image, from glory to glory, by His Spirit (2 Cor. 3:18).

So the Word of Christ resides in our heart, in all its richness (Col. 3:16). In it we are rooted, on it we are founded, by it we order our conduct in life, and all the time we overflow with praise and thanksgiving (Col. 2:6–7). This eucharist-thanksgiving has now become our life (Col. 3:15), the superabundance of our heart, the liturgy of the new world that deep within us we already celebrate. We are in fact temples of the Spirit (1 Cor. 6:19).

BIBLE SELECTIONS
Romans 8:19; 2 Corinthians 3:18; Colossians 3:16; Colossians 2:6–7;
Colossians 3:15; 1 Corinthians 6:19

For the creation waits with eager longing for the revealing of the children of God.

And all of us, with unveiled faces, seeing the glory of the Lord as though reflected in a mirror, are being transformed into the same image from one degree of glory to another; for this comes from the Lord, the Spirit.

Let the word of Christ dwell in you richly; teach and admonish one another in all wisdom; and with gratitude in your hearts sing psalms, hymns, and spiritual songs to God.

As you therefore have received Christ Jesus the Lord, continue to live your lives in him, rooted and built up in him and established in the faith, just as you were taught, abounding in thanksgiving.

And let the peace of Christ rule in your hearts, to which indeed you were called in the one body. And be thankful.

Or do you not know that your body is a temple of the Holy Spirit within you, which you have from God, and that you are not your own?

DISCUSSION QUESTIONS

The following can be used for discussion within a small group, or used for journal reflections by individuals:

1. Do I view prayer more as a burdensome duty or an obligation? What can help me view it as a gift of grace?
2. How can I use the prayerful imagination to think of my heart as a lute and God's word as a way of strumming?
3. Do I work too hard at prayer? What steps can I take to cultivate the art of letting go, yielding easily to prayer as something that flows readily from within?
4. In what ways have I allowed myself to experience the "superabundance of the heart"?

SUGGESTED EXERCISES

The following exercises can be done by individuals, shared between spiritual friends, or used in the context of a small group. Choose one or more of the following:

1. Choose a prayer place that is especially pleasant for you. You may want to walk in a nearby park or where the ducks and swans are swimming. Let your prayer bubble up from your natural joy in these surroundings.
2. Practice *lectio divina* (sacred reading) by taking a Bible text that you love, reading it over attentively, then entering into prayer through a single word or phrase. Dwell inside the text, experiencing God's love for you abundantly.
3. Pray with music playing in the background. Allow the Lord to play divine music in the lute of your heart.

REFLECTIONS

André Louf gives us a most clever and penetrating answer to the age-old question, "Is praying difficult?" even as he confesses that no definitive answer is possible. The reason no one can give a definitive answer is because we are here dealing with the infinite complexity of every individual in dynamic relationship with the infinite Reality of the universe.

But Father Louf's answer is indeed a helpful one. He simply turns our attention to the image of the lute player, and we catch the idea immediately. You see, for the beginning musician playing the lute is difficult indeed. The beginner faces a host of issues all at once: how to hold the lute, how to manipulate the plectrum, what tune to play and the need to memorize it, and so forth. But for the master musician playing the lute is sheer ease and joy. All of the actions necessary to make a beautiful melody flow effortlessly from ingrained habits of mind and muscle. As Father Louf notes, the accomplished lute player "is taken out of himself, for the music is soft and entrancing."

With this image Father Louf is helping us see that prayer is both difficult and easy. In the beginning we are struggling with a host of issues: how we as finite creatures approach the infinite God, what we are to say and how we are to say it, how we are to listen in return, and so forth. But we can rest easy with these difficulties of ours, for we know that over time a kind of practiced experience will develop within us deeply ingrained habits of prayer—"the superabundance of the heart" as Father Louf puts it. As this develops deep within then prayer is indeed easy, for "It bubbles up, it flows, it runs like living water."

RICHARD J. FOSTER

GOING DEEPER

ANDRÉ LOUF, *The Cistercian Way* (Kalamazoo, MI: Cistercian Publications, 1983). In this book Louf goes into great detail about how Cistercians live, work, and pray in Europe.

MICHAEL DOWNEY, *Trappist: Living in the Land of Desire* (New York: Paulist, 1997). This coffee-table book describes in paragraphs and photographs the daily life of an American Trappist (Cistercian), which mirrors the sort of life that André Louf has led. It's a life of prayer and work. "We earn to make a living," one monk is quoted as saying. "We do not live to make money. Choir comes before cake. Prayer comes before cheese, not to mention fudge."

Centering Prayer in Daily Life and Ministry, edited by Gustave Reiniger (New York: Continuum, 1998). This book contains a series of essays by such experts as Trappists Thomas Keating and Basil Pennington as well as Episcopal clergy Paul David Lawson and Thomas R. Ward Jr.

HENRI J. M. NOUWEN, *The Way of the Heart* (San Francisco: HarperSanFrancisco, 1981). This book by the renowned Dutch-born priest centers on desert spirituality and contemporary ministry.

The Sayings of the Desert Fathers, translated by Benedicta Ward (Kalamazoo, MI: Cistercian Publications, 1975). Ward, a Sister of the Love of God (an Anglican community), introduces us to the windswept heartfelt spirituality of, among many others, such crusty figures as Anthony the Great, Gregory the theologian, John the Dwarf, Paul the Barber.

THELMA HALL, *Too Deep for Words: Rediscovering Lectio Divina* (New York: Paulist Press, 1998). The author is a Religious of the Cenacle, a community engaged in giving retreats and running retreat houses called The Cenacle. In her book she explains this ancient method of prayer and offers five hundred Scripture texts that may be prayed in this manner.

Agnes Sanford

(1897–1982)

———

Agnes Sanford, born in China as the daughter of a Presbyterian missionary, lived for years in New Jersey as the wife of an Episcopalian rector. Her approach to healing through prayer has been uncomplicated and very confident of God's loving power to heal. She does not concern herself with complex questions of creed, denomination, or belief structure. Her approach is Christ-centered and church-centered. She has taught widely in many settings; she has been the instrument of many healings; and her books on healing prayer have sold in the millions around the English-speaking world.

In the following selection, taken from her much-loved book, *The Healing Light*, notice how Agnes Sanford concentrates on the practicality of prayer. Her recommendations are not ethereal and fanciful but exceedingly down to earth. When she recommends that we conduct experiments in prayer, she is not suggesting that we put God to the test. Instead, she wants us to put our own wavering faith to the test. She knows that we are afraid to petition God for specific things because we are afraid of being disappointed. Therefore, she gently guides us through an orderly process that requires us, at least for the moment, to have faith and to exercise that faith in a disciplined way. At the same time her approach is wonderfully childlike. Follow her, as she follows Jesus, in the experience of healing prayer.

THE HEALING LIGHT

Experiments in Prayer

The One who knew said, "Blessed are the poor in spirit, for theirs is the Kingdom of Heaven." Happy, that is, are those people who know that their spiritual power is small, that their creeds are imperfect, that their instruction concerning God and man is incomplete. Happy are those who know that they do not know all of truth. For only those who admit their spiritual poverty are willing to learn.

One way to understand a hitherto unexplored force of nature is to experiment with that force intelligently and with an open mind. This book suggests, for those willing to learn, a method so simple that it is childlike, as the more profound truths are apt to be. It is an experimental method. One decides upon a definite subject for prayer, prays about it and then decides whether or not the prayer-project succeeds. If it does not succeed, one seeks a better adjustment with God and tries again.

Producing results

"Blessed are the meek, for they shall inherit the earth." The attitude of perfect meekness consists of an unshakable faith in the laws of nature combined with perfect humility toward those laws and a patient determination to learn them at whatever cost. Through this meekness we have learned how to conform to the laws of nature, and by so doing have achieved great results. Through the same meekness those who seek God can produce results by learning to conform to His laws of faith and love.

Four simple steps into prayer

The first step in seeking to produce results by any power is to contact that power. The first step then in seeking help from God is to contact God. "Be still and know that I am God."

Let us then lay aside our worries and cares, quiet our minds and concentrate upon the reality of God. We may not know who God is or what God is, but we know that there is something that sustains this universe, and that something is not ourselves. So the first step is to relax and to remind ourselves that there is a source of life outside of ourselves.

The second step is to connect with this life by some such prayer as this: "Heavenly Father, please increase in me at this time your life-giving power."

The third step is to believe that this power is coming into use and to accept it by faith. No matter how much we ask for something it becomes ours only as we accept it and give thanks for it. "Thank you," we can say, "that your life is *now* coming into me and increasing life in my spirit and in my mind and in my body."

And the fourth step is to observe the operations of that light and life. In order to do so, we must decide on some tangible thing that we wish accomplished by that power, so that we can know without question whether our experiment succeeded or failed.

The value of specific requests

Many Christians are afraid to do this. A working woman once told me that she asked God to send her two pairs of rubbers for her sons, to protect their feet from rain and slush. That night, she said, the ground froze over solid and for two days the boys walked to school dry-shod. Upon the third day a neighbor gave her two pairs of rubbers for her sons.

"Oh, but I would never *dare* do that," cried a young man to whom I repeated this. "Because—what if the rubbers didn't come?"

If the rubbers weren't forthcoming, he implied—there was no God. But if he had turned on an electric light and it had failed to shine, he would not have said, "There is no electricity!" He would have said, "There is something wrong with this lamp."

Let us understand, then, that if our experiment fails, it is not due to a lack in God, but to a natural and understandable lack in ourselves. What scientist would be discouraged if his first experiment failed? Since we intend with His help to heal our shortcomings, to repair our wiring, we need not fear to test His power by prayer.

A pair of rubbers might not be the simplest objective, nor a new coat, nor a larger home. We might be mistaken concerning our need of these things. Moreover, the attaining of such things in prayer involves the swaying of more minds than ours, and is rather difficult for a first experiment. Let us choose one of the very simplest of prayer-experiments, remembering always that it must be tangible; that is, it must be something that we can put the finger on and say either "This has been done," or "This has not been done."

How strange it is that people who fear to do this do not hesitate to pray for the most difficult objectives of all, such as the peace of the world or the salvation of their souls! If they have so little confidence in prayer that they do not dare to test their powers of contacting God by praying for an easy thing, it is probable that their cosmic intercessions are of little force. If everyone who prayed for the peace of the world had enough prayer-power to accomplish the healing of a head cold, this would be a different world within twenty-four hours.

An objective that is simple and personal

All the cattle on a thousand hills are His, all the rubbers in all the world are under His control, and sufficient power to heal the head colds of all humanity flows at His command. Let us not be afraid then, to choose for our first prayer-experiment an objective that is simple and personal. This objective must of course be in accordance with God's will, for it is as difficult to make God's power operate contrary to His will as it is to make water flow uphill. A wise engineer studies the laws of flowing water and builds his water system in accordance with those laws. A wise scientist studies the laws of nature and adapts his experiments to those laws. And a wise seeker after God had better study the laws of God and adapt his prayers to those laws.

There is no great mystery concerning the will of God, in so far as it applies to our small selves. God's will is written into His nature, and the nature of God is love. Therefore, when we pray in accordance with the law of love, we are praying in accordance with the will of God.

BIBLE SELECTION
Matthew 8:5–10, 13

When [Jesus] entered Capernaum, a centurion came to him, appealing to him, and saying, "Lord, my servant is lying at home paralysed, in terrible distress." And [Jesus] said to him, "I will come and cure him." The centurion answered, "Lord, I am not worthy to have you come under my roof; but only speak the word, and my servant will be healed. For I also am a man under authority, with soldiers under me; and I say to one, 'Go,' and he goes, and to another, 'Come,' and he comes, and to my slave, 'Do this,' and the slave does it." When Jesus heard him, he was amazed and said to those who followed him, "Truly I tell you, in no one in Israel have I found such faith". . . . And to the centurion Jesus said, "Go; let it be done for you according to your faith." And the servant was healed in that hour.

DISCUSSION QUESTIONS

The following can be used for discussion within a small group, or used for journal reflections by individuals:

1. What keeps me from voicing specific prayer requests? Fear? Unanswered prayers? Discouragement?
2. How can I embrace simple forms of healing prayer?
3. What sincere new experiment in prayer am I willing to undertake next week?

SUGGESTED EXERCISES

The following exercises can be done by individuals, shared between spiritual friends, or used in the context of a small group. Choose one or more of the following:

1. Conduct an "experiment in prayer" by asking God to grant some simple, very limited request. Possible options: relief from worry about a troubling situation; to find a misplaced article.
2. Pray very specifically for someone you know who is ill. Pray wholeheartedly for that person's recovery. Send her or him a card or note to say that you are praying for this.
3. If you are in a prayer group, ask the group to pray for a healing that you need. Be specific in describing the ailment you have. Consciously apply your own faith to the healing request.

REFLECTIONS

In the introduction Emilie Griffin speaks of Agnes Sanford using terms like "practicality," "down to earth," and "childlike." This I found to be true, not only in her writings, but in all she was and did. I had the privilege of being in Agnes Sanford's home and hearing her speak on numerous occasions, and I was always instructed by her good sense.

Once, for example, after a full and intensive week of teaching on healing prayer to a distinguished group of doctors and ministers she explained that she now intended to go home and work in her garden and urged us to engage in some similar task. We needed, she explained, rest from all our prayer work.

This kind of practicality is a special grace to us, for everyone who takes the ministry of prayer seriously is sorely tempted toward spiritual gluttony. Rest and play and good conversation are proper complements to the work of prayer.

More than once I saw Agnes Sanford praying with great intensity and power one moment and laughing at a homespun joke the next. Such experiences freed me to be at home with God. I believe it will do the same for you.

RICHARD J. FOSTER

GOING DEEPER

AGNES SANFORD, *The Healing Light* (New York: Ballantine Books, 1983). This is by far her best-known book. It took the issue of divine healing and made it accessible to ordinary people long before the subject was thought respectable. It is truly a pioneer book and continues to be well worth reading.

AGNES SANFORD, *The Healing Gifts of the Spirit* (Philadelphia: J. B. Lippincott, 1966). This is Agnes Sanford's most substantive book. She deals carefully with such a wide range of subjects: mental depression, the gifts of wisdom and knowledge, the discerning of spirits, and more. This book contains an extensive discussion of her most original contribution to the healing ministry—the healing of memories.

AGNES SANFORD, *The Healing Power of the Bible* (Philadelphia: J. B. Lippincott, 1969). This is a pleasant journey through many well-known stories in the Bible—Noah, Abraham, Moses, Elijah, and more—focusing upon the healing work of these champions of faith.

AGNES SANFORD, *Behold Your God* (St. Paul, MN: Macalester Park Publishing, 1958). This book is interesting because it is a running commentary on the Apostles' Creed with a view to the healing dimension to that ancient creed.

AGNES SANFORD, *Sealed Orders* (Plainfield, NJ: Logos International, 1972). This autobiography—a spiritual memoir really—gives Agnes Sanford the opportunity to employ her full powers of description. For those who are interested this book fills in many of the details of her manifold experience of God. Its descriptive powers also remind us that she was the author of several novels including *Oh, Watchman!*, *Lost Shepherd*, and *The Rising River*.

Author of

The Cloud of Unknowing

(14th Century)

———

The Cloud of Unknowing is generally considered the greatest spiritual classic to issue from the fourteenth-century English contemplative movement. The author's identity is unknown, but a number of things about him can be deduced from the text. It's written in an East Midlands dialect. It's easy to suppose that he was a spiritual director, probably a priest and a theologian. The work is written for the instruction of a spiritual disciple who has passed through the beginning stages of prayer and now finds himself in a patch of "unknowing" or darkness.

The author of the *Cloud* is clearly skilled in patristics and later theology; he is familiar with the prayer controversies of his own time and takes the point of view that prayer is a matter of the will (of love) rather than thought or intellect. The author is also deeply conversant with Scripture and uses biblical language and imagery in an easygoing and forceful way. His style is fresh and original; no doubt this is one reason why the work continues even today to be a very popular work on prayer.

writings of early Christian Fathers

In the first selection, which is not taken from *The Cloud of Unknowing*, but from a tiny treatise entitled "The Letter on Prayer," the author offers down-to-earth advice on how to pray in the present moment, being fully attentive to the prayer at hand.

The second selection, Chapter 38 of *The Cloud*, gives the Church's traditional teaching on short prayers like the "Our Father."

THE LETTER ON PRAYER

Starting to Pray

My dear spiritual friend in God,

Since you have asked me how you should control your feelings when you are praying, let me give you the best answer I can.

Let me start by saying that the best thing you can do when you start to pray, however long or short your time of prayer is to be, is to tell yourself, and mean it, that you are going to die at the end of your prayer. I am not joking when I tell you this: just think how impossible it is to tell yourself—or for anyone living to tell himself or herself—that you are certain of living longer than the time your prayer takes.

When you think of this, you will see that it is quite safe to tell yourself that you are going to die, and I advise you to do so. If you do, you will find that the combination of your general sense of your own unworthiness combined with this special feeling of how short a time you have left to make a firm purpose of amendment, will concentrate your mind wonderfully on a proper fear of the Lord.

You will find this feeling taking real hold of your heart, unless (which God forbid), you manage to coax and cajole your false heart of flesh with the false security (which can only be a false promise) that you are going to live longer. It may well be that you are going to live longer. It may well be that you are going to live beyond the time of your prayer, but it is always a false comfort to promise yourself that this will be the case and to persuade your heart to rely on it. This is because only God can know the truth of the matter, and all you can do is rely blindly on his will, without having any certainty beyond this for a moment, for the time it takes to blink an eye.

Praying wisely

So if you want to pray wisely, or "sing psalms with all your art" (Ps. 47:7), as the psalmist counsels you to do, make sure you work your mind into embracing this proper fear of the Lord, which, as the same psalmist tells you later on, is "the beginning of wisdom" (Ps. 111:10). But for all that this is a proper feeling, beware of relying on fear alone, in case you get depressed; so follow this first thought of your imminent death with another: think firmly that whether God's grace allows you to get through to the end of your prayer, dwelling on every word as you go, or whether you actually die before you get to the end, you are doing what is in you to do, and therefore God will accept it from you in full satisfaction of all the times you have wilfully strayed from the straight and narrow path from your birth till that moment.

What I mean is this: provided that you have previously, to the best of your ability and following the dictates of your conscience, confessed your faults as the Church requires, then this short prayer, however little a thing it may be, will be sufficient for God to bring you to salvation if you should die in the act of saying it; and, if you live longer, it will be a great increase of merit in you.

THE CLOUD OF UNKNOWING

How and Why Their Short Prayer Pierces Heaven

Why does this little prayer of one syllable [such as "Lord!" or "Father!" or "Jesus!"] pierce the heavens? Surely because it is offered with a full spirit, in the height and the depth, in the length and the breadth of the spirit of him who prays.

In the height: that is with the full might of the spirit; in the depth: for in this little syllable all the faculties of the spirit are contained; in the length: because if it could always be experienced as it is in that moment, it would cry as it does then; in the breadth: because it desires for all others all that it desires for itself.

It is in this moment that the soul comprehends with all the saints what is the length and the breadth, the height and the depth of the everlasting, all-loving, almighty and all-wise God, as Saint Paul teaches; not fully, but in some way and to some degree, as is proper to this work.

The eternity of God is his length; his love is his breadth; his power is his height, and his wisdom is his depth. No wonder, then, that the soul which is so nearly conformed by grace to the image and likeness of God his maker is immediately heard by God.

Yes, and even if it were a very sinful soul, one which is, as it were, God's enemy, as long as it should come, through grace, to cry out with such a little syllable from the height and the depth, the length and the breadth of its spirit, it would always be heard and helped by God in the very vehemence of its shriek.

BIBLE SELECTIONS
Ecclesiastes 7:1–4; Romans 8:37–39

A good name is better than precious ointment,
    and the day of death, than the day of birth.
It is better to go to the house of mourning
    than to go to the house of feasting;
for this is the end of everyone,
    and the living will lay it to heart.
Sorrow is better than laughter,   *bearing or conduct*
    for by sadness of countenance the heart is made glad.
The heart of the wise is in the house of mourning;
    but the heart of fools is in the house of mirth.

No, in all these things we are more than conquerors through him who loved us. For I am convinced that neither death, nor life, nor angels, nor rulers, nor things present, nor things to come, nor powers, nor height, nor depth, nor anything else in all creation, will be able to separate us from the love of God in Christ Jesus our Lord.

DISCUSSION QUESTIONS

The following can be used for discussion within a small group, or used for journal reflections by individuals:

1. What little worries do I have about prayer? How can I get beyond such conflicts?
2. What can help me to plunge into prayer with a willing attitude?

SUGGESTED EXERCISES

The following exercises can be done by individuals, shared between spiritual friends, or used in the context of a small group. Choose one or more of the following:

1. Write down the "little worries" that get in the way of your prayer. Do you fret that you are not right with God? That you may lose control when you pray? That you may have left the water boiling on the stove? Or, even worse, that you may not be qualified to pray? Ancient teachers on prayer referred to these little worries as scruples, or little pebbles, that intrude upon our ability to walk confidently in the way of Christ. Perhaps, by naming them, you may be able to discard them or move beyond them in a more confident way.
2. Choose an image of grandeur that helps you to remember the vastness of God's power and love for you; for example, Isaiah 43:4. You may find this image within a scriptural text or possibly in the natural world: waves rolling in over the beach; sky and clouds; a river or stream; the exquisite beauty of a rose or a rose garden; the paternal wisdom of an enormous oak tree, stretching its arms far and wide. Dwell with this image, allowing it to remind you of the eternity of God and the breadth of his love.

REFLECTIONS

We moderns are absolutely shocked by the counsel that as we start to pray we should assume that we will die by the end of the prayer. What could be more out of step with the contemporary mood of self-actualization and self-affirmation? Of course, I would take that as a fairly strong argument in its favor.

The notion of reflecting on our own demise is actually an ancient spiritual discipline. Its intention is to remind us in the most vivid way possible that God is the One in charge of our days. Our hopes and dreams are in his hands and not ours. As a result we can at last lay down the crushing burden of trying to be CEO of the universe.

You notice that the author is answering the specific question of how to control our feelings when we are praying. Feelings or desires are not wrong in themselves, but they must be disciplined if they are to be kept from running wild. In short, this is the discipline for controlling your feelings: assume you will die soon. In this way feelings or desires that are not congenial with eternal life in the heaven—lies, anger, revenge, hatred, and the like—are shown to be unworthy of our indulgence, and they can gently but firmly be set aside. Likewise, feelings or desires that are genuinely congenial with such a life—love, joy, peace, and the like—are welcomed and nurtured. So, you see, a well-reasoned reflection upon our demise will wonderfully clear the mind and purify the feelings.

RICHARD J. FOSTER

GOING DEEPER

The Cloud of Unknowing, edited by James Walsh (New York: Paulist, 1981). Editor Walsh is a British Jesuit priest and a scholar of the period; he offers extensive historical background. Simon Tugwell, a British Dominican priest and scholar on prayer, has written the preface. This was the first volume in the publisher's highly acclaimed series *The Classics of Western Spirituality*, which now runs to more than a hundred volumes. Others in the series will be cited here and there in the rest of this book.

Simone Weil

(1909–1943)

Simone Weil (pronounced like "veil") was a French social activist and political radical who is now thought to be a remarkable twentieth-century mystic. Born a Jew, the daughter of a middle-class Parisian doctor, she was sensitized to political issues by World War I and was involved in a variety of pro-worker movements throughout the 1930s.

In 1938, on a visit to the Trappist Abbey at Solemnes, she reported that "Christ took hold of" her. From then on she believed in the love of Jesus and in his divinity; she was deeply influenced by the meaning of the Passion.

Driven by the anti-Semitic persecutions of that era, she went to Provence, where she worked as an agricultural laborer on the Thibon farm; there she discovered the relationship between prayer, God, and Eucharist but hesitated to become a formal Christian because of her solidarity with persecuted Judaism.

Educated in philosophy and experienced as a schoolteacher, Weil did not hesitate to comment on her experience of Jesus Christ. Her many essays on prayer, fidelity to Christ, and contemplative experience have been variously collected. Her best-known work is called *Waiting for God*.

The following selection is taken from a meditation on the prayer of prayers.

CONCERNING THE OUR FATHER

Our Father which art in heaven
He is our Father. There is nothing real in us which does not come from him. We belong to him. He loves us, since he loves himself and we are his. . . . We do not have to search for him, we only have to change the direction in which we are looking. It is for him to search for us. We must be happy in the knowledge that he is infinitely beyond our reach. Thus we can be certain that the evil in us, even if it overwhelms our whole being, in no way sullies the divine purity, bliss, and perfection.

Hallowed be thy name
God alone has the power to name himself. His name is unpronounceable for human lips. His name is his word. It is the Word of God. . . . Man has access to

48

this name, although it also is transcendent. It shines in the beauty and order of the world and it shines in the interior light of the human soul. This name is holiness itself; there is no holiness outside it; it does not therefore have to be hallowed. In asking for its hallowing we are asking for something that exists eternally, with full and complete reality, so that we can neither increase nor diminish it, even by an infinitesimal fraction. To ask for that which exists, that which exists really, infallibly, eternally, quite independently of our prayer, that is the perfect petition.

Thy kingdom come

This concerns something to be achieved, something not yet here. The Kingdom of God means the complete filling of the entire soul of intelligent creatures with the Holy Spirit. The Spirit bloweth where he listeth? We can only invite him. We must not even try to invite him in a definite and special way to visit us or anyone else in particular, or even everybody in general; we must just invite him purely and simply, so that our thought of him is an invitation, a longing cry. It is as when one is in extreme thirst, ill with thirst; then one no longer thinks of the act of drinking in relation to oneself, or even of the act of drinking in a general way. One merely thinks of water, actual water itself, but the image of water is like a cry from our whole being.

Thy will be done

We are only absolutely, infallibly certain of the will of God concerning the past. Everything that has happened, whatever it may be, is in accordance with the will of the almighty Father. That is implied by the notion of almighty power. The future also, whatever it may contain, once it has come about, will have come about in conformity with the will of God. We can neither add to nor take from this conformity. In this clause, therefore, after an upsurging of our desire toward the possible, we are once again asking for that which is. Here, however, we are not concerned with an eternal reality such as the holiness of the Word, but with what happens in the time order. Nevertheless we are asking for the infallible and eternal conformity of everything in time with the will of God. . . . We have to desire that everything that has happened should have happened, and nothing else. We have to do so, not because what has happened is good in our eyes, but because God has permitted it, and because the obedience of the course of events to God is in itself an absolute good.

On earth as it is in heaven

The association of our desire with the almighty will of God should be extended to spiritual things. Our own spiritual ascents and falls, and those of the beings we love, have to do with the other world, but they are also events that take place here below, in time. On that account they are details in the immense sea of events and are tossed about with the ocean in a way conforming to the will of God. Since our failures of the past have come about, we have to desire that they should have come about. We have to extend this desire into the future, for the day when it will have become the past. It is a necessary correction of the petition that the kingdom of God should come. We have to cast aside all other desires for the sake of our desire for eternal life, but we should desire eternal life itself with renunciation. We must not even become attached to detachment.

Give us this day our daily bread—

—the bread which is supernatural. Christ is our bread. We can only ask to have him now. Actually he is always there at the door of our souls, wanting to enter in, though he does not force our consent. If we agree to his entry, he enters; directly we cease to want him, he is gone. We cannot bind our will today for tomorrow; we cannot make a pact with him that tomorrow he will be within us, even in spite of ourselves. Our consent to his presence is the same as his presence. Consent is an act; it can only be actual, that is to say in the present. We have not been given a will that can be applied to the future. . . .

Bread is a necessity for us. We are beings who continually draw our energy from outside, for as we receive it we use it up in effort. If our energy is not daily renewed, we become feeble and incapable of movement. Besides actual food, in the literal sense of the word, all incentives are sources of energy for us. Money, ambition, consideration, decorations, celebrity, power, our loved ones, everything that puts into us the capacity for action is like bread. . . . All these objects of attachment go together with food, in the ordinary sense of the word, to make up the daily bread of this world. . . .

There is a transcendent energy whose source is in heaven, and this flows into us as soon as we wish for it. It is a real energy; it performs actions through the agency of our souls and of our bodies.

We should ask for this food. At the moment of asking, and by the very fact that we ask for it, we know that God will give it to us. . . .

And forgive us our debts, as we also forgive our debtors
At the moment of saying these words we must have already remitted everything that is owing to us. This not only includes reparation for any wrongs we think we have suffered, but also gratitude for the good we think we have done, and it applies in a quite general way to all we expect from people and things, to all we consider as our due and without which we should feel ourselves to have been frustrated. All these are the rights that we think the past has given us over the future. . . . That is the claim we have to renounce.

justice, too?

To have forgiven our debtors is to have renounced the whole of the past in a lump. It is to accept that the future should still be virgin and intact, strictly united to the past by bonds of which we are ignorant, but quite free from the bonds our imagination thought to impose upon it. It means that we accept the possibility that this will happen, and that it may happen to us in particular; it means that we are prepared for the future to render all our past life sterile and vain. In renouncing at one stroke all the fruits of the past without exception, we can ask of God that our past sins may not bear their miserable fruits of evil and error. . . .

The forgiveness of debts is spiritual poverty, spiritual nakedness, death. If we accept death completely, we can ask God to make us live again, purified from the evil in us. For to ask him to forgive us our debts is to ask him to wipe out the evil in us. Pardon is purification.

And lead us not into temptation, but deliver us from evil
After having contemplated the name, the kingdom, and the will of God, after having received the supernatural bread and having been purified from evil, the soul is ready for that true humility which crowns all virtues. Humility consists of knowing that in this world the whole soul, not only what we term the ego in its totality, but also the supernatural part of the soul, which is God present in it, is subject to time and to the vicissitudes of change. There must be absolute acceptance . . .

The Our Father contains all possible petitions; we cannot conceive of any prayer not already contained in it. It is to prayer what Christ is to humanity. It is impossible to say it once through, giving the fullest possible attention to each word, without a change, infinitesimal perhaps but real, taking place in the soul.

BIBLE SELECTION
Luke 11:1–9

[Jesus] was praying in a certain place, and after he had finished, one of his disciples said to him, "Lord, teach us to pray, as John taught his disciples." He said to them, "When you pray, say:

"Father, hallowed be your name.
  Your kingdom come.
  Give us each day our daily bread.
  And forgive us our sins,
    for we ourselves forgive everyone indebted to us.
  And do not bring us to the time of trial."

And he said to them, "Suppose one of you has a friend, and you go to him at midnight and say to him, 'Friend, lend me three loaves of bread; for a friend of mine has arrived, and I have nothing to set before him.' And he answers from within, 'Do not bother me; the door has already been locked, and my children are with me in bed; I cannot get up and give you anything.' I tell you, even though he will not get up and give him anything because he is his friend, at least because of his persistence he will get up and give him whatever he needs.

"So I say to you; Ask, and it will be given you; search, and you will find; knock, and the door will be opened for you."

DISCUSSION QUESTIONS

The following can be used for discussion within a small group, or used for journal reflections by individuals:

1. Have I been open to the possibility of a direct encounter with God? If not, why?
2. How have I entered into an experience of work, prayerfully, in solidarity with those who are less fortunate than myself?
3. Have I reflected deeply on the sufferings of Christ?

SUGGESTED EXERCISES

The following exercises can be done by individuals, shared between spiritual friends, or used in the context of a small group. Choose one or more of the following:

1. Often we recite the Lord's Prayer in haste or thoughtlessly. As an exercise, slow down the Lord's Prayer, praying it phrase by phrase and word by word.
2. Interweave an experience of prayer with an experience of intense work or labor. Pray while running or exercising; pray while lifting or rowing a boat. Listen for God's word to you in the middle of such effort.
3. Learn the Lord's Prayer in a language other than your own: listen for the beauty and sweetness of the recited words: in French, in Greek, in Spanish.
4. Listen to chanted prayers (there are many good compact discs offering chant); experience the sweetness of Christ in this unusual way.

REFLECTIONS

The Lord's Prayer is, without question, the grandest prayer of all. Nothing has ever equaled it in sheer power and majesty. More has been written about it than any other prayer in the history of humankind.

And to think that this prayer is the result of a simple request by the disciples that Jesus would teach them to pray. By responding to their request with the "Our Father" Jesus shows himself to be the absolute Master of prayer, as he is of all matters of life. Instead of giving them (and us) a lecture on prayer, he prays a prayer that teaches them (and us) to pray. It encompasses everything necessary to our unfolding relationship with our heavenly Father. We only move beyond it to the extent that we stay within it.

I marvel at and learn from the many reflections that have been written on the Lord's Prayer, including these compassionate words of Simone Weil. To know even a little of the sad times (including the Nazi occupation of her French homeland) under which she had to live and write gives power and poignancy to her reflections on "forgive us our debts, as we also forgive our debtors." When Weil writes, "The forgiveness of debts is spiritual poverty, spiritual nakedness, death," she is speaking of a reality deeper than many of us can bear. Indeed, who could see what she saw and declare that "the future should still be virgin and intact"? Only by the grace of God, only by the grace of God.

RICHARD J. FOSTER

GOING DEEPER

The Simone Weil Reader, edited by George A. Panichas (New York: David McKay, 1977). This 500-page book contains a variety of selections that show her piety, her vitality, her intellectuality. In the introduction, Panichas writes, "When one considers the exigencies of the historical era into which she was 'thrown,' the barbarity and brutality that it occasioned, the explosive cruelty and ugly hatreds that it engendered; when one thinks, in short, of the terrible and terrifying conditions—the collective disadvantages—of life in the secular pagan world that is ours, Simone Weil remains for us an astonishing example, as well as a reminding criterion, of the courage of faith."

SIMONE WEIL, *Waiting for God*, translated by Emma Crauford (New York: Harper & Row, 1973). This volume includes some of Weil's best-known essays, including "Friendship," "Last Thoughts," "Concerning the Our Father," and "Spiritual Autobiography." Many consider it her most important work.

Simone Weil, writings selected and with an introduction by Eric O. Springsted (Maryknoll, NY: Orbis Books, 1998). The selections have all been taken from the latter part of her life and have been thematically arranged under such headings as the love of God, love and faith, justice and human society.

ERIC O. SPRINGSTED, *Simone Weil and the Suffering of Love* (Cambridge, MA: Cowley Publications, 1986). This is a study of Weil's account of the place of suffering in the world. She was one of the few modern intellectuals to worry herself about this pressing subject.

Fasting

———

Catherine Marshall

(1914–1983)

———

Catherine Marshall first came to national prominence after the death of her husband, Peter Marshall, a native of Scotland who was a well-known Presbyterian minister and preacher in the United States as well as Chaplain of the United States Senate. She wrote a memoir about him, *A Man Called Peter*, which became a best-seller.

Marshall had some training as a journalist. A gifted storyteller, she had great capacity for spiritual reflection and went on to write a large number of books on prayer and spirituality. Her books have sold in the millions. Her novel *Christy* has enjoyed wide popularity. After her second marriage, to Leonard LeSourd, Marshall continued writing and also became a publisher.

In this selection on fasting from criticalness, notice how vivid she makes the relationship with God. It seems clear that she and the Lord have a lively dialogue going, one that often involves some resistance on her part, a resistance that reminds us of the relationships Abraham and Moses had with the Almighty.

Notice, also, how willingly Catherine declares her faults in a public way. Because she does so here, we can learn something about our own sinfulness.

A CLOSER WALK

A *Fasting on Criticalness*

The Lord continues to deal with me about my critical spirit, convicting me that I have been wrong to judge any person or situation:

> Do not judge, or you too will be judged. For in the same way you judge others, you will be judged, and with the measure you use, it will be measured to you.
> (Matt. 7:1–2; NIV)

One morning last week He gave me an assignment: *for one day I was to go on a "fast" from criticism. I was not to criticize anybody about anything.*

Into my mind crowded all the usual objections. "But then what happens to value judgments? You Yourself, Lord, spoke of 'righteous judgment.' How could society operate without standards and limits?"

All such resistance was brushed aside. "Just obey Me without questioning: an absolute fast on any critical statements for this day."

As I pondered this assignment, I realized there was an even humorous side to this kind of fast. What did the Lord want to show me?

The experiment

For the first half of the day, I simply felt a void, almost as if I had been wiped out as a person. This was especially true at lunch with my husband, Len, my mother, son Jeff, and my secretary Jeanne Sevigny, present. Several topics came up (school prayer, abortion, the ERA amendment) about which I had definite opinions. I listened to the others and kept silent. Barbed comments on the tip of my tongue about certain world leaders were suppressed. In our talkative family no one seemed to notice.

Bemused, I noticed that my comments were not missed. The federal government, the judicial system, and the institutional church could apparently get along fine without my penetrating observations. But still I didn't see what this fast on criticism was accomplishing—until mid-afternoon.

For several years I had been praying for one talented young man whose life had gotten sidetracked. Perhaps my prayers for him had been too negative. That afternoon, a specific, positive vision for this life was dropped into my mind with God's unmistakable hallmark on it—joy.

Ideas began to flow in a way I had not experienced in years. Now it was apparent what the Lord wanted me to see. My critical nature had not corrected a single one of the multitudinous things I found fault with. What it *had* done was to stifle my own creativity—in prayer, in relationships, perhaps even in writing—ideas that He wanted to give me.

Last Sunday night in a Bible study group, I told of my Day's Fast experiment. The response was startling. Many admitted that criticalness was the chief problem in their offices, or in their marriages, or with their teenage children.

The result

My own character flaw here is not going to be corrected overnight. But in thinking this problem through the past few days, I find the most solid scriptural basis possible for dealing with it. (The Greek word translated "judge" in King James, becomes "criticize" in Moffatt.) All through the Sermon on the Mount, Jesus sets Himself squarely against our seeing other people and life situations through this negative lens.

What He is showing me so far can be summed up as follows:

1. A critical spirit focuses us on ourselves and makes us unhappy. We lose perspective and humor.
2. A critical spirit blocks the positive creative thoughts God longs to give us.
3. A critical spirit can prevent good relationships between individuals and often produces retaliatory criticalness.
4. Criticalness blocks the work of the Spirit of God: love, good will, mercy.
5. Whenever we see something genuinely wrong in another person's behavior, rather than criticize him or her directly, or—far worse—gripe about him behind his back, we should ask the Spirit of God to do the correction needed.

Convicted of the true destructiveness of a critical mind-set, on my knees I am repeating this prayer: "Lord, I repent of this sin of judgment. I am deeply sorry for having committed so gross an offense against You and against myself so continually. I claim Your promise of forgiveness and seek a new beginning."

BIBLE SELECTION
Isaiah 58:3–9

"Why do we fast, but you do not see?
    Why humble ourselves, but you do not notice?"
Look, you serve your own interest on your fast day,
    and oppress all your workers.
Look, you fast only to quarrel and to fight
    and to strike with a wicked fist.
Such fasting as you do today
    will not make your voice heard on high.
Is such the fast that I choose,
    a day to humble oneself?
Is it to bow down the head like a bulrush,
    and to lie in sackcloth and ashes?
Will you call this a fast,
    a day acceptable to the LORD?

Is not this the fast that I choose:
    to loose the bonds of injustice,
    to undo the thongs of the yoke,

to let the oppressed go free,
    and to break every yoke?
Is it not to share your bread with the hungry,
    and bring the homeless poor into your house;
when you see the naked, to cover them,
    and not to hide yourself from your own kin?
Then your light shall break forth like the dawn,
    and your healing shall spring up quickly;
your vindicator shall go before you,
    the glory of the LORD shall be your rear guard.
Then you shall call, and the LORD will answer;
    you shall cry for help, and he will say, Here I am.

DISCUSSION QUESTIONS

The following can be used for discussion within a small group, or used for journal reflections by individuals:

1. How can I enlarge my idea about fasting? Should I consider abstaining from certain practices (like watching television or reading news media or making frequent value judgments about other people, even when these may be legitimate opinions)?
2. Are there other valid kinds of fasting, not mentioned by Marshall, which could be considered?

SUGGESTED EXERCISES

The following exercises can be done by individuals, shared between spiritual friends, or used in the context of a small group. Choose one or more of the following:

1. Consider "a fast from criticalness" for one day.
2. Pray over a particular personality trait of yours, one from which you would like to "fast," and consider writing in your journal about it. Express your struggle as a dialogue between you and the Lord.

REFLECTIONS

The central idea in fasting is the voluntary denial of an otherwise normal function for the sake of intense spiritual activity. Now, when we understand fasting from this perspective we see its reasonableness as well as its broader dimensions. The Catherine Marshall reading helps us see these broader dimensions by teaching us about a way of fasting that is not from food but from a critical spirit. Then as she chronicles her day we see the intense spiritual activity she enters, especially as it relates to the young man for whom she was praying.

One of the first things we learn in experiences of fasting is how it reveals what controls us. You see, we cover up with food and other good things what is inside of us, but in experiences of fasting these come to the surface. Did you notice how true this was in Catherine Marshall's experiment? She learned how dependent she was on criticism even to feel like a whole person and how utterly bankrupt her critical insights were at creating positive change in anyone or anything. She saw what was controlling her, and this released her to begin moving in a new direction, a direction free from a critical spirit. The same will be true for you and for me.

RICHARD J. FOSTER

GOING DEEPER

CATHERINE MARSHALL, *A Closer Walk* (Old Tappan, NJ: Chosen Books/Revell, 1986). Drawn from Catherine's journals, this book offers practical wisdom on many aspects of Christian living. She is quick to admit her flaws, which is encouraging to the reader.

CATHERINE MARSHALL, *Something More* (New York: Avon, 1974). This book is an extended and very helpful discussion on how to rely on biblical support during times of disquieting change.

CATHERINE MARSHALL, *Meeting God at Every Turn* (Carmel, NY: Guideposts, 1980). This book is not quite a memoir, but in it Catherine uses her personal history, from early childhood through two marriages, to show how God was with her at every turn.

John Henry Newman

(1801–1890)

———

John Henry Newman is one of the most gifted and imaginative figures in English religious history. Over his long lifetime, first as an Anglican clergyman and later as a Roman Catholic priest, he spoke, wrote, and published on a wide variety of religious topics.

Newman was the first of six children born in London to middle-class parents. His father had a business crisis in 1816, from which the family never recovered. That same year Newman experienced a five-month conversion to faith; at this time he became convinced that God was calling him to a celibate life.

Also in 1816 Newman began his career at Oxford, where he soon distinguished himself; in 1822 he was elected a Fellow of Oriel College. As an Anglican preacher and writer of religious tracts, especially while serving as Vicar of St. Mary's, the University Church in Oxford, he had wide influence.

In the 1830s, while traveling in Italy, Newman was drawn to Catholicism. He later converted to Rome. He established a house of prayer on the outskirts of Oxford, at Littlemore. He also helped to found the first Oratory in England, at Birmingham, and the Oratory in London.

Newman's many works include *Essay on the Development of Christian Doctrine, Apologia Pro Vita Sua* (his spiritual autobiography), *A Grammar of Assent, The Idea of a University*, and a very important essay, *On Consulting the Faithful in Matters of Doctrine*. He also wrote fiction and poetry. His poem "Lead Kindly Light" became a well-known hymn. Although he never became a bishop, he was named a cardinal in 1879, at the age of 78.

Newman was intensely scriptural. In this selection on fasting, notice how he leads from scriptural examples: Jacob, Moses, and Daniel. Notice, too, how he continually focuses on Christ.

PAROCHIAL AND PLAIN SERMONS

Fasting, a Source of Trial

Since prayer is not only the weapon, ever necessary and sure, in our conflict with the powers of evil, but a deliverance from evil is ever implied as the object of prayer, it follows that all texts whatever which speak of our addressing and prevailing on Almighty God, with prayer and fasting, do, in fact, declare this conflict and promise this victory over the evil one.

Thus, in the parable, the importunate widow, who represents the Church in prayer, is not only earnest *with* God, but *against* her adversary. "Avenge me of mine adversary," she says and our "adversary" is "the devil, who, like a roaring lion, walketh about seeking whom he may devour; whom resist," adds St. Peter, "steadfast in the faith". . . .

Jacob, Moses, and Daniel

This too is signified to us in the account of Jacob's conflict. He, like our Saviour, was occupied in it *through* the night. Who it was whom he was permitted to meet in that solitary season, we are not told; but He with whom he wrestled gave him strength to wrestle, and at last left a token on him, as if to show that he had prevailed only by the condescension of Him over whom he prevailed. So strengthened, he persevered till the morning broke, and asked a blessing; and He whom he asked did bless him, giving him a new name, in memory of his success. "Thy name shall be called no more Jacob, but Israel; for as a prince hast thou power with God and with men, and hast prevailed" (Gen. 32:28).

In like manner, Moses passed one of his forty days' fasts in confession and intercession for the people, who had raised the golden calf. "Thus I fell down before the Lord forty days and forty nights, as I fell down at the first; because the Lord had said He would destroy you. I prayed therefore unto the Lord, and said, O Lord God, destroy not Thy people and Thine inheritance, which Thou hast redeemed through Thy greatness, which Thou hast brought forth out of Egypt with a mighty hand" (Deut. 9:25–26).

Again, both of Daniel's recorded fasts ended in a blessing. His first was intercessory for his people, and the prophecy of the seventy weeks was given him. The second was also rewarded with prophetical disclosures . . .

Angelic helpers

An Angel came to Daniel upon his fast; so too in our Lord's instance, Angels came and ministered unto Him; and so we too may well believe, and take comfort in the thought, that even now, Angels are especially sent to those who thus seek God. Not Daniel only, but Elijah too was, during his fast, strengthened by an Angel; an Angel appeared to Cornelius, while he was fasting, and in prayer, and I do really think, that there is enough in what religious persons may see around them, to serve to confirm this hope thus gathered from the word of God.

"He shall give His Angels charge over Thee, to keep Thee in all Thy ways" (Ps. 91:11); and the devil knows of this promise, for he used it in that very hour of temptation. He knows full well what our power is, and what is his own weakness. So we have nothing to fear while we remain within the shadow of the throne of the Almighty. "A thousand shall fall beside Thee, and ten thousand at Thy right hand, but it shall not come nigh Thee."

Secure in Christ

While we are found in Christ, we are partakers of His security. He has broken the power of Satan; He has gone "upon the lion and adder, the young lion and the dragon hath He trod under His feet"; and henceforth evil spirits, instead of having power over us, tremble and are affrighted at every true Christian. They know he has that in him which makes him their master, that he may, if he will, laugh them to scorn, and put them to flight. They know this well, and bear it in mind, in all their assaults upon him; sin alone gives them power over him; and their great object is, to make him sin, and therefore to surprise him into sin, knowing they have no other way of overcoming him. They try to scare him by the appearance of danger, and so to surprise him; or they approach stealthily and covertly to seduce him, and so to surprise him. But except by taking him at unawares, they can do nothing.

Therefore let us be, my brethren, "not ignorant of their devices"; and as knowing them, let us watch, fast, and pray, let us keep close under the wings of the Almighty, that He may be our shield and buckler. Let us pray Him to make known to us His will—to teach us our faults—to take from us whatever may offend Him—and to lead us in the way everlasting.

BIBLE SELECTION
Genesis 32:24–30

Jacob was left alone; and a man wrestled with him until daybreak. When the man saw that he did not prevail against Jacob, he struck him on the hip socket; and Jacob's hip was put out of joint as he wrestled with him. Then he said, "Let me go, for the day is breaking." But Jacob said, "I will not let you go, unless you bless me." So he said to him, "What is your name?" And he said, "Jacob." Then the man said, "You shall no longer be called Jacob, but Israel, for you have striven with God and with humans, and have prevailed." Then Jacob asked him, "Please tell me your name." But he said, "Why is it that you ask my name?" And there he blessed him. So Jacob called the place Peniel, saying, "For I have seen God face to face, and yet my life is preserved."

DISCUSSION QUESTIONS

The following can be used for discussion within a small group, or used for journal reflections by individuals:

1. How do I see the correlation between fasting and prayer?
2. What would make me more conversant with fasting as a spiritual practice?
3. Have I experienced "the adversary" during any times of intense prayer or fasting? How should I handle this experience?

SUGGESTED EXERCISES

The following exercises can be done by individuals, shared between spiritual friends, or used in the context of a small group. Choose one or more of the following:

1. Design and undertake a modest type of fasting or abstinence (from a specific food item or another form of activity), one that you feel will not be too burdensome for you to maintain. Designate the period of time you wish to continue the fast (again, not too long or too difficult). Now, connect this fasting with a special prayer intention. Observe the fast all the way through. If you break the fast at some point, don't give up, but resume it as soon as you can until the appointed time you had planned to end the fast.
2. Write a reflection on the meaning of the fast you have chosen. What made you choose this particular form of fasting? Are you in dialogue with God about it? If temptations or trials come, record and describe the experience.
3. While you are fasting, use the prayerful imagination to be conscious of God's protection for you during times of trial. You may wish to think of this in terms of angels or in another scriptural way.

REFLECTIONS

Spiritual warfare is a subject of much interest today. Of course, we blithely assume that we are the ones who have discovered the idea, totally oblivious to the fact that Christians throughout the centuries have known far more than we about this vital subject. The Newman essay should, therefore, humble us. Here a nineteenth-century figure shows a nuanced understanding of spiritual warfare. Notice, for example, that he sees fasting as an accompanying means to the work of prayer; that is to say prayer is the overarching category under which fasting functions. This is a vital corrective for us today. Often our renewed interest (should I say "fascination"?) in fasting has a tendency to exalt it beyond all Scripture and reason. No, fasting has a vital but always subordinate function in the ongoing life of prayer.

Newman also understood that fasting as intense spiritual activity has the ability to so enflame prayer that it generates the power to conquer evil. He writes, "all texts whatever which speak of our addressing and prevailing on Almighty God, with prayer and fasting, do, in fact, declare this conflict and promise this victory over the evil one." We too can know the same victory over the evil one.

RICHARD J. FOSTER

GOING DEEPER

JOHN HENRY NEWMAN, *Parochial and Plain Sermons* (San Francisco: Ignatius, 1987). Newman has several sermons in this volume on fasting, abstinence, and self-denial.

BRIAN MARTIN, *John Henry Newman: His Life and Work* (Mahwah, NJ: Paulist, 1990). This biographical volume contains a number of black-and-white illustrations.

Augustine of Hippo

(354–430)

———

Augustine of Hippo is arguably the most important convert to Christianity after St. Paul. Born in Numidia, North Africa, the child of a Christian mother and a pagan father, Augustine was reared as a Christian but did not accept Christian belief and was not baptized. His mother, Monica, a devout Christian, attempted to reform her son from his life of sexual excess—he had a long-standing liaison with a woman who bore him a son—but she was unsuccessful at this.

Educated in philosophy and rhetoric at Carthage, Augustine went to Rome as a teacher of rhetoric. A year later he was appointed a professor at Milan, where three factors led to his conversion: Bishop Ambrose of Milan, Neoplatonism, and reading St. Paul.

Eventually Augustine experienced the grace of conversion and was baptized, along with his son, Adeodatus, in 387. Augustine soon took on a monastic way of life. Then, under popular pressure, he became a priest but continued living as a monk. Finally he became a bishop.

As a bishop, Augustine made about forty to fifty journeys. He wrote almost one hundred treatises, 200 letters, and 500 sermons that survive. Much of his work consisted of combating various heresies. His best-known works are his spiritual autobiography, *Confessions*, and his large-scale philosophical work, *The City of God*.

Augustine's emphasis in the following instruction on fasting is a counsel against worldliness. He knows that we sometimes engage in spiritual practices to prove to ourselves and others how devoted we really are. Here Augustine encourages us to think of fasting in the same way Jesus did, as a matter of inward rejoicing. Apparently, though some things may have changed since the fourth century, this isn't one of them.

THE LORD'S SERMON ON THE MOUNT

Cleansing of the Heart

There follows a precept about fasting which has to do with that same cleansing of the heart now under discussion. For in this work, too, a person must take heed that no spirit of self-display creeps in, no craving for human applause, which divides the heart and prevents it from being pure and candid for acquiring knowledge of God.

And when you fast, He says, *be not as the hypocrites, sad. For they disfigure their face that they may appear unto men to fast. Amen, I say to you, they have received their reward. But you, when you fast, anoint your heads and wash your faces that you appear not to men to fast but to your Father who is in secret; and your Father who seeth in secret will repay you* (Matt. 6:16–18).

It is evident from these precepts that our entire striving is to be directed towards inward joys, to keep ourselves from seeking outward rewards and becoming conformed to this world and forfeiting the promise of a blessedness which is the more solid and enduring as it is interior, and by which God chose us *to be made conformable to the image of His Son.*

Ostentation has two faces

But in this section particular attention must be given to the fact that there can be ostentation not only amid the splendor and pomp of material things but, also in the drab of sackcloth itself; and this is all the more dangerous as it masquerades in the guise of service to God. Thus, when a person is loudly conspicuous by an extravagant care of the body and by a display of clothes or other things, there is no question but that these very things stamp him a worldling and that he deceives no one if he puts on an air of sanctimoniousness. But as to a person who in making profession of his Christianity draws the eyes of people to himself by his extraordinary show of sackcloth and ashes: when he does this of his own accord and not under the duress of necessity, it can be gathered from the rest of his behavior whether he does this from contempt of care that can be dispensed with, or merely to make an impression. Here also the Lord tells us to beware of wolves under a sheep's skin: *By their fruits,* He said, *you shall know them.*

For when by some situations those very things are being taken away or denied which they have realized or wish to realize in this guise, then of necessity it becomes apparent whether he is a wolf in a sheep's skin or a sheep in its own. On the other hand, a Christian must not intrigue the eyes of men by his elaborate dress simply because frauds, too, only too often put on other dress—that which serves bare necessity—to deceive the unwary: plainly, such sheep, too, must not lay aside their own skins merely because at times wolves use the same to cover themselves.

Be joyful while you fast

Hence the common question, what is meant by His statement: *But you, when you fast, anoint your heads and wash your faces that you appear not to men to fast?* For certainly a person would not be in the right, were he, while we do have the everyday practice of washing our face, to prescribe that we ought also to have our hair anointed when we fast. Granting that all find this most objectionable, the necessary conclusion is that this precept of oiling the hair and washing the face refers to the interior man. Now, then, putting oil on the head refers to joy; washing the face, to cleanness; and therefore a person anoints his head when he rejoices within, in his mind and reason. As to the head, we are right in regarding it as that which has the pre-eminence in the soul and by which all else that concerns man is governed and controlled. And he does this who does not seek joy from without for the purpose of realizing the joy of the flesh in human praise. For the flesh, which ought to be subordinated, is in no way the head of the whole man. *No one* indeed *ever hated his own flesh*, as the Apostle says in stating the precept about loving one's wife; *and the head of the woman is the man*, and of the man Christ is the head.

In his fasting, therefore, let a man rejoice inwardly in the very fact that by this his fasting he is turning away from the pleasures of the world to make himself subject to Christ, who in the words of this precept wants him to have his head anointed. With the same intent he will be washing his face, that is, cleansing his heart whereby he is to see God, with no veil intervening because of a beclouding infirmity—firm and unshaken because he is clean and upright. *Wash yourselves*, He said, *be clean. Take away the iniquities from your souls and from the sight of my eyes.* From this filth, then, our face must be washed, the filth that offends the eyes of God. For *we, beholding the glory of the Lord with open face, shall be transformed into the same image.*

The divided heart

Often, too, reflection upon the things we need for carrying on this life injures the eye of our spirit and bedims it; and for the most part it divides our heart, so that in the things which to all appearances we do rightly in our relations with our fellow men, we actually fail to do them with the intention the Lord demands, that is, not because we love them, but merely because we wish to obtain some advantage from them in view of the needs of the present life. But we ought to do good to them motivated by their eternal welfare, not by some temporal concern of our own. May God, therefore, incline our heart to His testimonies and not to gain. For *the end of the commandment is charity from a pure heart, a good conscience, and an unfeigned faith.* He who looks after the interests of a brother with a view to his own needs in this life, certainly is not acting in a spirit of love; for he is not looking after the interests of one whom he ought to love as he loves himself, but after his own; or rather, not even after his own, since he is thus making his heart a divided heart and so preventing himself from seeing God, in the vision of whom alone is certain and lasting blessedness.

BIBLE SELECTION
Matthew 4:1–6

Then Jesus was led up by the Spirit into the wilderness to be tempted by the devil. He fasted forty days and forty nights, and afterwards he was famished. The tempter came and said to him, "If you are the Son of God, command these stones to become loaves of bread." But he answered, "It is written,

'One does not live by bread alone,
but by every word that comes from the mouth of God.'"

Then the devil took him to the holy city and placed him on the pinnacle of the temple, saying to him, "If you are the Son of God, throw yourself down; for it is written,

'He will command his angels concerning you,'
and 'On their hands they will bear you up,
so that you will not dash your foot against a stone.'"

Jesus said to him, "Again it is written, 'Do not put the Lord your God to the test.'"

DISCUSSION QUESTIONS

The following can be used for discussion within a small group, or used for journal reflections by individuals:

1. Have I used fasting—or any other spiritual practice—as a way of getting attention or showing off? Explain.
2. What are the practical difficulties of fasting in an entirely private way?
3. What are the benefits of not publicizing our intention to fast? Are some of these more practical than spiritual? Are there some spiritual benefits, too?

SUGGESTED EXERCISES

The following exercises can be done by individuals, shared between spiritual friends, or used in the context of a small group. Choose one or more of the following:

1. One way of fasting is to abstain from a certain kind of food or treat over a given period of time. Often, during Lent, we hear that people give up chocolate, or soft drinks, or desserts. Another version of fasting might be giving up meat—becoming a vegetarian—for a given time. These forms of abstinence are so commonplace and socially acceptable that they need not be perceived as "fasting." Consider doing one or more of these things without explaining to others that you are "fasting."
2. Reflect in your journal, or with a spiritual confidant, about the effect of "fasting and praying in secret." Are you putting one over on somebody? Or are you following the will of Christ?

REFLECTIONS

In an outward sense fasting is one of those spiritual disciplines which deal almost exclusively with physical matters—food and drink, eating and abstaining. In this respect it is very unlike other disciplines such as prayer and worship. Now, because it is a spiritual discipline dealing with physical matters it is critical that we pay careful attention to Augustine's counsel that we stay focused on the interior reality in fasting. This interior reality he describes for us as "inward joys." I like that. What he is underscoring by saying this is that in fasting we are learning by experience that we do not "live by bread alone, but by every word that proceeds from the mouth of God." Anyone who has ever experienced this reality knows that "inward joys" is a good description.

Augustine further warns us of the ostentation of sackcloth. This warning against outward show is not a way of changing the subject, for, once again, <u>he is calling us back to the intents of the heart</u>. Next, he notes that fasting is "a turning away from the pleasures of the world." Once again we are right on the subject of "inward joys" for in fasting we are learning by experience how to be sustained by divine pleasures rather than human pleasures. Put another way, <u>fasting is feasting—feasting on God alone</u>.

All of this, concludes Augustine, purifies our motives so that we are freed to do good to others for their good alone. Did you have any idea that there could be so many interior benefits to such an exterior act?

RICHARD J. FOSTER

GOING DEEPER

St. Augustine: Confessions, translated by Richard Pine-Coffin (New York: Penguin, 1961). This contemporary rendering of Augustine's personal conversion story gives us a fine appreciation of the meaning of grace.

St. Augustine: City of God, translated by Gerald Walsh, Demetrius Zema, Grace Monahan, and Daniel J. Honan (New York: Doubleday/Image, 1958). This abridged version, with an introduction by the distinguished French philosopher Etienne Gilson, provides a good introduction to Augustine's thought.

Augustine: Major Writings, edited by Benedict J. Groeschel (New York: Crossroad, 1995). This volume in the *Spiritual Legacy* series introduces us to a good cross section of Augustine's thought and spiritual advice. His chapter on "Augustine as a Spiritual Guide" is quite useful.

PETER BROWN, *Augustine of Hippo: A Biography* (Berkeley, CA: University of California Press, 1969). This biography continues to be well regarded for its scholarship and interpretation.

William Law

(1686–1761)

William Law, a devout Anglican priest, lived during the eighteenth-century Enlightenment, when science and reason were bringing a serious challenge to Christian devotion. His exposure to earlier writers like John Tauler, John Ruusbroec, and Thomas à Kempis prompted Law's work, *A Serious Call to a Devout and Holy Life*, which appeared in 1728. It became popular and has remained so.

Later in life, William Law became involved with the writings of the Protestant mystic Jakob Boehme. This brought him to an even deeper appreciation of the indwelling of Christ in the soul and the importance of the Atonement. These concerns were reflected in a second major work, *The Spirit of Love* (1752–54). He was an important factor in the English Evangelical Revival.

In his counsel on fasting, Law encourages us in this practice. He repeats the teaching of Jesus in order to clarify it. Jesus doesn't want to make fasting difficult or impractical; he doesn't mean for us to deceive others, especially close family members. Law wants to remind us of what is central in Jesus' teaching: namely, that we are not supposed to get puffed up or put on airs about our prayer practices. Notice how he makes this vivid by mentioning Cornelius the centurion (Acts 10).

A SERIOUS CALL TO A DEVOUT AND HOLY LIFE

Prayer and Fasting, Public or Private?

Private prayer, as it is opposed to prayer in public, does not suppose that no one is to have any witness of it. For husbands and wives, brothers and sisters, parents and children, masters and servants, tutors and pupils, are to be witnesses to one another of such devotion as may truly and properly be called private. It is far from being a duty to conceal such devotion from such near relations.

No objection to the chanting of a hymn
In all these cases, therefore, where such relations sometimes pray together in private and sometimes apart by themselves, the chanting of a Psalm can have nothing objected against it.

Our blessed Lord commands us when we fast to anoint our heads and wash our faces that we appear not unto men to fast, but unto our Father which is in secret.

But this only means that we must not make public ostentation to the world of our fasting.

For if no one was to fast in private or could be said to fast in private but he that had no witnesses of it, no one could keep a private fast but he that lived by himself. For every family must know who fasts in it. Therefore the privacy of fasting does not suppose such a privacy as excludes everybody from knowing it, but such a privacy as does not seek to be known abroad.

Cornelius's fasting

Cornelius the devout centurion, of whom the scripture saith that he gave much and prayed to God always, saith unto St. Peter, "Four days ago I was fasting until this hour" (Acts 10:30).

Now that this fasting was sufficiently private and acceptable to God appears from the vision of an angel with which the holy man was blessed at that time.

But that it was not so private as to be entirely unknown to others appears as from the relation of it here, so from what is said in another place, that he "called two of his household servants, and a devout soldier of them that waited upon him continually" (Acts 10:7). So that Cornelius his fasting was so far from being unknown to his family that the soldiers and they of his household were made devout themselves by continually waiting upon him, that is, by seeing and partaking of his good works.

The whole of the matter is this. The greater part of the world can be as private as they please; therefore, let them use this excellent devotion between God and themselves.

BIBLE SELECTIONS
Matthew 6:16–18; Acts 10:30–31 (KJV)

"And whenever you fast, do not look dismal, like the hypocrites, for they disfigure their faces so as to show others that they are fasting. Truly, I tell you, they have received their reward. But when you fast, put oil on your head and wash your face, so that your fasting may be seen not by others but by your Father who is in secret; and your Father who sees in secret will reward you."

And Cornelius said, Four days ago I was fasting until this hour; and at the ninth hour I prayed in my house, and, behold, a man stood before me in bright clothing, and said, Cornelius, thy prayer is heard, and thine alms are had in remembrance in the sight of God.

DISCUSSION QUESTIONS

The following can be used for discussion within a small group, or used for journal reflections by individuals:

1. How can I include fasting in my life in ways that are more confident and cheerful?
2. What approaches could help me to be unselfconscious and simple about fasting, almsgiving, and prayer?

SUGGESTED EXERCISE

The following exercise can be done by individuals, shared between spiritual friends, or used in the context of a small group.

1. In your journal make a list of attachments that may be holding you back from easygoing, freewheeling service to God. These are not necessarily bad things, just things that may have gotten somewhat out of balance in your life. Are you overcommitted? Do you find it hard to say no to certain requests? Consider the possibility of changing your practice for a time.

REFLECTIONS

I am always moved by the way William Law is able to penetrate to the heart of a matter. In this seemingly simple selection on "private prayer" and how it can never really be private he is attacking the spirit of legalism that so permeated his day, as it does ours. You see, the legalist will read Jesus' words about going into our closet and praying to God in secret and turn it into an absurdity. And Law highlights this absurdity by taking the legalist's efforts at secrecy to its logical conclusion: "For if no one was to fast in private or could be said to fast in private but he that had no witnesses of it, no one could keep a private fast but he that lived by himself."

Next, Law uses the example of Cornelius to show that a private fast acceptable to God need not be hidden from everybody. Did you wonder why he chose the example of Cornelius? There are many other fine biblical illustrations of this point, including Jesus himself. Why Cornelius? Precisely because Cornelius was the kind of person—a Gentile—whom the legalists of that day felt simply could not be acceptable to God. So by using Cornelius as his illustration Law gently causes readers—you and me— to examine their own legalisms by considering whom they might find unacceptable to God.

RICHARD J. FOSTER

GOING DEEPER

William Law: A Serious Call to a Devout and Holy Life and The Spirit of Love, edited by Paul G. Stanwood (Ramsey, NJ: Paulist, 1978). A volume in *The Classics of Western Spirituality* series, this book provides excellent biographical material on William Law, together with both the important texts mentioned in the subtitle. Two other distinguished William Law scholars have contributed to this volume: Austin Warren is the author of the introduction, and John E. Booty contributed the preface. The bibliography and indexes provide added depth for one who wants to know more about William Law.

Study

George MacDonald

(1824–1905)

———

George MacDonald is one of the most engaging and prolific creative writers of the Victorian era. A native of Aberdeen, Scotland, he became a Congregational minister, then a freelance preacher and lecturer.

In 1855 he published a poetic tragedy, *Within and Without,* and afterward made literature his profession, writing novels, fairy tales, poetry, and Christian allegories of the quest for God.

Phantastes: A Faerie Romance for Men and Women (1858) and *Lilith* (1895) were influential to many other writers, among them C. S. Lewis, who cited MacDonald as an influence on his conversion and his literary pursuits.

His best-known book for children is *At the Back of the North Wind* (1871). Other enduring stories by MacDonald are *The Princess and the Goblin* (1872) and its sequel, *The Princess and Curdie* (1873).

His works of Christian reflection have been collected in three volumes under the title *Unspoken Sermons.*

Although MacDonald was plagued by failure, poverty, and ill health, he was said to have a deep trust in God and a sunny, playful disposition.

In the selection that follows, George MacDonald helps us to study the Gospels more easily by his creative storytelling and pointed interpretation of the feeding of the four thousand. Like the Gospel writers themselves, he is presenting us with a vivid picture of Jesus in action and his encounter with incomprehension—both from the Pharisees and the disciples. Then he leads us more deeply into the text with his interpretation, helping us to understand Jesus' miracles as "the ordinary works of His Father, wrought small and swift that we might take them in."

CREATION IN CHRIST

The Cause of Spiritual Stupidity

> Do you not yet understand? (Mark 8:21)

After feeding the four thousand with seven loaves and a few small fishes, on the east side of the Sea of Galilee, Jesus, having crossed the lake, was met on the other side by certain Pharisees, whose attitude towards Him was such that He went again to the boat, and recrossed the lake. On the way the disciples considered that they had in the boat but a single loaf. Probably while the Lord was occupied with the Pharisees, one of them had gone and bought it, little thinking they were about to start again so soon.

Jesus, still occupied with the antagonism of the leaders of the people, and desirous of destroying their influence on His disciples, began to warn them against them. In so doing He made use of a figure they had heard Him use before—that of leaven as representing a hidden but potent and pervading energy. The kingdom of heaven, He had told them, was like leaven hid in meal, gradually leavening the whole of it. He now tells them to beware of the leaven of the Pharisees.

The disciples, whose minds were occupied with their lack of provisions, the moment they heard the word leaven, thought of bread, concluded it must be because of its absence that He spoke of leaven, and imagined perhaps a warning against some danger of defilement from Pharisaical cookery: "It is because we have taken no bread!" A leaven like that of the Pharisees was even then at work in their hearts; for the sign the Pharisees sought in the mockery of unbelief, they had had a few hours before, and had already, in respect of all that made it of value, forgotten.

Recalling the miracle

He addresses Himself to rouse in them a sense of their lack of confidence in God, which was the cause of their blunder as to His meaning. He reminds them of the two miracles with the loaves, and the quantity of fragments left beyond the need. From one of these miracles they had just come. It was not a day behind them, yet here they were doubting already!

He makes them go over the particulars of the miracles—hardly to refresh their memories—but to make their hearts dwell on them. For they had already forgotten or had failed to see their central revelation—the eternal fact of God's love and care and compassion. They knew the number of the men each time, the number of the loaves each time, the number of the baskets of fragments they had each time taken up, but they forgot the Love that had so broken the bread that its remnants twenty times outweighed its loaves.

The lesson of the miracle

Having thus questioned them like children, and listened as to the answers of children, He turns the light of their thoughts upon themselves, and, with an argument to the man which overlaps all the links of its own absolute logic, demands,

"How is it that you do not understand?" Then they did understand, and knew that He did not speak to them of the leaven of bread, but of the teaching of the Pharisees and of the Sadducees. He who trusts can understand; he whose mind is set at ease can discover a reason.

The lesson He would have had them learn from the miracle, the natural lesson, the only lesson worthy of the miracle, was, that God cared for His children, and could, did, and would provide for their necessities. This lesson they had not learned. No doubt the power of the miracle was some proof of His mission, but the love of it proved it better, for it made it worth proving: it was a throb of the Father's heart.

The reason for the miracle

The ground of the Master's upbraiding is not that they did not understand Him, but that they did not trust God. After all they had seen, they yet troubled themselves about bread. Because we easily imagine ourselves in want, we imagine God ready to forsake us. The miracles of Jesus were the ordinary works of His Father, wrought small and swift that we might take them in. The lesson of them was that help is always within God's reach when His children want it. Their design [was] to show what God is—not that Jesus was God, but that His Father was God—that is, was what He was. No other kind of God could be, or be worth believing in, no other notion of God be worth having.

The mission undertaken by the Son, was not to show Himself as having all power in heaven and earth, but to reveal His Father, to show Him to men such as He is, that men may know Him, and knowing, trust Him. It were a small boon indeed that God should forgive men, and not give Himself. It would be but to give them back themselves, and less than God just as He is will not comfort men for the essential sorrow of their existence. Only God the gift can turn that sorrow into essential joy: Jesus came to give them God, who is eternal life.

The Father's provision

Those miracles of feeding gave the same lesson to their eyes, their hands, their mouths, that His words gave to their ears when He said, "Do not be anxious about what you shall eat, or what you shall drink. . . . your heavenly Father knows that you have need of these things. But seek first His kingdom and His righteousness, and all these things shall be yours as well." So little had they learned it yet, that they remembered the loaves but forgot the Father—as men in their theology forget the very Logos.

Thus forgetting, they were troubled about provision for the day, and the moment leaven was mentioned, thought of bread. "What else could He mean?" The connection was plain! The Lord reminds them of the miracle, which had they believed after its true value, they would not have been so occupied as to miss what He meant. It had set forth to them the truth of God's heart towards them; revealed the loving care without which He would not be God.

In God's care

The care of the disciples was care for the day, not for the morrow; the word *morrow* must stand for any and every point of the future. The next hour, the next moment, is as much beyond our grasp and as much in God's care, as that a hundred years away. Care for the next minute is just as foolish as care for the morrow, or for a day in the next thousand years—in neither can we do anything, in both God is doing everything. Those claims only of the morrow which have to be prepared today are of the duty of today. The moment which coincides with work to be done, is the moment to be minded; the next is nowhere till God has made it.

Their lack of bread seems to have come from no neglect, but from the immediacy of the Lord's re-embarkation. At the same time, had there been a want of foresight, that was not the kind of thing the Lord cared to reprove. It was not this and that fault He had come to set right, but the primary evil of life without God, the root of all evils, from hatred to discourtesy. Certain minor virtues also, prudence among the rest, would thus at length be almost, if not altogether, superseded.

The immediate duty

If a man forget a thing, God will see to that: man is not lord of his memory or his intellect. But man is lord of his will, his action; and is then verily to blame when, remembering a duty, he does not do it, but puts it off, and *so* forgets it. If a man lay himself out to do the immediate duty of the moment, wonderfully little forethought, I suspect, will be found needful. That forethought only is right which has to determine duty, and pass into action. To the foundation of yesterday's work well done, the work of the morrow will be sure to fit. Work done is of more consequence for the future than the foresight of an archangel.

BIBLE SELECTION
Mark 8:1–21

In those days when there was again a great crowd without anything to eat, he called his disciples and said to them, "I have compassion for the crowd, because they have been with me now for three days and have nothing to eat. If I send them away hungry to their homes, they will faint on the way—and some of them have come from a great distance." His disciples replied, "How can one feed these people with bread here in the desert?" He asked them, "How many loaves do you have?" They said, "Seven." Then he ordered the crowd to sit down on the ground; and he took the seven loaves, and after giving thanks he broke them and gave them to his disciples to distribute; and they distributed them to the crowd. They had also a few small fish; and after blessing them, he ordered that these too should be distributed. They ate and were filled; and they took up the broken pieces left over, seven baskets full. Now there were about four thousand people. And he sent them away. And immediately he got into the boat with his disciples and went to the district of Dalmanutha.

The Pharisees came and began to argue with him, asking him for a sign from heaven, to test him. And he sighed deeply in his spirit and said, "Why does this generation ask for a sign? Truly I tell you, no sign will be given to this generation." And he left them, and getting into the boat again, he went across to the other side.

Now the disciples had forgotten to bring any bread; and they had only one loaf with them in the boat. And he cautioned them, saying, "Watch out—beware of the yeast of the Pharisees and the yeast of Herod." They said to one another, "It is because we have no bread." And becoming aware of it, Jesus said to them, "Why are you talking about having no bread? Do you still not perceive or understand? Are your hearts hardened? Do you have eyes, and fail to see? Do you have ears, and fail to hear? And do you not remember? When I broke the five loaves for the five thousand, how many baskets full of broken pieces did you collect?" They said to him, "Twelve." "And the seven for the four thousand, how many baskets full of broken pieces did you collect?" And they said to him, "Seven." Then he said to them, "Do you not yet understand?"

DISCUSSION QUESTIONS

The following can be used for discussion within a small group, or used for journal reflections by individuals:

1. What lesson do I take from the feeding of the four thousand? What does this long-ago miracle say to me about my relationship to Jesus now?
2. Do I have the same weakness of faith that the disciples show in the Gospel story?

SUGGESTED EXERCISES

The following exercises can be done by individuals, shared between spiritual friends, or used in the context of a small group. Choose one or more of the following:

1. The central image in Jesus' teaching is that of bread. In particular he singles out the yeast, or leaven, which makes the bread rise, in order to teach about the reign of God. Consider having your group actually make a loaf of bread together, pounding the bread down and watching it rise. Because this is sometimes a lengthy process, perhaps one member could volunteer to get the process started, but have the group arrive in time to participate. This activity can become a form of study, just as MacDonald's creative interpretation of the Gospel story heightens our awareness of meaning.

2. Design a reflection around a single loaf of bread. In a group setting, break the bread and pass it around so that everyone can have a share. Let individuals comment on bread as a source of life and as a way of understanding God's providence and presence in our lives.

REFLECTIONS

The Scripture passage that George MacDonald unpacks for us is so instructive when we consider the spiritual discipline of study. We have a tendency to confine study to classrooms and books, but here Jesus is urging his disciples to study their experience so that they might come to trust in God. If they had simply studied what they had seen—Jesus' feeding of the five thousand and of the four thousand—they would have known that God is the One who gives in abundance and truly the One—the only One—they can trust to supply all their needs. But they did not study and so they could not trust.

In the Scripture lesson Jesus' final question to the disciples haunts us: "Do you not yet understand?" It is a question that searches us all through our days and creeps into our dreams at night: "Do you not yet understand?"

Have we not received rain and sunshine day after day? "Do you not yet understand?" Are we not blessed daily with the beauty and order of sky and sea, leaf and flower? "Do you not yet understand?" Do not our children show us the face of faith and trust? "Do you not yet understand?"

RICHARD J. FOSTER

GOING DEEPER

George MacDonald: Creation in Christ, edited by Rolland Hein (Wheaton, IL: Harold Shaw, 1976). This is an excellent collection of devotional writings by MacDonald, focusing on the figure of Jesus Christ.

George MacDonald: An Anthology, edited by C. S. Lewis (New York: Simon and Schuster, 1996). In the preface to this anthology, Lewis says of MacDonald, "I know hardly any other writer who seems closer, or more continually close, to the spirit of Christ himself."

GEORGE MACDONALD, *Diary of an Old Soul* (Minneapolis, MN: Augsburg, 1975). This is a collection of MacDonald's devotional poetry.

GEORGE MACDONALD, *Life Essential: The Hope of the Gospel* (Wheaton, IL: Harold Shaw, 1974). A short work on the Gospels that has inspired many generations of Christians.

Lilias Trotter

(1853–1928)

Lilias Trotter led a remarkable life that took her far beyond the boundaries of her London upbringing. Born to a wealthy family, she had every advantage of education, travel, and culture. She also had a strong sense of Christian compassion for the poor.

During her twenties, Trotter showed promise as a visual artist. Her mentor, the distinguished painter and illustrator John Ruskin, believed she was a significant talent.

Meanwhile Trotter flung herself into volunteer work with the Young Women's Christian Association (YWCA) and the Welbeck Street Institute. There, she opened the first public restaurant in London for women and transformed a discarded nightclub into a hostel for women of the street, offering both shelter and training for wholesome employment.

But no one in London was fully prepared for Trotter's next amazing venture. In 1888, when she was thirty-four, she set out for North Africa with two women friends to organize a mission to the poor of Algeria. She did this, relying entirely on her personal means, independent of any organization, and not knowing one person nor a single sentence of Arabic. This was Christian zeal, indeed.

Within a decade, Trotter's North African ministry was well established, and she was known among the Algerians as a compassionate figure who cared for children and the sick. But even more remarkable, she was welcomed as a spiritual authority figure by Arab leaders. In 1902, at the age of forty-nine, she paid a historic visit to the *zaouria*, a fraternity house of the Sufi brotherhood, to discuss contemplative prayer with them.

For the rest of her life, Trotter pursued both a life of Christian discipline and creative artistry. Her illustrated books and pamphlets, among them *Parables of the Cross* and *Master of the Impossible*, spoke to her generation eloquently about the radical love of Jesus Christ. In *The Desert and the Sea*, her sketches and watercolors capture her almost forty-year love affair with Algeria.

In the selection that follows, taken from *The Way of the Sevenfold Secret*, which was published first in Arabic and then in English, Persian, and French, Trotter is encouraging her readers to study carefully the notion of leadership exemplified in Christ the Good Shepherd. Notice how she seems to be addressing not only her English readers but her Algerian readers with such phrases as "O brothers of the Road" and "You feel that your sheikh knows you through and through . . . ," yet her message is entirely Christian, <u>concentrating on the centrality of Jesus Christ</u>.

THE WAY OF THE SEVENFOLD SECRET

The Secret of Leadership

If we go back to the end of the last chapter, we shall see that there is a link between that one and this one. ["I am come that they might have life, and that they might have it more abundantly" (John 10:10).] We have seen there that the first stage is to be led forth by the Shepherd. We need more than safety, we need a Saviour. . . .

In this new chapter we see a new step, for under the similitudes of the Bread and the Light and the Door, Christ the Lord invites those who are unsaved to be partakers of His salvation, but in these words on the Shepherd and His sheep He speaks to those who have crossed the threshold of salvation, and have entered His kingdom.

God has been preparing you

In this as in other things, O brothers of the Road, we recognise that God has been preparing you through many centuries, that you should have your share in His secrets, which He has revealed in these names of Jesus Christ.

For you are men who feel that you need leadership. When you have found a leader who is after your own heart, you yield yourselves to follow him. You yield this obedience, first to the founder (*waly*) of your order, and under him to the sheikh representing him, who can interpret his teaching into your daily life. Each one in starting on the inward journey, puts himself under the leadership of his director, and yields him an obedience that is complete. Nothing is accounted too hard that his wisdom and his will appoint to the disciple. You feel that your sheikh knows you through and through, and into his hands you deliver yourself, as you express it, as a corpse into the hands of the washer, that he may rid you of all impurity. For this you desire a leader who is wholly trustworthy, for it is a great trust that you put in him, even the well-being of your soul during the time of its probation here on earth.

God chose Christ our Lord

God Most High, who created us and you, knows that it is in our hearts to seek a Leader. He knows that this Leader must be a man like ourselves, who has trodden the path by which He would lead us: but it is also in the counsels of God, that this Leader, to lead us aright must be more than man, even as the sheep, who have like ourselves the inclination to follow are not safe when they are following other sheep, but only when they are following the shepherd.

Therefore, God Chose Christ our Lord, before He was born on the earth, because in Him the Divine Leadership and the human leadership meet in one, for He is *"declared to be the Son of God with power"* (Rom. 1:4), in the Spirit; while in the flesh—He is *"the Son of Man"* (John 5:27). God spoke of Him in the prophecy of Isaiah—*"Behold I have given Him for a Leader and Commander to the people"* (Isa. 55:4). He is by the authority of God the true subduer by constraint, but the constraint of love, and whenever in His days upon earth He called to one or another, "Follow Me," it is told us that they arose and left all, to follow Him. . . .

Not *afraid for His sheep*

Now the first thing that we are told about the leadership of the Shepherd in the passage before us, is that He is not afraid for His sheep. He knows the dangers, around them, but He calls them out. He goes to the fold in the early morning, where they lie sheltered and secure, and he goes out at the head of them, out into the wilderness. . . .

Therefore, my brother, for this first step of the way in which He calls you to walk with Him, put your hands by faith into His hands, and, though you cannot see Him, let Him look into your eyes and read your heart, and transfer to Him the true surrender that you have learned in the path of the Brotherhood, and that without a fear or a misgiving, for He can make no mistake. A new and wonderful longing will arise in your heart to know and do His will. And not only will your own faith and love be established by going forth with Him, but it is by witnessing to Him that you are able to draw others to seek His salvation.

Temptations *that meet the soul*

Now this tenth chapter of St. John tells us of the different temptations that meet the soul when it has set out in this path of obedience: they are described under the image of the dangers that beset the sheep.

First comes the similitude of a stranger who gives a countercall—that is, one who, under the pretence of friendship, would lure you from following Christ. It may well be that these whom God counts as strangers, may be the nearest in earthly relationship, for it is often these who try to draw the soul away. As it is written—*"A man's foes shall be they of his own household."* Whoever he be, this stranger, *flee from him* (Matt. 10:36).

Next, this chapter speaks of danger to the sheep under the figure of a thief ["The thief cometh not but for to steal and to kill and to destroy" (John 10:10)]. Satan is like the thief, for he comes silently and secretly, without warning, to rob us of God's grace and joy and strength, and to seek to destroy His life in our souls.

Then we see another danger under the figure of the hireling. The hireling is a picture of the world, that is only friendly while all is prosperous ["The hireling leaveth the sheep and fleeth" (John 10:12)], and leaves us carelessly to be a prey when distress comes. Foolish is the sheep that trusts this hireling.

Lastly, there is the danger of the wolf ["The wolf catcheth them, and scattereth the sheep" (John 10:12)]. The wolf stands for outward trouble that comes with violence, as persecution that is set on by the powers of hell to scatter Christ's followers. If it finds them close to the Good Shepherd they have nothing to fear in this, not even death itself, for as David said in the 23rd Psalm, *"The Lord is my Shepherd, I shall not want. Yea, though I walk through the valley of the shadow of death, I will fear no evil, for Thou art with me"* (Ps. 23:1,4). But if they are trusting the hireling, that is the world, to protect them, they are in an evil case.

Look at the Good Shepherd

Now we turn from all these enemies, the stranger, the thief, the hireling, and the wolf, who endanger those who follow afar off ["I am the Good Shepherd and know my sheep and am known of mine" (John 1:14)], and look at the Good Shepherd and the sheep who stay in His care. They are "His own," not by force, but because He has paid the price of His life for them, and none shall pluck them out of His Hand.

Instead of listening to the call of the stranger who tempts them, or the cry of the wolf which terrifies them, His sheep pay heed to His voice.

This means that you must look up with the vision of the heart to the Person of Christ, and listen for the impress of His will on your will through His words ["The words that I speak unto you, they are spirit, and they are life" (John 6:63)], that is, through the Book of the Gospel that was written to be the means of communication with the souls of His people. As you become familiar with them He will by His Spirit bring them to your memory as you need them, to be your defence in the dangers of the way, even as David said in the Psalms: *"Thy word have I hid in my heart that I might not sin against Thee"* (Ps. 119:11). You may grow so to follow His voice that even your thoughts will be brought *"into captivity to the obedience of Christ"* (2 Cor. 10:5). This bondage is perfect freedom, for we desire, He and we, only one and the same thing, and the true heartlove makes it all joy to follow, even if the path is narrow and rough.

BIBLE SELECTION
John 10:1–14, 27–28

"Very truly, I tell you, anyone who does not enter the sheepfold by the gate but climbs in by another way is a thief and a bandit. The one who enters by the gate is the shepherd of the sheep. The gatekeeper opens the gate for him, and the sheep hear his voice. He calls his own sheep by name and leads them out. When he has brought out all his own, he goes ahead of them, and the sheep follow him because they know his voice. They will not follow a stranger, but they will run from him because they do not know the voice of strangers." Jesus used this figure of speech with them, but they did not understand what he was saying to them.

So again Jesus said to them, "Very truly, I tell you, I am the gate for the sheep. All who came before me are thieves and bandits; but the sheep did not listen to them. I am the gate. Whoever enters by me will be saved, and will come in and go out and find pasture. The thief comes only to steal and kill and destroy. I came that they may have life, and have it abundantly.

"I am the good shepherd. The good shepherd lays down his life for the sheep. The hired hand, who is not the shepherd and does not own the sheep, sees the wolf coming and leaves the sheep and runs away—and the wolf snatches them and scatters them. The hired hand runs away because a hired hand does not care for the sheep. I am the good shepherd. I know my own and my own know me. . . . My sheep hear my voice. I know them, and they follow me. I give them eternal life, and they will never perish. No one will snatch them out of my hand."

DISCUSSION QUESTIONS

The following can be used for discussion within a small group, or used for journal reflections by individuals:

1. What kinds of study and reflection will best enable us to "enter in" to the understanding of leadership presented by Christ as Shepherd?
2. Consider the dangers that Trotter discerns in the passage from John: the stranger who under the guise of friendship would lure us away from God, the thief who seeks to rob us, the hireling who can't be trusted, the wolf. How can we discern these enemies in our own Christian path? What does Trotter suggest about the power of Jesus Christ as leader in helping us?

SUGGESTED EXERCISES

The following exercises can be done by individuals, shared between spiritual friends, or used in the context of a small group. Choose one or more of the following:

1. Identify and discuss styles of leadership that you yourself have observed: in your church, in your community, in your neighborhood. Does the Christian notion of Shepherd leadership have meaning in these situations? Discuss.
2. Without looking at the Scripture text, retell the story of the Good Shepherd in your own words. Can you remember the four kinds of dangerous characters who try to destroy the sheep? How does the Good Shepherd protect his flock? What are the lessons to be learned from this story, now that you have "taken it out of the Bible" and retold it in your own terms?

REFLECTIONS

Lilias Trotter uses a highly culture-sensitive teaching technique in the selection you have just read. She was writing to people who understood leadership in a way that Westerners never can. Our unconscious push toward democratic egalitarianism inevitably tempers the authority of the leader. But Trotter's readers understood leadership in terms of absolute monarchy. The sheikh, and the waly over him, were given unquestioned obedience. But even such allegiance—perhaps especially such allegiance—can instantly recognize the difference between a tyrant and a benevolent autocrat.

So Trotter asks her readers simply to study Jesus as a leader. Look at him and see how he functions as the Good Shepherd and how he contrasts with "the stranger, the thief, the hireling, the wolf"—all examples of leadership with which they were undoubtedly well acquainted. Consider Jesus, says Trotter, the Good Shepherd who protects his sheep, who feeds his sheep, who lays down his life for his sheep. Here is a leader worthy of your unqualified obedience. Yes, and even we who instinctively fear such monocratic leadership, we too can give Jesus our life, our all.

RICHARD J. FOSTER

GOING DEEPER

Lilias Trotter's many books, sadly, are long out of print. An extensive collection of them is housed at the Trotter Archives in the Arab World Ministries headquarters in Loughborough, UK. Among the best known of these titles are *Between the Desert and the Sea, Parables of the Cross, Parables of the Christ-Life, The Master of the Impossible,* and *The Way of the Seven-Fold Secret.* The address of this collection is AWM, PO Box 51, Loughborough, Leics, LE11 0ZQ, England. The e-mail address is 74754.1321@compuserve.com.

MIRIAM HUFFMAN ROCKNESS, *A Passion for the Impossible: The Life of Lilias Trotter* (Wheaton, IL: Harold Shaw Publishers, 1999). This recent biography brings a fresh eye to Lilias Trotter's life achievement. It contains a complete bibliography of Trotter's works. It also includes a number of her drawings and paintings, some of which are in color.

ELISABETH ELLIOT, *A Path Through Suffering* (Ann Arbor, MI: Vine Books, 1992). (See the meditation on Lilias Trotter's works.)

J. B. Phillips

(1906–1982)

John Bertram Phillips was an Anglican clergyman best known for his contemporary translation of the New Testament. A Cambridge graduate with honors in classics, he worked as a curate (and subsequently a vicar) in wartime London.

In his dialogues with young people, Phillips became concerned that many of them could not understand or relate to the venerable King James Bible. Responding pastorally, he tried his hand at a new translation of one of Paul's letters, using contemporary language and tone.

Parishioners young and old were delighted. Said his friend C. S. Lewis, "It's like looking at an old picture after it's been cleaned." Encouraged by such reactions, and by his own experience in the translation process, Phillips went on to put the entire New Testament into modern English, a translation that became internationally popular.

In addition, Phillips also wrote books to evangelize and teach. Among these were *Your God Is Too Small* (1953) and *Plain Christianity* (1957). His series of twenty-six radio plays about the life of Christ was collected as *A Man Called Jesus* (1959).

In the following selection, which is taken from *Ring of Truth: A Translator's Testimony,* Phillips tells his personal response to the work of translating the letters of Paul, James, and others.

Clearly, he is on a personal journey of discovery, dealing with things in the Bible that may have baffled him in earlier translations.

He is delighted to get in closer touch with first-century Christians. He also is glad that he can bring his readers closer to Jesus Christ.

In particular, he devotes one chapter to nine serendipities he found in the New Testament. Here are three of them.

RING OF TRUTH

Three New Testament Serendipities

Just over two hundred years ago, in 1754 to be precise, Horace Walpole coined the word "serendipity," which has now come to be accepted into our language. The word, which is derived from the ancient name for Ceylon, is defined as "the faculty of making happy and unexpected discoveries by accident." Before I go on to discuss the work of translating the Gospels I feel I must mention some of the "happy and unexpected discoveries" which I made in the translation of the Epistles.

Serendipity 1

The first one I will mention, which of course may all the time have been no secret to anybody else, was the expression "rich in mercy" (Eph. 2:4). This struck me as a positive jewel. Just as we might say that a Texas tycoon is "rich in oil," so Paul writes it as a matter of fact that God is "rich in mercy." The pagan world was full of fear, and the Christian gospel set out to replace that fear of the gods or the fates, or even life itself, with love for and trust in God. "Rich in mercy" was good news to the ancient world and it is good news today. . . .

Serendipity 3

I had for some time been worried about the expression "fear and trembling." It did not seem likely to me that Paul in writing to the Philippians could have meant literally that they were to work out their salvation in a condition of anxiety and nervousness. We all know that fear destroys love and spoils relationships, and a great deal of the New Testament is taken up with getting rid of the old ideas of fear and substituting the new ideas of love and trust.

I realised that the Greek word translated "fear" can equally well mean "reverence" or "awe" or even "respect," but I was bothered about the "trembling." Surely the same Spirit who inspired Paul to write to Timothy that "God hath not given us the spirit of fear; but of power and of love and of a sound mind" could not also have meant us to live our entire lives in a state of nervous terror. I came to the conclusion, a little reluctantly, that the expression "in fear and trembling" had become a bit of a cliché, even as it has in some circles today.

As I went on translating I found that this must be the case. For when Paul wrote to the Corinthians and reported that Titus had been encouraged and refreshed by their reception of him, he then went on to say that the Corinthian Christians received him with "fear and trembling" (2 Cor. 7:15)! Now this makes nonsense, unless it is a purely conventional verbal form implying proper respect. For, little as we know of Titus, we cannot imagine any real Christian minister being encouraged and refreshed by a display of nervous anxiety.

We get the same phrase occurring again in Paul's advice to Christian slaves (Eph. 6:5), where the context makes it quite clear that faithfulness and responsibility are much more what Paul means than "fear and trembling." This much became plain, and then I realised that when Paul really did mean the words to be taken literally he amplified them to make sure they would be properly understood.

I think we sometimes imagine that the incredibly heroic Paul suffered from no human weaknesses, except for the "thorn in the flesh" about which all New Testament commentators have written (2 Cor. 12:7). But if we turn to 1 Corinthians 2:3, we find Paul writing that "I was with you in weakness, and in fear, and in much trembling." Now this is a different thing altogether. Here we have a man honest enough to admit that he was frightened and that he was, or had been, ill. "Fear and trembling" here are perfectly legitimate. It is only when they are used as a phrase almost without literal meaning that we begin to feel uncomfortable. . . .

Serendipity 9

There are naturally many more happy and unexpected discoveries which I made over the years, some of them perhaps merely revealing how superficial must have been my previous knowledge of the New Testament letters. But since this is a personal testimony, I have felt it right to mention some of the things which came to me with fresh and startling clarity. I have kept the best until last.

It occurs in John's first letter, chapter 3, verse 20. Like many others, I find myself something of a perfectionist, and if we don't watch ourselves this obsession for the perfect can make us arrogantly critical of other people and, in certain moods, desperately critical of ourselves. In this state of mind it is not really that I cannot subscribe to the doctrine of the Forgiveness of Sins, but that the tyrannical super-Me condemns and has no mercy on myself.

Now John, in his wisdom, points out in inspired words, "If our heart condemn us, God is greater than our heart, and knoweth all things." This is a gentle but salutary rebuke to our assumption that we know better than God! God, on any showing, is infinitely greater in wisdom and love than we are and, unlike us, knows all the factors involved in human behaviour.

We are guilty of certain things, and these we must confess with all honesty, and make reparation where possible. But there may be many factors in our lives for which we are not really to blame at all. We did not choose our heredity; we did not choose the bad, indifferent, or excellent way in which we were brought up.

This is naturally not to say that every wrong thing we do, or every fear or rage to which we are subject today, is due entirely to heredity, environment, and upbringing. But it certainly does mean that we are in no position to judge ourselves; we simply must leave that to God, who is our Father and "is greater than our heart, and knoweth all things." It is almost as if John is saying, "If God loves us, who are we to be so high and mighty as to refuse to love ourselves?"

BIBLE SELECTION
2 Corinthians 7 (Phillips's Translation)

With these promises ringing in our ears, dear friends, let us keep clear of anything that smirches body or soul. Let us prove our reverence for God by consecrating ourselves to him completely.

Do make room in your hearts again for us! Not one of you has ever been wronged or ruined or cheated by us. I don't say this to condemn your attitude, but simply because, as I said before, whether we live or die, you live in our hearts. To your face I talk to you with utter frankness; behind your back I talk about you with deepest pride. Whatever troubles I have gone through, the thought of you has filled me with comfort and deep happiness.

For even when we arrived in Macedonia, we had a wretched time with trouble all round us—wrangling outside and anxiety within. Not but what God, who cheers the depressed, gave us the comfort of the arrival of Titus. And it wasn't merely his coming that cheered us, but the comfort you had given him, for he could tell us of your eagerness to help, your deep sympathy and keen interest on my behalf.

All that made me doubly glad to see him. For although my letter had hurt you, I don't regret it now (as I did, I must confess, at one time). I can see that the letter did upset you, though only for a time, and now I am glad I sent it, not because I want to hurt you, but because it made you grieve for things that were wrong. In other words, the result was to make you sorry as God would have had you sorry, and not merely to make you offended by what we said. The sorrow which God uses means a change of heart and leads to salvation—it is the world's sorrow that is such a deadly thing. You can look back now and see how the hand of God was in that sorrow. Look how seriously it made you think, how eager it made you to prove your innocence, how indignant it made you and, in some cases, how afraid! Look how it made you long for my presence, how it stirred up your keenness for the faith, how ready it made you to punish the offender! Yes, that letter cleared the air for you as nothing else would have done.

Now I did not write that letter really for the sake of the man who sinned, or even for the sake of the one who was sinned against, but to let you see for yourselves, in the sight of God, how deeply you really do care for us. That is why we now feel so deeply comforted, and our sense of joy was greatly enhanced by the satisfaction that your attitude had obviously given Titus. You see, I had told him of my pride in you, and you have not let me down. I have always spoken the truth to you, and this proves that my proud words about you were true as well. Titus himself has a much greater love for you, now that he has seen for himself the obedience you gave him, and the respect and reverence with which you treated him. I am profoundly glad to have my confidence in you so fully proved.

DISCUSSION QUESTIONS

The following can be used for discussion within a small group, or used for journal reflections by individuals:

1. What is the importance to me of the biblical translation that I use? What are the advantages and disadvantages of the more traditional as opposed to the more contemporary translations?
2. What specific phrases in Scripture are stumbling blocks for me, as "fear and trembling" was for J. B. Phillips? How have I used the discipline of study as a way of working through these difficult phrases?

SUGGESTED EXERCISES

The following exercises can be done by individuals, shared between spiritual friends, or used in the context of a small group. Choose one or more of the following:

1. In a group setting, list the biblical translations that are being used by different members. Have people changed translations for a particular reason? Discuss.
2. Consider swapping Bibles for a week—or if that's too difficult, for a day or so—just to gain a different perspective. At the next session, report on the difference you felt.
3. Read aloud from J. B. Phillips or an even more contemporary translation of the New Testament, like Eugene Peterson's *The Message*.
4. If anyone in the group knows New Testament Greek, have him or her read aloud the passages from 2 Corinthians 7:15 and Ephesians 6 that Phillips mentions and comment on the "feel" of the Greek texts.

REFLECTIONS

The serendipities that J. B. Phillips experienced in his translation work afford us a helpful insight into study as a spiritual discipline. Did you notice that the insights he gained came simply by paying attention to the words of Scripture? Now, this matter of attention is so important for us who live in the wordy world of high-tech telecommunication systems. We now have the dubious distinction of being able to communicate more and say less than any civilization in history. We have become, as Clement of Alexandria says, like old shoes—all worn out except for the tongue. And because so many words bombard us from so many media we tend to pay little attention to them. Can you or I remember even a single full sentence from the last movie we saw, or the last e-mail we received?

What we must learn, therefore, is discernment. Some words deserve sustained attention, others do not. The phrase that Phillips took such delight in—"rich in mercy"—is a reality we all could soak in for a very long time. In contrast, we should probably speed-read the latest book from the New York Times best-seller list, for likely it deserves no more than five or ten minutes of our attention. In fact, it is a positive virtue for us to remain ignorant of much of the attention-getting, ego-driven, greed-motivated words that whiz by on the information superhighway. We do so in order to be attentive to words that speak life into our souls. This, too, is a discipline.

RICHARD J. FOSTER

GOING DEEPER

J. B. PHILLIPS, *The Ring of Truth: A Translator's Testimony* (New York: Macmillan, 1967). This book provides genuine insight into the thought of Paul, James, and other New Testament writers. Most important of all, it is a testimony of faith, in which Phillips says how much more the authenticity of the New Testament came home to him as he labored over his translations.

The Newborn Christian: 114 Readings from J. B. Phillips, edited by William Griffin (New York: Macmillan, 1978.) This devotionally styled anthology offers brief readings from a broad variety of works by J. B. Phillips.

Phoebe Palmer

(1807–1874)

―――

Born in New York City to a devout Methodist family, Phoebe Worrall Palmer was one of the first women of the nineteenth century to become a celebrated public figure and speaker. Her work as a poet, humanitarian, evangelist, and social reformer had impact on a number of communities: American social activism, the Wesleyan spiritual tradition of which she was a part, and numerous other holiness movements.

Her small book, *The Way of Holiness* (1843), became (much to her own amazement) a huge best-seller, influencing hundreds of thousands of readers, bringing her suddenly into the public eye, and opening doors previously closed to women. From then on she was constantly on the road, speaking in such places as Chicago, London, and Glasgow. By 1867 the book had gone through fifty editions.

Through her leadership in American Methodism, missions were begun, camp meetings initiated, hymns composed, and thousands upon thousands aroused by God's grace. Four years of her amazing ministry (1859–63) were spent in Ireland and in the Newcastle neighborhood of England.

Palmer did not advocate "women's rights" or even preaching by women. Yet her powerful example inspired the Women's Temperance Movement and many other humanitarian causes led by women. Her 1857 series of essays, "A Laity for the Times," helped bring about a strong lay-influenced revival on both sides of the Atlantic. She is considered one of the best spiritual writers of the American tradition.

While you are reading this selection from *The Way of Holiness*, bear in mind that Palmer wrote her book out of deep biblical study. She is not advocating "short cuts" in the spiritual life. Instead, the "shorter way" she speaks of is one of total responsiveness to God's grace.

THE WAY OF HOLINESS

Is There Not a Shorter Way?

"Be always ready to give an answer to every man that asketh you a reason of the hope that is within you, with meekness and fear" (1 Pet. 3:15)

"I have thought," said one of the children of Zion to the other, as in love they journeyed onward in the way cast up for the ransomed of the Lord to walk in; "I have thought," said he, "whether there is not *a shorter way* of getting into this way of holiness than some of our brethren apprehend?"

"Yes," said the sister addressed, who was a member of the denomination alluded to; "Yes, brother, THERE IS A SHORTER WAY! O! I am sure this long waiting and struggling with the powers of darkness is not necessary. There is a shorter way." And then, with a solemn feeling of responsibility, and with a realizing conviction of the truth uttered, she added, "But, brother, there is but one way."

How many, whom Infinite Love would long since have brought into this state, instead of seeking to be brought into the possession of the blessing at once, are seeking a preparation for the reception of it! They feel that their *convictions* are not deep enough to warrant an approach to the throne of grace, with the confident expectation of receiving the blessing now. Just at this point some may have been lingering months and years. Thus did the sister, who so confidently affirmed "there is a shorter way." And here, dear child of Jesus, permit the writer to tell you just how that sister found the "shorter way."

On looking at the requirements of the word of God, she beheld the command, "Be ye holy" (1 Pet. 1:16). She then began to say in her heart, "Whatever my former deficiencies may have been, God requires that I should now be holy. Whether *convicted*, or otherwise, *duty is plain*. God requires *present* holiness." On coming to this point, she at once apprehended a simple truth before unthought of, i.e., *Knowledge is conviction.* She well knew that, for a long time, she had been assured that God required holiness. But she had never deemed this knowledge a sufficient plea to take to God—and because of present need, to ask a present bestowment of the gift. . . .

Deeply conscious of past unfaithfulness, she now determined that the time past should suffice, and with a humility of spirit, induced by a consciousness of not having lived in the performance of such a "reasonable service" (Rom. 12:1), she was enabled, through grace, to resolve, with firmness of purpose, that entire devotion of heart and life to God should be the absorbing subject of the succeeding pilgrimage of life.

How shall I know?

After having thus resolved on devoting the entire service of her heart and life to God, the following questions occasioned much serious solicitude: How shall I know *when* I have consecrated all to God? And how ascertain whether God *accepts* the sacrifice—and how know the manner of its acceptance? Here again the blessed Bible which she had now taken as her counselor, said to her heart,

"We have received not the spirit of the world, but the Spirit which is of God, that we might know the things freely given to us of God" (1 Cor. 2:12).

It was thus she became assured that it was her privilege to *know when she* had consecrated all to God, and also to know that the sacrifice was *accepted*, and the resolve was solemnly made that the subject should not cease to be absorbing until this knowledge was obtained. . . .

From a sense of responsibility thus imposed, she began to be more abundant in labors, "instant in season and out of season" (2 Tim. 4:2).

While thus engaged in active service, another difficulty presented itself. How much of self in these performances? said the accuser. For a moment, almost bewildered at being thus withstood, her heart began to sink. . . .

It was here again that the blessed word sweetly communed with her heart, presenting the marks of the way, by a reference to the admonition of Paul. "Therefore, my beloved brethren, be ye steadfast and unmovable, always abounding in the work of the Lord, forasmuch as ye know that your labor is not in vain in the Lord. . . ." (1 Cor. 15:58).

Growing in grace daily
. . . So far from having those overwhelming perceptions of guilt, on which she afterward saw she had been too much disposed to place reliance, as somewhat meritorious, she was constantly and *consciously* growing in grace daily—yea, even hourly her heavenward progress seemed marked as by the finger of God.

No gloomy fears that she was *not a child of God* dimmed her spiritual horizon, presenting fearful anticipations of impending wrath. There had been a period in her experience, some time previous to that under present consideration, from which she had not *one lingering doubt of her acceptance with God, as a member of the household of faith* (see Eph. 2:19). But, [she was] conscious that she had *not the witness of entire consecration to God*, neither the assurance that the great deep of her heart, the fountain from whence action emanates, was pure, which at this time stood before the vision of her mind as two distinct objects (yet which, as she afterward perceived, most clearly merged in *one*), and impelled onward also by such an intense desire to be *fruitful in every good work* (see Col. 1:10). . . . Conscious that she had submitted herself to the dictations of the Spirit, a sacred conviction took possession of her mind that she was being led into all truth.

"Stand still, and see the salvation of God" (see Exod. 14:13), was now the listening attitude in which her soul eagerly waited before the Lord, and it was but a few hours after the above encouraging admonition had been spoken to her heart that she set apart a season to wait before the Lord, especially for the bestowment of the object, or rather the two distinct objects previously stated.

On first kneeling, she thought of resolving that she would continue to wait before the Lord until the desire of her heart was granted. But the adversary, who had stood ready to withstand every progressive step, suggested, "Be careful, God may disappoint your expectations, and suppose you should be left to wrestle all night; ay, and all the morrow too?" . . .

And here most emphatically could she say, she was led by a "way she knew not" (see Josh. 3:4); so simple, so clearly described, and urged by the word of the Lord, and yet so often overlooked, for want of that childlike simplicity which, without reasoning, takes God at his word. It was just while engaged in the act of preparing the way, as she deemed, to some great and undefinable exercise, that the Lord, through the medium of faith in his *written word*, led her astonished soul directly into the "way of holiness," where, with unutterable delight, she found the comprehensive desires of her soul blended and satisfied in the fulfillment of the command, *"Be ye holy."*

It was thus, waiting child of Jesus, that this traveler in the King's highway was directed onward, through the teachings of the word of God and induced so confidently to affirm, in reply to the brother, *"There is a shorter way."*

Counting the cost

. . . It was on this wise that the word of the Lord, the "Book of books," as a "mighty counselor," urged her onward, and by unerring precept directed every step of the way. And as each progressive step by which she was ushered into the enjoyment of this blessed state of experience was as distinctly marked, by its holy teachings, as those already given, may it not be presumed, that some heretofore wavering one may be induced to rest more confidently in the assurance that "the word of the Lord is tried," and is the same in its immutable nature as the Faithful and True, by stating, as nearly as will comport with the brevity required, the steps as successively taken by which this disciple of Jesus entered?

Over and again, previous to the time mentioned, had she endeavored to give herself away in covenant to God. But she had never, till this hour, deliberately resolved on counting the cost, with the solemn intention to "reckon herself dead *indeed* unto sin, but alive unto God through Jesus Christ our Lord"; to account herself permanently the Lord's, and in verity no more at *her own* disposal, but *irrevocably the Lord's property*, for time and eternity. Now, in the name of the Lord Jehovah, after having deliberately "counted the cost," she resolved to enter into the bonds of an everlasting covenant, with the fixed purpose to *count all things loss* for the excellency of the knowledge of Jesus, that she might know him and the power of his resurrection, by being made conformable to his death, and raised to an entire newness of life. . . .

On doing this a hallowed sense of consecration took possession of her soul; a divine conviction that the covenant was recognized in heaven, accompanied with the assurance that the seal, proclaiming her wholly the Lord's, was set; while a consciousness, deep and abiding, that she had been but a co-worker with God in this matter, added still a greater confirmation to her conceptions of the extent and permanency of those heaven-inspired exercises, by which a mighty work had been wrought in and for her soul, which she felt assured would tell on her eternal destiny, even after myriads of ages had been spent in the eternal world.

But she did not at the moment regard the state into which she had been brought as the "way of holiness," neither had the word holiness been the most prominent topic during this solemn transaction. *Conformity to the will of God in all things* was the absorbing desire of her heart. Yet after having passed through these exercises she began to give expression to her full soul thus: "I am wholly thine!—Thou dost reign unrivaled in my heart! There is not a tie that binds me to earth; every tie has been severed, and now I am wholly, wholly thine!" While lingering on the last words, the Holy Spirit appealingly repeated the confident expressions to her heart, thus: What! wholly the Lord's? Is not this the holiness that God requires? What have you more to render? Does God require more than all? Hath he issued the command "Be ye holy," and not given the ability, with the command, for the performance of it? Is he a hard master, unreasonable in his requirements? She now saw, in a convincing light, her error in regarding holiness as an attainment beyond her reach, and stood reproved, though consciously shielded by the atonement from condemnation, and enjoying the blessedness of that soul "to whom the Lord will not impute sin." And now the eyes of her understanding were more fully opened, and founded on eternal faithfulness did she find the words of the Saviour, *"If any man will do his will he shall know of the doctrine"* (John 7:17).

BIBLE SELECTION
Romans 8:24–35

For in hope we were saved. Now hope that is seen is not hope. For who hopes for what is seen? But if we hope for what we do not see, we wait for it with patience.

Likewise the Spirit helps us in our weakness; for we do not know how to pray as we ought, but that very Spirit intercedes with sighs too deep for words. And God, who searches the heart, knows what is the mind of the Spirit, because the Spirit intercedes for the saints according to the will of God.

We know that all things work together for good for those who love God, who are called according to his purpose. For those whom he foreknew he also predestined to be conformed to the image of his Son, in order that he might be the firstborn within a large family. And those whom he predestined he also called; and those whom he called he also justified; and those whom he justified he also glorified.

What then are we to say about these things? If God is for us, who is against us? He who did not withhold his own Son, but gave him up for all of us, will he not with him also give us everything else? Who will bring any charge against God's elect? It is God who justifies. Who is to condemn? It is Christ Jesus, who died, yes, who was raised, who is at the right hand of God, who indeed intercedes for us. Who will separate us from the love of Christ? Will hardship, or distress, or persecution, or famine, or nakedness, or peril, or sword?

DISCUSSION QUESTIONS

The following can be used for discussion within a small group, or used for journal reflections by individuals:

1. What reactions do I have to the intense revival feelings that Phoebe Palmer describes? Am I aware of the biblical foundations of these forms of intense spirituality?
2. What would help me give in to Phoebe Palmer's "shorter way"?

SUGGESTED EXERCISES

The following exercises can be done by individuals, shared between spiritual friends, or used in the context of a small group. Choose one or more of the following:

1. Phoebe Palmer's writing is rooted in the Bible. After almost every sentiment she voices, she quotes a short biblical text. Have members of your group identify and chase down the many Bible references in the passage above. Then read the texts aloud, noticing what a picture is formed of the experience of God's grace by the verses that influenced Palmer.
2. Many of the church movements influenced by Phoebe Palmer and mid-nineteenth-century Methodism are still going strong today. Among these are The Church of the Nazarene, The Salvation Army, the Church of God, and

the Pentecostal-Holiness Church. Reflect on the power of movements like these to help the afflicted and to effect social change. Name and mention other groups in your community that may be empowered by the same intense feelings of religious and charitable zeal. Be encouraged by this ongoing and recurring witness to the power of God in contemporary life.

REFLECTIONS

To us today Phoebe Palmer's "shorter way" seems terribly convoluted and torturous. We simply do not have the history of searching and struggling to enter "the way of holiness" that characterized the "saints" of Palmer's day. As you were reading the selection, did you realize you were listening in on Palmer's own arduous search for "entire sanctification" written in that modest third-person way characteristic of the nineteenth century?

Her personal diary "Notes" are even more revealing. Listen to her describe the events of July 26, 1837—what she called her "day of days": "Between the hours of eight and nine (in the evening)—while pleading at the throne of grace for a present fulfilment of the exceeding great and precious promises; pleading also the fulness and freeness of the atonement, its unbounded efficacy, and making an entire surrender of body, soul, and spirit; time, talents, and influence; and also of the dearest ties of nature, my beloved husband and child; in a word, my earthly all—I received the assurance that God the Father, through the atoning Lamb, accepted the sacrifice; my heart was emptied of self, and cleansed of all idols, from all filthiness of the flesh and spirit, and I realized that I dwelt in God, and felt that he had become the portion of my soul, my ALL IN ALL."

RICHARD J. FOSTER

GOING DEEPER

Phoebe Palmer: Selected Writings, edited by Thomas C. Oden (New York: Paulist, 1988). This fine volume in *The Classics of Western Spirituality* series provides selections from the very large number of influential writings by Phoebe Palmer, including her poetry, hymns, theological essays, correspondence with various prominent individuals, and published books. It also provides in-depth scholarship and a clear vision of Palmer's life achievement.

CHARLES EDWARD WHITE, *The Beauty of Holiness: Phoebe Palmer as Theologian, Revivalist, Feminist, and Humanitarian* (Grand Rapids, MI: Zondervan, 1986). A fine interpretation of Palmer's contribution in four distinct dimensions of her extensive ministry.

Outward Disciplines

SIMPLICITY

SOLITUDE

SUBMISSION

SERVICE

Simplicity

A. W. Tozer

(1897–1963)

———

Born in the hills of western Pennsylvania, Aiden W. Tozer was reared in hardship and poverty. He came to Christ at the age of fifteen and shortly thereafter became an active Methodist lay preacher. Soon he entered the ministry despite his lack of both high school and college training. Before long, in disfavor with the Methodists, he joined the Christian and Missionary Alliance where his preaching gift gained wide attention.

Tozer pastored churches in West Virginia, Ohio, and Indiana, then accepted a call (1928) to the Southside Alliance Church in Chicago, where he stayed thirty-one years. Avenue Road Alliance Church in Toronto, Ontario, was his last pastorate.

Tozer also preached on the Moody Bible Institute radio station, WMBI (Chicago), offering biblically based "Talks from a Pastor's Study." His best-known book, *The Pursuit of God* (1948), gained an international readership. In 1950 he became editor of *The Alliance Witness*, a position he held until his death.

A man of intense prayer who cultivated solitude, Tozer was said to read and even to write while actually on his knees. He was also something of a twentieth-century prophet calling the church back to simplicity and godliness.

The following selection came out of Tozer's personal struggle to turn his only daughter over to God. When he surrendered her to God at last, he experienced a sense of complete peace.

THE PURSUIT OF GOD

The Blessedness of Possessing Nothing

Blessed are the poor in spirit: for theirs is the kingdom of heaven. (Matt. 5:3)

Before the Lord God made man upon the earth He first prepared for him a world of useful and pleasant things for his sustenance and delight. In the Genesis account of the creation these are called simply "things." They were made for man's use, but they were meant always to be external to the man and subservient to him. In the deep heart of the man was a shrine where none but God was worthy to come. Within him was God; without, a thousand gifts which God had showered upon him.

But sin has introduced complications and has made those very gifts of God a potential source of ruin to the soul.

Our woes began when God was forced out of His central shrine and things were allowed to enter. Within the human heart things have taken over. Men have now by nature no peace within their hearts, for God is crowned there no longer, but there in the moral dusk stubborn and aggressive usurpers fight among themselves for first place on the throne.

This is not a mere metaphor, but an accurate analysis of our real spiritual trouble. . . .

The tyranny of things

Our Lord referred to this tyranny of things when He said to His disciples, "If any man will come after me, let him deny himself, and take up his cross, and follow me. For whosoever will save his life shall lose it: and whosoever shall lose his life for my sake shall find it" (Matt. 16:24–25).

Breaking this truth into fragments for our better understanding, it would seem that there is within each of us an enemy which we tolerate at our peril. Jesus called it "life" and "self," or as we would say, the *self-life*. Its chief characteristic is its possessiveness: the words *gain* and *profit* suggest this. To allow this enemy to live is, in the end, to lose everything. To repudiate it and give up all for Christ's sake is to lose nothing at last, but to preserve everything unto life eternal. And possibly also a hint is given here as to the only effective way to destroy this foe: it is by the cross. "Let him take up his cross and follow me." . . .

Uncleansed love

As is frequently true, this New Testament principle of spiritual life finds its best illustration in the Old Testament. In the story of Abraham and Isaac we have a dramatic picture of the surrendered life as well as an excellent commentary on the first Beatitude.

Abraham was old when Isaac was born, old enough indeed to have been his grandfather, and the child became at once the delight and idol of his heart. From the moment he first stooped to take the tiny form awkwardly in his arms, he was an eager love slave of his son. God went out of His way to comment on the strength of this affection. And it is not hard to understand. The baby represented everything sacred to his father's heart: the promises of God, the covenants, the hopes of the years and the long messianic dream. As he watched him grow from babyhood to young manhood, the heart of the old man was knit closer and closer with the life of his son, till at last the relationship bordered upon the perilous. It was then that God stepped in to save both father and son from the consequences of an uncleansed love.

"Take now thy son," said God to Abraham, "thine only son Isaac, whom thou lovest, and get thee into the land of Moriah; and offer him there for a burnt-offering upon one of the mountains which I will tell thee of" (Gen. 22:2). The sacred writer spares us a close-up of the agony that night on the slopes near Beersheba when the aged man had it out with his God, but respectful imagination may view in awe the bent form wrestling convulsively alone under the stars. Possibly not again until One greater than Abraham wrestled in the Garden of Gethsemane did such mortal pain visit a human soul. If only the man himself might have been allowed to die. That would have been a thousand times easier, for he was old now, and to die would have been no great ordeal for one who had walked so long with God. Besides, it would have been a last, sweet pleasure to let his dimming vision rest upon the figure of his stalwart son who would live to carry on the Abrahamic line and fulfil in himself the promises of God made long before in Ur of the Chaldees.

Obedient love

How should he slay the lad! Even if he could get the consent of his wounded and protesting heart, how could he reconcile the act with the promise, "In Isaac shall thy seed be called"? This was Abraham's trial by fire, and he did not fail in the crucible. While the stars still shone like sharp white points above the tent where the sleeping Isaac lay, and long before the gray dawn had begun to lighten the east, the old saint had made up his mind. He would offer his son as God had directed him to do, and *then trust God to raise him from the dead*. This, says the writer to the Hebrews, was the solution his aching heart found sometime in the dark night, and he rose "early in the morning" to carry out the plan. It is beautiful to see that, while he erred as to God's method, he had correctly sensed the secret of His great heart. And the solution accords well with the New Testament Scripture "Whosoever will lose for my sake shall find."

God let the suffering old man go through with it up to the point where He knew there would be no retreat, and then forbade him to lay a hand upon the boy. To the wondering patriarch He now says in effect, "It's all right, Abraham. I never intended that you should actually slay the lad. I only wanted to remove him from the temple of your heart that I might reign unchallenged there. I wanted to correct the perversion that existed in your love. Now you may have the boy, sound and well. Take him and go back to your tent. Now I know that thou fearest God, seeing that thou hast not withheld thy son, thine only son, from me."

Then heaven opened and a voice was heard saying to him, "By myself have I sworn, saith the Lord, for because thou hast done this thing, and hast not withheld thy son, thine only son: that in blessing I will bless thee, and in multiplying I will multiply thy seed as the stars of the heaven, and as the sand which is upon the seashore; and thy seed shall possess the gate of his enemies; and in thy seed shall all the nations of the earth be blessed; because thou hast obeyed my voice" (Gen. 22:16–18).

Surrendered love

The old man of God lifted his head to respond to the Voice, and stood there on the mount strong and pure and grand, a man marked out by the Lord for special treatment, a friend and favorite of the Most High. Now he was a man wholly surrendered, a man utterly obedient, a man who possessed nothing. He had concentrated his all in the person of his dear son, and God had taken it from him. God could have begun out on the margin of Abraham's life and worked inward to the center. He chose rather to cut quickly to the heart and have it over in one sharp act of separation. In dealing thus, He practiced an economy of means and time. It hurt cruelly, but it was effective.

I have said that Abraham possessed nothing. Yet was not this poor man rich? Everything he had owned before was his still to enjoy: sheep, camels, herds, and goods of every sort. He had also his wife and his friends, and best of all he had his son Isaac safe by his side. He had everything, *but he possessed nothing*. There is the spiritual secret. There is the sweet theology of the heart which can be learned only in the school of renunciation. The books on systematic theology overlook this, but the wise will understand.

After that bitter and blessed experience I think the words *my* and *mine* never again had the same meaning for Abraham. The sense of possession which they connote was gone from his heart. Things had been cast out forever. They had now become external to the man. His inner heart was free from them. The world said, "Abraham is rich," but the aged patriarch only smiled. He could not explain it, but he knew that he owned nothing, that his real treasures were inward and eternal. . . .

The way of renunciation

If we would indeed know God in growing intimacy, we must go this way of renunciation. And if we are set upon the pursuit of God, He will sooner or later bring us to this test. Abraham's testing was, at the time, not known to him as such, yet if he had taken some course other than the one he did, the whole history of the Old Testament would have been different. God would have found His man, no doubt, but the loss to Abraham would have been tragic beyond the telling. So we will be brought one by one to the testing place, and we may never know when we are there. At that testing place there will be no dozen possible choices for us—just one and an alternative—but our whole future will be conditioned by the choice we make.

Father, I want to know Thee, but my cowardly heart fears to give up its toys. I cannot part with them without inward bleeding, and I do not try to hide from Thee the terror of the parting. I come trembling, but I do come. Please root from my heart all those things which I have cherished so long and which have become a very part of my living self, so that Thou mayest enter and dwell there without a rival. Then shalt Thou make the place of Thy feet glorious. Then shall my heart have no need of the sun to shine in it, for Thyself wilt be the light of it, and there shall be no night there. In Jesus' name, Amen.

BIBLE SELECTION
Genesis 22:1–18

After these things God tested Abraham. He said to him, "Abraham!" And he said, "Here I am." He said, "Take your son, your only son Isaac, whom you love, and go to the land of Moriah, and offer him there as a burnt offering on one of the mountains that I shall show you." So Abraham rose early in the morning, saddled his donkey, and took two of his young men with him, and his son Isaac; he cut the wood for the burnt offering, and set out and went to the place in the distance that God had shown him. On the third day Abraham looked up and saw the place far away. Then Abraham said to his young men, "Stay here with the donkey; the boy and I will go over there; we will worship, and then we will come back to you." Abraham took the wood of the burnt offering and laid it on his son Isaac, and he himself carried the fire and the knife. So the two of them walked on together. Isaac said to his father Abraham, "Father!" And he said, "Here I am, my son." He said, "The fire and the wood are here, but where is the lamb for a burnt offering?" Abraham said, "God himself will provide the lamb for a burnt offering, my son." So the two of them walked on together.

When they came to the place that God had shown him, Abraham built an altar there and laid the wood in order. He bound his son Isaac, and laid him on the altar, on top of the wood. Then Abraham reached out his hand and took the knife to kill his son. But the angel of the LORD called to him from heaven, and said, "Abraham, Abraham!" And he said, "Here I am." He said, "Do not lay your hand on the boy or do anything to him; for now I know that you fear God, since you have not withheld your son, your only son, from me." And Abraham looked up and saw a ram, caught in a thicket by its horns. Abraham went and took the ram and offered it up as a burnt offering instead of his son. So Abraham called that place "The LORD will provide"; as it is said to this day, "On the mount of the LORD it shall be provided."

The angel of the LORD called to Abraham a second time from heaven, and said, "By myself I have sworn, says the LORD: Because you have done this, and have not withheld your son, your only son, I will indeed bless you, and I will make your offspring as numerous as the stars of heaven and as the sand that is on the seashore. And your offspring shall possess the gate of their enemies, and by your offspring shall all the nations of the earth gain blessing for themselves, because you have obeyed my voice."

DISCUSSION QUESTIONS

The following can be used for discussion within a small group, or used for journal reflections by individuals:

1. How can I evaluate the "things" in my life to which I am inordinately attached—whether people, places, or possessions?
2. What makes us so uncomfortable about admitting our "attachments" to another person? What qualities should a person have to assist us in dealing with "the tyranny of things"?

SUGGESTED EXERCISES

The following exercises can be done by individuals, shared between spiritual friends, or used in the context of a small group. Choose one or more of the following:

1. Have each person in the group bring an object that symbolizes a relationship of overattachment. It might be a picture of something; it might be a keepsake associated with someone; it could be money, jewelry, or some other object. (Possibly the meaning of this symbolic object may be known only to the person who brought it.) First, have everyone place these objects within the circle, where they are clearly within view. Have each individual pray in his or her own words to be released from overattachment to this particular object. After the prayer, have each individual place the same object behind him or her. Now, say a prayer of gratitude that God's power is great

enough to relieve us of such attachments. (Yes, you can retrieve the object and take it home with you. The object is not the problem in and of itself, but what it stands for, a kind of spiritual bondage you are asking to be set free from.)

2. Tell stories about ways you have been released in the past from excessive attachments. Appreciate that deliverance.

REFLECTIONS

This selection from Tozer is one of my favorite passages in all his writings. Somehow he makes Abraham's dilemma live for me. I think the key is that he never allows me off the hook. Under Tozer's watchful eye I cannot read the Abraham story at arm's length. He refuses to let me say, in effect, "I'm certainly glad that I'm not in Abraham's shoes!" No, Tozer presses me into the story, declaring, "You are in Abraham's shoes. God is asking you to sacrifice your most prized possession. What will you answer?" That is how his writing affects me.

Did you notice that Tozer calls our perennial passion to possess, "the self-life"? In another of his writings he expands on this idea. Here he uses the metaphor of the veil in the Holy of Holies to describe for us "the veil in our hearts . . . the close-woven veil of the self-life." His powers of description are so telling that they cannot be improved upon. Listen. "It is woven of the fine threads of the self-life, the hyphenated sins of the human spirit. They are not something we do, they are something we are, and therein lies both their subtlety and their power."

"To be specific, the self-sins are these: self-righteousness, self-pity, self-confidence, self-sufficiency, self-admiration, self-love and a host of others like them . . . . Self is the opaque veil that hides the Face of God from us. . . . We must bring our self-sins to the cross for judgment. We must prepare ourselves for an ordeal of suffering in some measure like that through which our Savior passed when He suffered under Pontius Pilate." This is Tozer at his best calling us to the obedience of the cross life, which he reminds us is "the blessedness of possessing nothing."

RICHARD J. FOSTER

GOING DEEPER

Tozer wrote more than forty books, tracts, and booklets. Hopefully, these three will encourage you to discover more of his writings.

A. W. TOZER, *The Pursuit of God* (Camp Hill, PA: Christian Publications, 1982). Originally published in 1948, this book gained wide popularity and was translated into many different languages. Written out of a deep personal devotion, the book also shows Tozer's gifts as a writer, gained by prayerful reading of such writers as Shakespeare and the evangelical mystics.

A. W. TOZER, *The Knowledge of the Holy* (San Francisco: Harper & Row, 1961). This book discusses the attributes of God and their meaning for our life today. While considering the standard theological themes such as God's immutability and transcendence, it looks at other characteristics like his mercy, grace, and love.

A. W. TOZER, *Worship: The Missing Jewel* (Camp Hill, PA: Christian Publications, 1992). This booklet—a series of lectures on worship—shows Tozer at his prophetic best. He saw the lack of heart worship among many churches (in the sense of the *Mysterium Tremendum*) and sought to address this lack. In doing so, he anticipated the worship renewal occurring in our day.

Martin Luther

(1483–1546)

Martin Luther is preeminent among the Protestant Reformers. His extensive writings include not only theology but works of doctrine, sermons, and treatises on spiritual formation, and he is a person of spiritual depth and intensity.

Luther was born in Eisleben, a Saxon mining town in Germany. His parents gave him a good education, hoping their son would become a prosperous lawyer and town leader. Instead, he became an Augustinian monk (1505), a life he pursued for twenty years until his extensive and controversial writings brought him into vigorous conflict with Church and secular authorities.

Standing by his work, Luther voiced principles—especially the primacy of Scripture—that would drive the entire Protestant cause. He was extreme in language and passionate. Much of his writing and opinion was forged in the crucible of theological conflict. For example, his famous tract "On the Bondage of the Human Will" was a defense against the views of Erasmus.

One of his most enduring ideas, simply stated, *Simul Justus et Peccator*, is that the Christian is at once justified and sinful, an idea that has helped many people to deal with and understand the Christian's ongoing tendency toward sin.

Luther's writing has had profound impact throughout the generations. He influenced the conversion of John Bunyan and both John and Charles Wesley as well as such key figures as Søren Kierkegaard and Dietrich Bonhoeffer.

In the selection that follows, *The Place of Trust*, which brings together passages from Luther's preaching on the Sermon on the Mount, the reader can see how personal Luther's approach is. In speaking about spiritual freedom he is clearly drawing on his own intense struggle against anxiety and fear.

THE PLACE OF TRUST

Do Not Be Anxious About Your Life
(on Matthew 6:25–7:11)

> *Therefore I tell you, do not be concerned about your life, what you shall eat or what you shall drink, nor about your body, what you shall put on. Is not life more than food, and the body more than clothing? (6:25)*

Listen . . . to what serving *Mammon* [the god of possession] means. It means being concerned about our life and our body, about what we should eat and drink and put on. It means thinking only about this life, about how to get rich here and how to accumulate and increase our money and property, as though we were going to stay here forever. The sinful worship of Mammon does not consist in eating and drinking and wearing clothes, nor in looking for a way to make a living and working at it; for the needs of this life and of the body make food and clothing a requirement. But the sin consists in being concerned about it and making it the reliance and confidence of your heart. Concern does not stick to clothing or to food, but directly to the heart, which cannot let a thing go and has to hang on to it. As the saying goes, "Property makes a person bold." Thus "being concerned" means clinging to it with your heart. I am not concerned about anything that my heart does not think about, but I must have a heart for anything about which I am concerned.

You must not tighten this text too much, however, as if it prohibited any kind of concern at all. Every office and station involves taking on certain concerns, especially being in charge of other people. As St. Paul says about spiritual offices in Christendom (Rom. 12:8): "He who rules, let him be careful." In this sense the head of a household has to be concerned about whether his children are being brought up properly; . . . if he neglects this, he does wrong. . . .

Christ is not talking here about this sort of concern. This is an official concern, which must be sharply distinguished from greed. It is not concerned for its own sake but for the neighbor's sake; it does not seek its own interests (1 Cor. 13:5), but even neglects them and forgets them in order to serve somebody else. Therefore it may be called a concern of love, something divine and Christian, not a concern devoted to its own advantage or to Mammon, militating against faith and love, and even interfering with the official concern. The man whose money is dear to him and who is on the lookout for his own advantage will not have much regard for his neighbor or for the office that involves his neighbor. . . .

Christ has forbidden this greedy concern and worship of Mammon as an idolatry that makes men enemies of God. Now He goes on with many statements, examples, and illustrations. . . .

The birds, our schoolmasters

Look at the birds of the air; they neither sow nor reap nor gather into barns, and yet your heavenly Father feeds them. Are you not of more value than they? And which of you by being anxious can add one cubit to his stature? (6:26–27)

You see, He is making the birds our schoolmasters and teachers. It is a great and abiding disgrace to us that in the Gospel a helpless sparrow should become a theologian and a preacher to the wisest of men, and daily should emphasize this to our eyes and ears, as if he were saying to us: "Look, you miserable man! You have house and home, money and property. Every year you have a field full of grain and other plants of all sorts, more than you ever need. Yet you cannot find peace, and you are always worried about starving. If you do not know that you have supplies and cannot see them before your very eyes, you cannot trust God to give you food for one day. Though we are innumerable, none of us spends his living days worrying. Still God feeds us every day." In other words, we have as many teachers and preachers as there are little birds in the air. Their living example is an embarrassment to us. Whenever we hear a bird singing toward heaven and proclaiming God's praises and our disgrace, we should feel ashamed and not even dare to lift up our eyes. But we are as hard as stone, and we pay no attention even though we hear the great multitude preaching and singing every day.

Look at what else the dear little birds do. Their life is completely unconcerned, and they wait for their food solely from the hands of God. Sometimes people cage them up to hear them sing. Then they get food in abundance, and they ought to think: "Now I have plenty. I do not have to be concerned about where my food is coming from. Now I have a rich master, and my barns are full." But they do not do this. When they are free in the air, they are happier and fatter. Their singing of Lauds and of Matins to their Lord early in the morning before they eat is more excellent and more pleasant. Yet none of them knows of a single grain laid away in store. They sing a lovely, long *Benedicite* and leave their cares to our Lord God, even when they have young that have to be fed.

Whenever you listen to a nightingale, therefore, you are listening to an excellent preacher. He exhorts you with this Gospel, not with mere simple words but with a living deed and an example. He sings all night and practically screams his lungs out. He is happier in the woods than cooped up in a cage, where he has to be taken care of constantly and where he rarely gets along very well or even stays alive. It is as if he were saying: "I prefer to be in the Lord's kitchen. He has made heaven and earth, and He Himself is the cook and the host. Every day He feeds and nourishes innumerable little birds out of His hand. For He does not have merely a bag full of grain, but heaven and earth."

Now Christ says: "Every day you see before your very eyes how the heavenly Father feeds the little birds in the field, without any concern on their part. Can you not trust Him to feed you as well, since He is your Father and calls you His children? Shall He not be concerned about you, whom He has made His children and to whom He gives His Word and all creatures, more than about the little birds, which are not His children but your servants? And yet He thinks enough of them to feed them every day, as if they were the only thing He is concerned about. And He enjoys it when they fly around and sing without a care in the world, as if they were saying: 'I sing and frolic, and yet I do not know of a single grain that I am to eat. My bread is not baked yet, and my grain is not planted yet. But I have a rich Master who takes care of me while I am singing or sleeping. He can give me more than all my worries and the worries of all people could ever accomplish.'"

Now, since the birds have learned so well the art of trusting Him and of casting their cares from themselves upon God, we who are His children should do so even more. Thus this is an excellent illustration that puts us all to shame. We, who are rational people and who have the Scriptures in addition, do not have enough wisdom to imitate the birds. When we listen to the little birds singing every day, we are listening to our own embarrassment before God and the people. But after his fall from the word and the commandment of God, man became crazy and foolish; and there is no creature alive which is not wiser than he. A little finch, which can neither speak nor read, is his theologian and master in the Scriptures, even though he has the whole Bible and his reason to help him. . . .

The lilies, our theologians

> And why are you anxious about clothing? Consider the lilies of the field, how they grow; they neither toil nor spin; yet I tell you, even Solomon in all his glory was not arrayed like one of these. But if God so clothes the grass of the field, which today is alive and tomorrow is thrown into the oven, will He not much more clothe you, O men of little faith? (6:28–30)

Here you have another example and analogy; according to it, the little flowers in the field, which cattle trample and eat, are to become our theologians and masters and to embarrass us still further. Just look at them grow, all adorned with lovely colors! Yet not one of them is anxious or worried about how it should grow or what color it should have, but it leaves these anxieties to God. And without any care or effort on its part God dresses it up in such lovely and beautiful colors that, as Christ says, King Solomon in all his glory was not so beautiful as one of these— indeed, no empress with all her ladies-in-waiting, with all her gold, pearls, and jewels. No king He could name was so rich or so glorious or so beautifully adorned as was Solomon. But with all his magnificent pomp and splendor, the king is nothing when compared with a rose or a pink or a violet in the field. In this way our Lord God can adorn anyone whom He chooses to adorn. That is really an adornment, a color that no man can make or match, an adornment that no one could or would surpass. Though they were to be covered with pure gold and satin, they would still say: "I prefer the adornment of my Master up there in heaven, who adorns the little birds, to that of all the tailors and embroiderers on earth."

Now, since He dresses and adorns so many flowers with such a variety of colors, and each has its own coat, more splendid than all the adornment in the world, why is it that we cannot have faith that He will dress us as well? What are the flowers and the grass in the field when compared with us? And what were they created for except to stand there for a day or two, to let themselves be looked at, and then to wither and turn into hay? Or as Christ says, they are "thrown into the oven" to be burned and to heat the oven. Yet our Lord God regards these tiny and transient things so highly that He lavishes His gifts upon them and adorns them more beautifully than any earthly king or other human being. Yet they do not need this adornment; indeed, it is wasted upon them, since, with the flower, it soon perishes. But we are His highest creatures, for whose sakes He made all things and to whom He gives everything. We matter so much to Him that this life is not to be the end of us, but after this life He intends to give us eternal life. Now, should we not trust Him to clothe us as He clothes the flowers of the field with so many colors and the birds of the air with their lovely feathers? He is speaking satirically, in order to describe how abominable our unbelief is and to make it look as ridiculous as possible. . . . They sing and preach to us and smile at us so lovingly, just to have us believe. And yet we go right on letting them preach and sing, while we remain as greedy and selfish as ever. But to our eternal shame and disgrace each individual flower is a witness against us to condemn our unbelief before God and all the creatures until the Last Day. . . .

Forget your anxieties

> *Therefore do not be anxious, saying, "What shall we eat?" or, "What shall we drink?" or, "What shall we wear?" For the Gentiles seek all these things, and your heavenly Father knows that you need them all (6:31–32).*

Every day you see these illustrations before your very eyes, how God nourishes and feeds everything that lives and grows from the earth, clothes and adorns it so beautifully. Now let these illustrations persuade you to lay aside your anxiety and your unbelief and to remember that you are Christians and not heathen. Such anxiety and greed are appropriate to heathen, who do not know God or care about Him. It is really idolatry, as St. Paul says (Eph. 5:5; Col. 3:5) . . . .

"Since you are Christians," He says, "you dare not doubt that your Father is well aware of your need for all this, of the fact that you have a belly that needs food and drink and a body that needs clothing. If He did not know it, you would have reason to be concerned and anxious about how to provide for yourselves. But since He does know it, He will not forsake you. He is faithful and willing to take special care of you Christians, because, as has been said, He cares for the birds of the air as well. So forget your anxieties, since you cannot accomplish anything by them. It does not depend upon your anxiety but upon His knowledge and concern." If nothing grew in the field unless we were anxious about it, we would all have died in our cradles; and during the night, while we are lying asleep, nothing could grow. Indeed, even by worrying ourselves to death we could not make a single blade of grass grow in the field. We really ought to see and understand that God gives everything without any anxiety on our part, and yet we are such godless people that we refuse to give up our anxiety and our greed. Though it is up to Him to be concerned, as a father is concerned for his children, we refuse to leave it to Him.

BIBLE SELECTION
Matthew 6:25–34; 7:7–11

"Therefore I tell you, do not worry about your life, what you will eat or what you will drink, or about your body, what you will wear. Is not life more than food, and the body more than clothing? Look at the birds of the air; they neither sow nor reap nor gather into barns, and yet your heavenly Father feeds them. Are you not of more value than they? And can any of you by worrying add a single hour to your span of life? And why do you worry about clothing? Consider the lilies of the field, how they grow; they neither toil nor spin, yet I tell you, even Solomon in all glory was not clothed like one of these. But if God so clothes the grass of the field, which is alive today and tomorrow is thrown into the oven, will he not much more clothe you—you of little faith? Therefore do not worry, saying, 'What will we eat?' or 'What will we drink?' or 'What will we wear?' For it is the Gentiles who strive for all these things; and indeed your heavenly Father knows that you need all these things. But strive first for the kingdom of God—and his righteousness, and all these things will be given to you as well.

"So do not worry about tomorrow, for tomorrow will bring worries of its own. Today's trouble is enough for today. . . .

"Ask, and it will be given you; search, and you will find; knock, and the door will be opened for you. For everyone who asks receives, and everyone who searches finds, and for everyone who knocks, the door will be opened. Is there anyone among you who, if your child asks for bread, will give a stone? Or if the child asks for a fish, will give a snake? If you then, who are evil, know how to give good gifts to your children, how much more will your Father in heaven give good things to those who ask him!"

DISCUSSION QUESTIONS

The following can be used for discussion within a small group, or used for journal reflections by individuals:

1. Are there times when I am crippled by anxiety and stress? Do I sometimes take my feeling of worry and anxiety out on other people in my circle? How can Jesus' counsel help me with this?
2. What concrete steps might I take to develop a deeper trust in God?

SUGGESTED EXERCISES

The following exercises can be done by individuals, shared between spiritual friends, or used in the context of a small group. Choose one or more of the following:

1. During the next week spend some time listening to and watching the birds. Take into account the simplicity of their lives: fed with what they find, clothed with their own feathers, and sheltered in a rather haphazard way. Their alertness and vitality seem to suggest a confidence in God's plan. What can we learn from our observations?
2. Plan to visit a garden, if possible a really spectacular one where many different kinds of flowers are in bloom. Or, for a group meeting, buy a lovely bunch of flowers and display them for the group's reflection. What do these blooms have to say to us about our anxieties?

REFLECTIONS

I find Luther's distinction between "the concern of love" and "greedy concern" instructive. He is trying, of course, to help us understand Jesus' teaching: "Be not concerned . . ." Now, we all know that we cannot live without concern. Human existence simply cannot go on without it, and so Luther is helping us to distinguish between the concern that is necessary and good for human life and the concern that is destructive to it.

I like Luther's phrase "the concern of love" and I like what he says about it; namely, that it is a focused concern for the well-being of others. And I like his emphasis that "greedy concern" is tied to the issue of "the reliance and confidence of your heart." But I wish he would have unpacked it all a bit more. For example, am I expressing "greedy concern" when I take out a life insurance policy or set up a retirement plan? What about setting aside monies for the kids' college education? And what about . . . oh, hundreds of similar questions abound.

But then I realize that neither Jesus' words nor Luther's commentary upon them are meant to absolve me of wrestling with these issues for myself. They simply give me the idea of a life free from ulcer-generating anxiety and leave me with the responsibility of translating the reality into my life circumstances. Besides, as Luther reminds us, we have as many teachers and preachers as there are birds in the air, as many theologians and masters as there are flowers in the field.

RICHARD J. FOSTER

GOING DEEPER

JOHN DILLENBERGER, *Martin Luther: Selections from His Writings* (Garden City, NY: Doubleday, 1961). An excellent introduction to Luther's best work.

Martin Luther's Basic Theological Writings, edited by Timothy F. Lull (Minneapolis, MN: Fortress, 1989). A fine compendium of some of Luther's best theological writing, chosen and interpreted by one who understands Luther's relevance to many of the current theological debates.

MARTIN E. MARTY, *The Place of Trust: Martin Luther* (San Francisco: Harper & Row, 1983). This volume brings together passages from Luther's preaching on the Sermon on the Mount. As he reflects on Jesus' images and teaching, he speaks warmly and directly and brings parallels from his own experience to bear. Marty has arranged these selections under three main headings: trust, prayer, and the Beatitudes.

ROLAND BAINTON, *Here I Stand* (New York: Abingdon–Cokesbury, 1950). A classic and readable account of Luther's life and the circumstances that shaped it.

George Fox

(1624–1691)

———

George Fox was born and raised in the turmoil of seventeenth-century Puritan England. He became the founder and most prominent leader of the Quakers (the Society of Friends). He was a bold and passionate man who acted with the certainty of one who knows God firsthand, not by hearsay. He was quick to confront those who "did not possess what they professed." He laid bare pomposity and pretense. He also called thousands to a direct, intimate knowledge of Christ, who was present to teach and empower them. For his witness he was thrown into prison numerous times.

Fox's *Journal* initiated a new literary genre and is the first of a long line of religious journals, *The Journal of John Wesley* and *The Journal of John Woolman* being among the better known.

The selections that follow, taken from *The Journal of George Fox*, focus on his early prophetic "openings." Notice the ways in which these "openings" interface with the theme of Christian simplicity. There is something amazingly clear-cut and simple (in the best sense of that word) about true prophetic ministry.

THE JOURNAL OF GEORGE FOX

The Lord Opened unto Me

At another time, as I was walking in a field on a First-day morning, the Lord opened unto me that being bred at Oxford or Cambridge was not enough to fit and qualify men to be ministers of Christ; and I stranged at it [i.e., thought it strange] because it was the common belief of the people. But I saw clearly, as the Lord opened it to me, and was satisfied, and admired the goodness of the Lord who had opened this thing unto me that morning.

Then I heard a voice

Now after I had received that opening from the Lord that to be bred at Oxford or Cambridge was not sufficient to fit a man to be a minister of Christ, I regarded the priests less, and looked more after the dissenting people. And among them I saw there was some tenderness, and many of them came afterwards to be convinced, for they had some openings. But as I had forsaken all the priests, so I left the separate preachers also, and those called the most experienced people; for I saw there was none among them all that could speak to my condition. And when all my hopes in them and in all men were gone, so that I had nothing outwardly to help me, nor could tell what to do, then, Oh then, I heard a voice which said, "There is one, even Christ Jesus, that can speak to thy condition," and when I heard it my heart did leap for joy. . . . And this I knew experimentally.

Great openings, yet great troubles

Now though I had great openings, yet great trouble and temptations came many times upon me, so that when it was day I wished for night, and when it was night I wished for day; and by reason of the openings I had in my troubles, I could say as David said, "Day unto day uttereth speech, and night unto night showeth knowledge." And when I had openings, they answered one another and answered the Scriptures, for I had great openings of the Scriptures; and when I was in troubles, one trouble also answered to another.

But my troubles continued, and I was often under great temptations; and I fasted much, and walked abroad in solitary places many days, and often took my Bible and went and sat in hollow trees and lonesome places till night came on; and frequently in the night walked mournfully about by myself, for I was a man of sorrows in the times of the first workings of the Lord in me.

An ocean of light and love

The Lord shewed me that the natures of those things which were hurtful without were within, in the hearts and minds of wicked men. . . . The natures of these I saw within, though people had been looking without. And I cried to the Lord, saying, "Why should I be thus, seeing I was never addicted to commit those evils?" And the Lord answered that it was needful I should have a sense of all conditions, how else should I speak to all conditions; and in this I saw the infinite love of God. I also saw that there was an ocean of darkness and death, but an infinite ocean of light and love, which flowed over the ocean of darkness. And in that also I saw the infinite love of God, and I had great openings.

A great shaking

In the year 1648, as I was sitting in a Friend's house in Nottinghamshire . . . I saw there as a great crack to go throughout the earth, and a great smoke to go as the crack went, and that after the crack, there should be a great shaking. This was the earth in people's hearts, which was to be shaken before the Seed of God was raised out of the earth. And it was so; for the Lord's power began to shake them, and great meetings we began to have, and a mighty power and work of God there was amongst people, to the astonishment of both people and priests.

A *living hope arose in me*

One morning, as I was sitting by the fire, a great cloud came over me, and a temptation beset me; but I sat still. And it was said, "All things come by nature"; and the elements and stars came over me so that I was in a manner quite clouded with it. But inasmuch as I sat, still and silent, the people of the house perceived nothing. And as I sat still under it and let it alone, a living hope arose in me, and a true voice, which said, "There is a living God who made all things." And immediately the cloud and temptation vanished away, and life rose over it all, and my heart was glad, and I praised the living God.

A *briery, thorny wilderness*

And on a certain time, as I was walking in the fields, the Lord said unto me, "Thy name is written in the Lamb's book of life, which was before the foundation of the world"; and as the Lord spoke it I believed, and saw it in the new birth. Then, some time after, the Lord commanded me to go abroad into the world, which was like a briery, thorny wilderness, and when I came in the Lord's mighty power with the word of life into the world, the world swelled and made a noise like the great raging waves of the sea. Priests and professors, magistrates and people, were all like a sea, when I came to proclaim the day of the Lord amongst them and to preach repentance to them.

A *great people to be gathered*

At night we came to a country house; and there being no alehouse near they desired us to stay there all night, where we had a good service for the Lord, declaring his Truth amongst them; for the Lord had said unto me if I did but set up one in the same spirit that the prophets and apostles were in that gave forth the Scriptures, he or she should shake all the country in their profession ten miles about them . . .

And the next day we passed on, warning people as we met them of the day of the Lord that was coming upon them. As we went I spied a great high hill called Pendle Hill, and I went on the top of it with much ado, it was so steep; but I was moved of the Lord to go atop of it; and when I came atop of it I saw Lancashire sea; and there atop of the hill I was moved to sound the day of the Lord; and the Lord let me see a-top of the hill in what places he had a great people to be gathered. As I went down, on the hill side I found a spring of water and refreshed myself, for I had eaten little and drunk little for several days.

Many great and wonderful things

After I was set at liberty from Nottingham jail, where I had been kept prisoner a pretty long time, I travelled as before, in the work of the Lord.

Coming to Mansfield-Woodhouse, I found there a distracted woman under a doctor's hand, with her hair loose about her ears. He was about to let her blood, she being first bound, and many people about her, holding her by violence; but he could get no blood from her.

I desired them to unbind her and let her alone, for they could not touch the spirit in her by which she was tormented. So they did unbind her; and I was moved to speak to her, and in the name of the Lord to bid her be quiet; and she was so. The Lord's power settled her mind, and she mended. Afterwards she received the truth, and continued in it to her death; and the Lord's name was honoured.

Many great and wonderful things were wrought by the heavenly power in those days; for the Lord made bare His omnipotent arm, and manifested His power, to the astonishment of many, by the healing virtue whereby many have been delivered from great infirmities. And the devils were made subject through His name; of which particular instances might be given, beyond what this unbelieving age is able to receive or bear.

BIBLE SELECTION
Acts 8:4–8, 26–31, 35–39

Now those who were scattered went from place to place, proclaiming the word. Philip went down to the city of Samaria and proclaimed the Messiah to them. The crowds with one accord listened eagerly to what was said by Philip, hearing and seeing the signs that he did, for unclean spirits, crying with loud shrieks, came out of many who were possessed; and many others who were paralyzed or lame were cured. So there was great joy in that city.

Then an angel of the Lord said to Philip, "Get up and go toward the south to the road that goes down from Jerusalem to Gaza." (This is a wilderness road.) So he got up and went. Now there was an Ethiopian eunuch, a court official of the Candace, queen of the Ethiopians, in charge of her entire treasury. He had come to Jerusalem to worship and was returning home; seated in his chariot, he was reading the prophet Isaiah. Then the Spirit said to Philip, "Go over to this chariot and join it." So Philip ran up to it and heard him reading the prophet Isaiah. He asked, "Do you understand what you are reading?" He replied, "How can I, unless someone guides me?" And he invited Philip to get in and sit beside him.

Then Philip began to speak, and starting with this scripture, he proclaimed to him the good news about Jesus. As they were going along the road, they came to some water; and the eunuch said, "Look, here is water! What is to prevent me from being baptized?" He commanded the chariot to stop, and both of them, Philip and the eunuch, went down into the water, and Philip baptized him. When they came up out of the water, the Spirit of the Lord snatched Philip away; the eunuch saw him no more, and went on his way rejoicing.

DISCUSSION QUESTIONS

The following can be used for discussion within a small group, or used for journal reflections by individuals:

1. Where do I see evidences of a Pentecostal spirit in contemporary life?
2. Are there some examples of Pentecostal or prophetic ministries that I find disturbing? What are the reasons for this?

SUGGESTED EXERCISES

The following exercises can be done by individuals, shared between spiritual friends, or used in the context of a small group. Choose one or more of the following:

1. List, or name, examples of prophetic ministry either in our own time or in the last 200 to 300 years. What major social changes have been brought about by such prophetic events or ministries?
2. Share your experiences of Christian healing, especially any that may resemble the story George Fox tells.

REFLECTIONS

We have a tendency to think that, outside of the early church, true prophetic ministry is unique to us, with the early twentieth-century Pentecostal explosion or the slightly more refined charismatic renewal that broke out at mid-century in mainline churches. Basically this reflects historical ignorance combined with a touch of modern arrogance. *Prophetic ministry has been going on all through the history of the Church in both healthy and unhealthy ways.* Studying these sample "openings" of George Fox can yield useful insights into a more biblical and healthy form of prophetic witness. (Incidentally, as far as I know, describing prophetic insights as "openings" is unique to George Fox.)

One of the very first things we notice is how many of Fox's prophetic openings were tied to ethical and moral sensibilities. These insights were not centered on good feelings or personal spiritual goose bumps, but were *a call to righteous living.* In this Fox was standing squarely in the tradition of Isaiah and Jeremiah and Amos. And note how the message was first applied to the prophet himself. When Fox heard a voice saying, "There is one, even Christ Jesus, that can speak to thy condition," he understood this to be a call to Christian discipleship, to holy obedience.

Then notice that the prophetic witness focuses much more on "forth telling" than it does on "foretelling." To be sure, there is an element of predicting future events, as was true of Fox's experience on Pendle Hill, but being tantalized by the next revelation or end-times scenario is simply not the center of attention in any genuine prophetic ministry. No, *the center of attention is always upon proclaiming the good news of the kingdom of God and calling people to turn and walk in holiness of life.*

Third, prophetic ministry does not insulate the prophet from personal struggle. We see this especially in Fox's experience of "great openings, yet great trouble and temptations . . . upon me." Yet another example (which certainly has contemporary application) was his experience of being tempted by a kind of naturalism and how he was given to see that "there is a living God who made all things."

Finally, prophetic openings result in a call to mission. These openings are not merely for our own personal enjoyment or for our own private club. No, *prophets are called out for the good of others.* Following his vision on Pendle Hill of a "great people to be gathered" Fox launched into extensive preaching and teaching missions. One of these was "a-top of a rock" on Firbank Fell, a rock that to this day is known as "Fox's Pulpit." About a thousand people gathered around Fox as he was perched on a rock, and he preached for some three hours; "For the Lord had sent me with his everlasting gospel to preach . . . so that they might all come to know Christ their teacher, their counselor, their shepherd to feed them, and their bishop to oversee them and their prophet to open to them, and to know their bodies to be the temples of God and Christ for them to dwell in." Consider also the tender ministry Fox gave to the distraught woman and how God "settled her mind, and she mended." Would to God that we could have a similar effect upon those around us.

RICHARD J. FOSTER

GOING DEEPER

The Journal of George Fox, edited by John L. Nickalls (Cambridge: Cambridge University Press, 1952). Reprinted with corrections, London: London Yearly Meeting, 1986. Fox's *Journal* is prototypical of modern religious journal writing: powerful, cryptic, insightful, and compassionate all at once.

T. CANBY JONES, *George Fox's Attitude Toward War* (Annapolis, MD: Academic Fellowship, 1972). This is an excellent study of the background to the Quaker peace testimony with special attention given to what Fox himself said and believed about war. One special feature of this book is Dr. Jones's study of the distinctively Quaker notion of "The Lamb's War" and the final victory of God over all evil.

GEORGE FOX, *Narrative Papers of George Fox*, edited by Henry J. Cadbury (Richmond, IN: Friends United Press, 1972). An interesting collection of fragmentary *Journal* sources, letters to Margaret Fell, and a kind of "lives of the saints" of Quaker ministers.

EDMUND GOERKE, *The Gift of Healing in the Life of George Fox* (Gloucester, UK: Fellowship Press, 1972). A booklet highlighting the healing ministry of George Fox. It seeks to make a case for Pentecostal-style works in the beginnings of the Quaker movement.

Clare of Assisi

(1194–1253)

Clare of Assisi is the founder of the Poor Clares, a community dedicated to poverty, simplicity, and service. Born to a noble family in Assisi in 1194, she was converted under the influence of Francis of Assisi in 1211. She escaped from her parental home and received the habit from Francis on March 18–19, 1212, in the Church of the Portiuncula. Soon her sister Agnes followed her into the religious life, as did her mother, Ortolana, and her sister Beatrice. In 1215–16 Pope Innocent III granted Clare's community the privilege of taking the vow of poverty.

Although Clare was ill and confined to a sickbed from 1224 until her death (the exact nature of her illness is not known), she was widely recognized for her holiness and exerted great influence. Because of her devotion to the Holy Eucharist it was said that she helped to spare Assisi from the assault of the Saracens.

After many difficulties, the Rule of her community was approved on August 9, 1253, just two days before her death. Two short years after her death she was proclaimed a saint by the Roman Catholic Church.

The following short reading, which is taken from a letter, contains counsels directed to Blessed Agnes of Prague. They develop the notion of God-centered poverty, not as a lack of material goods, but as a spiritual discipline of simplicity and detachment of heart.

LETTERS TO BLESSED AGNES OF PRAGUE

All for Nothing, Nothing for All

> O blessed poverty,
>> who bestows eternal riches on those who love and
>> embrace her!
> O holy poverty,
>> to those who possess and desire you
>> God promises *the kingdom of heaven*
>> and offers, indeed, eternal glory and blessed life!
> O God-centered poverty,

whom the Lord Jesus Christ
Who ruled and now rules heaven and earth,
Who spoke and things were made,
condescended to embrace before all else!

The foxes have dens, He says, *and the birds of the air have nests, but the Son of Man,* Christ, *has nowhere to lay His head* (Matt. 8:20), but *bowing His head gave up His spirit* (John 19:30).

If so great and good a Lord, then, on coming into the Virgin's womb, chose to appear despised, needy, and *poor* in this world, so that people who were in utter poverty and want and in absolute need of heavenly nourishment might become *rich* (cf. 2 Cor. 8:9) in Him by possessing the kingdom of heaven, then *rejoice and be glad* (Hab. 3:18)! Be filled with a remarkable happiness and a spiritual joy! Contempt of the world has pleased You more than [its] honors, poverty more than earthly riches, and You have sought to store up greater *treasures in heaven* rather than on earth, *where rust does not consume nor moth destroy nor thieves break in and steal* (Matt. 6:20). *Your reward,* then, *is very great in heaven* (Matt. 5:12)! And You have truly merited to be called a *sister, spouse, and mother* (2 Cor. 11:2; Matt. 12:50) of the Son of the Father of the Most High and of the glorious Virgin.

The trouble with temporal things
You know, I am sure, that the kingdom of heaven is promised and given by the Lord only to the poor (see Matt. 5:3): for he who loves temporal things loses the fruit of love. Such a person *cannot serve God and Mammon,* for *either the one is loved and the other hated,* or *the one* is served *and the other despised* (Matt. 6:24).

You also know that one who is clothed cannot fight with another who is naked, because he is more quickly thrown who gives his adversary a chance to get hold of him; and that one who lives in the glory of earth cannot rule with Christ in heaven.

Again, [you know] that it is easier for *a camel to pass through the eye of a needle than for a rich man to enter the kingdom of heaven* (Matt. 19:24). Therefore, you have cast aside Your garments, that is, earthly riches, so that You might not be overcome by the one fighting against You, [and] that You might enter the kingdom of heaven *through the straight path and the narrow gate* (Matt. 7:13–14).

What a great laudable exchange:

to leave the things of time for those of eternity,
to choose the things of heaven for the goods of earth,
to receive the hundred-fold in place of one,
and *to possess* a blessed and eternal *life.*

Because of this I have resolved, as best I can, to beg Your excellency and Your holiness by my humble prayers in the mercy of Christ, to be strengthened in His holy service, and to progress from good to better, *from virtue to virtue* (Ps. 83:8), so that He Whom You serve with the total desire of Your soul may bestow on You the reward for which You long.

BIBLE SELECTION
Matthew 8:18–22

Now when Jesus saw great crowds around him, he gave orders to go over to the other side. A scribe then approached and said, "Teacher, I will follow you wherever You go." And Jesus said to him, "Foxes have holes, and birds of the air have nests; but the Son of Man has nowhere to lay his head." Another of his disciples said to him, "Lord, first let me go and bury my father." But Jesus said to him, "Follow me, and let the dead bury their own dead."

DISCUSSION QUESTIONS

The following can be used for discussion within a small group, or used for journal reflections by individuals:

1. Joining a vowed religious community is one way that Christians may follow the evangelical counsels of poverty, chastity, and obedience. Are there other ways to make such a commitment in contemporary life?
2. Do we need to rid ourselves of all our possessions and become materially poor in order to practice simplicity? If we do not, what other ways can we practice simplicity of life?

SUGGESTED EXERCISES

The following exercises can be done by individuals, shared between spiritual friends, or used in the context of a small group. Choose one or more of the following:

1. Make a list of the possessions you have that you find burdensome and would be better off without. Do you wish you could dump them all in one spot? Or are some of these possessions necessary to the fulfilment of your obligations as worker, parent, householder, and citizen? Discuss.

2. Make a list of the possessions you have that you treasure. Are your material "treasures" (family keepsakes, portraits, photograph albums) in some way connected to your spiritual development? Or are they getting in the way of it? How?

3. Think of one realistic step you could take in your own life to practice the discipline of simplicity. You may wish to outline several options (giving unwanted possessions to a thrift shop, donating a car that you don't need to an organization or a needy person, cutting down on the number of organizations you belong to or the number of activities you engage in each week or month). Write the step down in your journal or somewhere else as a real commitment, and stick to it.

REFLECTIONS

I have always been intrigued by the vows of poverty, chastity, and obedience, though I have never been tempted toward a monastic community life myself—Carolynn, my wife, would never hear of it! Why, I wondered, these particular three vows? Why not some others? Or why not vows to deal with other areas of life? Why poverty, chastity, and obedience?

Then one day (I well remember the day) it dawned on me that these vows were designed to respond to the three great ethical issues of human life: money, sex, and power. These are the crucial themes all of us struggle with throughout our lives. Nor are these just individual matters; they are issues with profound social implications. The social dimension to money is business; for sex it is marriage; for power it is government.

These vowed communities then were attempting to give an answer to the question of how we might live in right relationship toward these most important of issues: money, sex, and power. Now, we may feel that their answer was inadequate in certain respects, or at least that it was an answer that few of us can follow, but we must admire their courage to take on the three great issues of life. And this selection from Clare of Assisi shows us something of the beauty of such efforts.

Most of us, however, will never live as Clare lived. We could not do so even if we wanted to. And yet, we too must give an answer to how we will live in relationship to these three great issues of life. My own answer, in brief, is this: in response to the issue of money we learn to live in simplicity; in response to the issue of sex we learn to live in fidelity; in response to the issue of power we learn to live in service. What would your answer be?

RICHARD J. FOSTER

GOING DEEPER

Francis and Clare: The Complete Works, translated with an introduction by Regis J. Armstrong and Ignatius C. Brady, preface by John Vaughan (New York: Paulist, 1982); a volume in *The Classics of Western Spirituality* series. This book allows us to see the close relationship between two holy lives, that of Francis of Assisi and Clare. The biographical material shows how, despite their differences of age and class, the two were able to influence each other and guide many others toward holiness of life.

FRANCO ZEFFIRELLI, *Brother Sun, Sister Moon* (UK/Italy: Paramount/Vic Films/ Euro International, 1972). This feature film presents an attractive and engaging view of the spiritual friendship and collaboration of Francis and Clare. Available for rental at video stores and for purchase on the Internet.

Solitude

———

Anne Morrow Lindbergh

(1907–)

———

Anne Morrow and her husband, Charles Lindbergh, were both children of United States senators. He is best remembered for the first transatlantic solo flight on May 20–21, 1927. The Lindberghs were married in 1928 and made aviation history through worldwide transoceanic travels. She served as navigator and radio operator on these flights, one of which took them from the United States to Labrador, Greenland, Iceland, Africa, and South America, traversing a total of 29,081 miles and touching twenty-one countries. Anne wrote and published popular accounts of their journeys.

Always in the spotlight, the Lindberghs were the object of much media attention and sympathy when their first son, an infant born in 1930, was kidnapped and later found dead. They had a second son, born in 1932.

The Christian faith dimension became more apparent in Anne Lindbergh's later writing. _A Gift from the Sea,_ a meditation on marriage, is perhaps her most enduring work. She wrote it during a month of complete solitude on an island on the Atlantic shore. Her rich insights acquaint us with the spiritual value of solitude, which is not practiced for its own sake but in order to gain clarity in our own lives and relationships.

In the following selection, notice how Anne Lindbergh expresses herself in terms suggested by the seashore in which she is having her solitary time. She mentions "the common sea of the universal," the "eternal ebb and flow," linking these sea images to human images, the movements of dancers who move closer together and then farther apart. Since she herself is on an island, the idea of an island is explored as well. An ongoing motif is that of the argonauta, which is a sea creature named after the famous argonaut in ancient mythology, Jason, who went in search of the golden fleece.

THE GIFT FROM THE SEA

The Silent Beach, the Bowl of Stars

Relationship is not strangled by claims. Intimacy is tempered by lightness of touch. We have moved through our day like dancers, not needing to touch more than lightly because we were instinctively moving to the same rhythm.

A good relationship has a pattern like a dance and is built on some of the same rules. The partners do not need to hold on tightly, because they move confidently in the same pattern, intricate but gay and swift and free, like a country dance of Mozart's. To touch heavily would be to arrest the pattern and freeze the movement, to check the endlessly changing beauty of its unfolding. There is no place here for the possessive clutch, the clinging arm, the heavy hand; only the barest touch in passing. Now arm in arm, now face to face, now back to back—it does not matter which. Because they know they are partners moving to the same rhythm, creating a pattern together, and being invisibly nourished by it.

The joy of such a pattern is not only the joy of creation or the joy of participation, it is also the joy of living in the moment. Lightness of touch and living in the moment are intertwined. . . .

When the heart is flooded with love

But how does one learn this technique of the dance? Why is it so difficult? What makes us hesitate and stumble? It is fear, I think, that makes one cling nostalgically to the last moment or clutch greedily toward the next. . . . But how to exorcize it? It can only be exorcized by its opposite, love. When the heart is flooded with love there is no room in it for fear, for doubt, for hesitation. And it is this lack of fear that makes for the dance. When each partner loves so completely that he has forgotten to ask himself whether or not he is loved in return; when he only knows that he loves and is moving to its music—then, and then only, are two people able to dance perfectly in tune to the same rhythm.

But is this all to the relationship of the argonauta—this private pattern of two dancers perfectly in time? Should they not also be in tune with a larger rhythm, a natural swinging of the pendulum between sharing and solitude; between the intimate and the abstract; between the particular and the universal, the near and the far? And is it not the swinging of the pendulum between these opposite poles that makes a relationship nourishing? Yeats once said that the supreme experience of life was "to share profound thought and then to touch." But it takes both.

Separating and uniting

First touch, intimate touch of the personal and particular (the chores in the kitchen, the talk by the fire); then the loss of intimacy in the great stream of the impersonal and abstract (the silent beach, the bowl of stars overhead). Both partners are lost in a common sea of the universal which absorbs and yet frees, which separates and yet unites. Is this not what the more mature relationship, the meeting of two solitudes, is meant to be? The double-sunrise stage was only intimate and personal. The oyster bed was caught in the particular and the functional. But the argonauta, should they not be able to swing from the intimate and the particular and the functional out into the abstract and the universal, and then back to the personal again?

And in this image of the pendulum swinging in easy rhythm between opposite poles, is there not a clue to the problem of relationships as a whole? Is there not here even a hint of an understanding and an acceptance of the wingèd life of relationships, of their eternal ebb and flow, of their inevitable intermittency? . . .

The ebb and flow of life

When you love someone you do not love them all the time, in exactly the same way, from moment to moment. It is an impossibility. It is even a lie to pretend to. And yet this is exactly what most of us demand. We have so little faith in the ebb and flow of life, of love, of relationships. We leap at the flow of the tide and resist in terror its ebb. We are afraid it will never return. We insist on permanency, on duration, on continuity; when the only continuity possible, in life as in love, is in growth, in fluidity—in freedom, in the sense that the dancers are free, barely touching as they pass, but partners in the same pattern.

The only real security is not in owning or possessing, not in demanding or expecting, not in hoping, even. Security in a relationship lies neither in looking back to what it was in nostalgia, nor forward to what it might be in dread or anticipation, but living in the present relationship and accepting it as it is now. For relationships, too, must be like islands. One must accept them for what they are here and now, within their limits—islands, surrounded and interrupted by the sea, continually visited and abandoned by the tides. . . .

The most important thing

How can one learn to live through the ebb-tides of one's existence? How can one learn to take the trough of the wave? It is easier to understand here on the beach, where the breathlessly still ebb-tides reveal another life below the level which mortals usually reach. In this crystalline moment of suspense, one has a sudden revelation of the secret kingdom at the bottom of the sea. Here in the shallow flats one finds, wading through warm ripples, great horse-conchs pivoting on a leg; white sand dollars, marble medallions engraved in the mud; and log myriads of bright-colored cochina-clams, glistening in the foam, their shells opening and shutting like butterflies' wings. So beautiful is the still hour of the sea's withdrawal, as beautiful as the sea's return when the encroaching waves pound up the beach, pressing to reach those dark rumpled chains of seaweed which mark the last high tide.

Perhaps this is the most important thing for me to take back from beach-living: simply the memory that each cycle of the tide is valid; each cycle of the wave is valid; each cycle of a relationship is valid. And my shells? I can sweep them all into my pocket. They are only there to remind me that the sea recedes and returns eternally.

BIBLE SELECTION
Proverbs 31:10–31

A capable wife who can find?
  She is far more precious than jewels.
The heart of her husband trusts in her,
  and he will have no lack of gain.
She does him good, and not harm,
  all the days of her life.
She seeks wool and flax,
  and works with willing hands.
She is like the ships of the merchant,
  she brings her food from far away.
She rises while it is still night
  and provides food for her household
  and tasks for her servant girls.
She considers a field and buys it;
  with the fruit of her hands she plants a vineyard.
She girds herself with strength,
  and makes her arms strong.
She perceives that her merchandise is profitable.
  Her lamp does not go out at night.
She puts her hands to the distaff,
  and her hands hold the spindle.
She opens her hand to the poor,
  and reaches out her hands to the needy.
She is not afraid for her household when it snows,
  for all her household are clothed in crimson.
She makes herself coverings;
  her clothing is fine linen and purple.
Her husband is known in the city gates,
  taking his seat among the elders of the land.
She makes linen garments and sells them;
  she supplies the merchant with sashes.

Strength and dignity are her clothing,
   and she laughs at the time to come.
She opens her mouth with wisdom,
   and the teaching of kindness is on her tongue.
She looks well to the ways of her household,
   and does not eat the bread of idleness.
Her children rise up and call her happy;
   her husband too, and he praises her:
"Many women have done excellently,
   but you surpass them all."
Charm is deceitful, and beauty is vain,
   but a woman who fears the LORD is to be praised.
Give her a share in the fruit of her hands,
   and let her works praise her in the city gates.

DISCUSSION QUESTIONS

The following can be used for discussion within a small group, or used for journal reflections by individuals:

1. How can I arrange for times of quiet and separation from daily obligations? What will point to God in such times?
2. Which relationships in my life could be strengthened by a time of solitude?

SUGGESTED EXERCISES

The following exercises can be done by individuals, shared between spiritual friends, or used in the context of a small group. Choose one or more of the following:

1. Devote a portion of your week to solitude; say, half an hour during lunchtime, or several hours on a Saturday afternoon. During this time reflect on one important relationship in your life. Write in your journal about the experience.
2. Remember a time of solitude that benefited you in the past. Share this with others in your group (or another spiritual friend) with a view to continuing the benefits of solitude at a future time.
3. Daydream about going to an "island," as Anne Morrow Lindbergh did. Is there some place that is within your power to visit in search of spiritual

time, if only you would actually plan it? Consider planning a formal or
informal retreat time in such a place.

4. Plan a day of complete solitude close to home, or if it can be accomplished,
within your own home. Treat this solitude as sacred time. Turn off the
phones (or plan not to answer them); cherish the beauty of solitude within
your own walls. Afterward, reflect on the difficulties and blessings of this
experience. What did you learn about yourself and your relationships (to
God and others) during this solitary time?

REFLECTIONS

*Isn't it interesting that in a prolonged time of solitude Anne Morrow Lindbergh
decided to write on marriage, relationship, and intimacy. You see, being completely
alone in solitude can often heighten our understanding of those we love most. A
companion to solitude is silence, and together they enable us to value people for
who they are, not for what they say.*

*It is interesting to me how deeply the setting of Lindbergh's island retreat worked
itself into her insights into relationships. I am thinking especially about her discussion of the ebb and flow of relationships, obviously suggested to her by the coming
and going of the tides upon the shore that she observed day after day. "We have so
little faith," she writes, "in the ebb and flow of life, of love, of relationships. We leap
at the flow of the tide and resist in terror its ebb." This stress upon the fluidity and
growth of relationships is perhaps her most valuable insight.*

*And, notice, she has done little more than a thoughtful, prayerful meditation
upon the creation. We might call it a bit of nature theology, believing that God has
placed in his created order certain truths about the reality of life under God. Then
she uses this understanding to help us through the ebb tides of our relationships. Just
as the ebb tides of the ocean reveal "the secret kingdom at the bottom of the sea" so
the ebb tide periods in our marriage or other relationships can uncover for us a richer
understanding of ourselves and others.*

RICHARD J. FOSTER

GOING DEEPER

ANNE MORROW LINDBERGH, *A Gift from the Sea* (New York: Pantheon Books, 1975). This edition has Lindbergh's eight original chapters (first published in 1955) and a twentieth-anniversary commentary by the author.

RICHARD FOSTER, "The Discipline of Solitude," in *Celebration of Discipline: The Path to Spiritual Growth* (San Francisco: Harper & Row, revised edition, 1988), pp. 96–109. Richard Foster explores solitude and silence as graced opportunities, using evocative language to invite us deeper into the heart of God.

EMILIE GRIFFIN, *Wilderness Time: A Guide to Spiritual Retreat* (San Francisco: HarperSanFrancisco, 1997). Emilie Griffin's guide offers practical suggestions on what to do with our solitude when making a retreat.

Thomas à Kempis

(c. 1379–1471)

———

Thomas à Kempis was a member of the Brethren of the Common Life, a religious community in Holland devoted to education and the care of the poor. Well educated himself, he spent his life as a copyist of manuscripts both sacred and secular, and as a spiritual director to young men wanting to join his order, a branch of the Augustinians.

His book, _The Imitation of Christ,_ first published in 1441, has become a classic devotional work with multicentury impact like John Bunyan's _The Pilgrim's Progress_. The _Imitation_ has been called the perfect expression of a spiritual movement known as _devotio moderna_ (modern devotion), which swept Roman Catholicism through the fourteenth to sixteenth centuries. It stressed meditation and the inner life and cautioned against the outer life of much busyness and occupation.

In the selection that follows, Kempis develops the importance of solitude and silence for one who would follow Jesus. He consistently counterpoints life outside the monastery with life inside, much to the advantage of the latter.

For those outside the monastery who cannot fully adopt a monastic style of life, Kempis's ideas are nevertheless useful. From time to time we can place ourselves in the cloister in a spiritual way, to gain the benefits of the monk's singleness of heart.

As you read the following selection, which is Book One, Chapter 20, imagine that you are a resident of a fifteenth-century monastery or convent. Each person there has a private room (cell or cubicle) that has in it a cot, a kneeler, possibly even a chair. The room may have a door or curtain. The rest of the religious house included rooms used in common: chapel, dining hall, library, and kitchen. Monasteries and convents today are similarly arranged, but usually with less austere furnishings and more relaxed rules for daily living.

THE IMITATION OF CHRIST

Solitude and Silence

Plan to take some time off, and give some thought as to what you'd do with that time; hopefully, you'll spend part of it reviewing God's favors to you in the past. What else? Lock up ye olde curiosity shop. Devote more time to reading your spiritual books than your survival manuals. Withdraw from casual conversations and leisurely pursuits. Don't contract for new ventures, and don't gossip about old ones. All these having been done, you'll find more than enough time to undertake a program of meditation. Most of the Saints did just that, avoided collaborative projects whenever they could, choosing instead to spend some private time with God.

Leave the crowd behind

Seneca, that old pagan philosopher and playwright, had it right so many centuries ago. When he went out with the intelligentsia or hung about with the entertainment crowd, he returned home utterly talked out and terribly hoarse, or so he said in one of his letters (Letter 7). Quite often we have the same experience when we horse around with our friends and associates for hours, even days, on end.

What's the remedy for a talkathon? It's easier to cut out the conversation altogether than it is to cut it down. What's the wisdom? It's easier to stay at home alone than to stroll the rialto with a bodyguard. What's certain? The person who wants to arrive at interiority and spirituality has to leave the crowd behind and spend some time with Jesus.

Nobody's comfortable in public unless he's spent a good deal of time in the quiet of his home. Nobody speaks with assurance who hasn't learned to hold his tongue. Nobody's a success as general who hasn't already survived as a soldier. Nobody respects decrees who hasn't already obeyed writs.

Feeling anything but secure

If a person wants to feel secure, then he has to have a good conscience. That's how the Saints did it. Virtue and grace shone from their very faces, but the fear of God ran in their very veins; even then they were subject to fits of spiritual anxiety and secular stress.

As for the depraved, what security they do feel in their being rises from a swamp of pride and presumption resolving itself into a pool of despond.

What's the moral? On the outside you may appear modest as a monk or holy as a hermit; but on the inside, at least while you're on this earth, you're seething and insecure.

Temptation helps

More often than they might suspect, people of reputation have been in grave danger and didn't know it; they're good people, but they've extended their self-confidence beyond its natural limit. From this one could draw the conclusion that it's helpful to be tempted from time to time. One might even say that to be tempted to the point of endurance could help deflate interior desolations and deflect exterior consolations.

Who doesn't seek transitory joy? Who doesn't occupy himself with the world! We all do, but the one who has a good conscience, severs all tentacles to attachment, and meditates on divine and salutary things, he's the one who places his whole hope in God. He's the one who sails his boats on a sea of calm.

Sorrow helps

No one can ascend to heavenly consolation. That's because there's no sure stair. One solid step, though, is our heart's true sorrow. And where else can this sorrow be found but in one's cubicle; there you can shut out the hubbub of the world. "In your cubicles, work out your sorrowful contrition," says the psalmist (4:4). More often than not, you'll find in your cell what you lost in the streets.

A cell that's much prayed in is a pleasant spot. A cell that's rarely prayed in is a forbidding place. In the first blush of your conversion, you did what you were supposed to do, cultivate the solitude of your cell, and guard against the invasions of your quietude. Now you find it comfortable, welcoming, like an old dog or an old shoe.

Silence and quiet

In quiet and silence the faithful soul makes progress, the hidden meanings of the Scriptures become clear, and the eyes weep with devotion every night. Even as one learns to grow still, he draws closer to the Creator and farther from the hurly-burly of the world. As one divests himself of friends and acquaintances, he is visited by God and his holy angels.

Two courses of action. Better, to lie still in one's cubicle and worry about one's spiritual welfare. Worse, to roam the streets a wonderworker for others to the neglect of one's own spiritual life. Laudable it is for the religious to go to market only rarely. Laudable too is that, even when the religious goes, he refrains from meeting the eyes of others; from his very mien they know that he lives in another world.

Sickness and sadness

Why do you want to go out and see what you really shouldn't need to see? "The world passes, as does its concupiscence," wrote the Evangelist John (2:17). Our sensual desires promise us a promenade, but deliver us only a dragonnade. A sprightly step in the forenoon turns into a draggled tail in the afternoon. All-nighters of roister-doistery lead only to mornings of huggermuggery; that is to say, of sickness and sadness. Need I speak it? Every carnal joy begins with a caress, but in the end curls up into a ball and dies. I ask the question again. What can you see outside the monastery walls that you can't see inside? Behold heaven and earth and all the elements; from these all things are made.

Peace and quiet
What can you see on the outside that will survive the sun? Perhaps you believe you can find satisfaction out there somewhere, but truth to tell, you still can't reach it. If you were to cram all the things of the world into one still life, no matter how large the canvas, you'd still be no better off.

"Raise your eyes to God in the highest," says the psalmist (122:1). Pray for your own sins and negligences. Forgive the vain things the vain people have done.

Look to the precepts God gave you. "Shut the door behind you," wrote the Evangelist Matthew (6:6). Call Jesus, your beloved friend, to join you. Remain with him in your cell because you won't find such peace elsewhere.

As for the common wisdom, if you hadn't gone out, you wouldn't have heard the disturbing rumors; better for you to have stayed at home in blissful ignorance. From which it follows that you may delight in hearing the latest news on the strand, but you'll surely have to deal with the sense of dislocation that results.

BIBLE SELECTION
Ecclesiastes 1:1–14

The words of the Teacher, the son of David, king in Jerusalem.
Vanity of vanities, says the Teacher,
  vanity of vanities! All is vanity.
What do people gain from all the toil
  at which they toil under the sun?
A generation goes, and a generation comes,
  but the earth remains forever.
The sun rises and the sun goes down,
  and hurries to the place where it rises.
The wind blows to the south,
  and goes around to the north;

round and round goes the wind,
and on its circuits the wind returns.
All streams run to the sea,
but the sea is not full;
to the place where the streams flow,
there they continue to flow.
All things are wearisome;
more than one can express;
the eye is not satisfied with seeing,
or the ear filled with hearing.
What has been is what will be,
and what has been done is what will be done;
there is nothing new under the sun.
Is there a thing of which it is said,
"See, this is new"?
It has already been,
in the ages before us.
The people of long ago are not remembered,
nor will there be any remembrance
of people yet to come
by those who come after them.

I, the Teacher, when king over Israel in Jerusalem, applied my mind to seek and to search out by wisdom all that is done under heaven; it is an unhappy business that God has given to human beings to be busy with. I saw all the deeds that are done under the sun; and see, all is vanity and a chasing after wind.

DISCUSSION QUESTIONS

The following can be used for discussion within a small group, or used for journal reflections by individuals:

1. What kinds of overactivity affect me? Do the demands of the telephone overload my day? Are my letters and correspondence (however welcome in one sense) stacking up? Are there any blank spaces left on my appointment calendar? How does Thomas à Kempis's concern about overinvolvement in the "outer life" apply to me?
2. In what realistic ways can I gain the benefits of solitude and silence?

SUGGESTED EXERCISES

The following exercises can be done by individuals, shared between spiritual friends, or used in the context of a small group. Choose one or more of the following:

1. Set up a prayer space in your home, and plan to use it regularly for a month to six weeks on a specified schedule. Arrange this space with encouragements to prayer: an extra Bible, postcards with visuals of religious subjects, a book of meditations. Dialogue with others about the good effects of doing this.

2. During the coming week enter into the cubicle or cell of your heart, that interior space where you can pursue your friendship with Jesus. Enjoy and delight in his conversation and company.

3. List in your journal (or with your group) two or three practical steps you can take to stop rushing around, spinning your wheels, and running scared from life pressures. (What about taking a day off from local, national, and international news?) Don't try to reinvent the monastic life; but absorb into your heart and your thought the real wisdom of what Thomas à Kempis has to say.

REFLECTIONS

Please don't try to find this Thomas à Kempis selection in any of your standard editions of the Imitation. *It is an original translation by William Griffin, a fellow writer who possesses an exceptional facility with both Latin and English. He's quite serious and sensible, and at the same time an extremely funny chap.*

I mean, only Bill Griffin, an old friend of mine, would have the imagination (and the daring) to translate "Trahunt desideria sensualitatis ad spatiandum: sed cum hora transierit, quid nisi gravitatem conscientiae, et cordis dispersionem, reportas?" (Literally, "The desires of sensuality draw us to take a walk; but when the hour shall have passed, what do you have to report except a heaviness of conscience and a scattering of the heart?") as "Our sensual desires promise us a promenade, but deliver us only a dragonnade."

And then, I all but fell out of my chair when I came upon this line: "All-nighters of roister-doistery lead only to mornings of huggermuggery." Funny, but at the same time right to the point because such behavior does indeed produce only sickness and sadness. I love Mr. Griffin's translation, scholarly and urbane.

Now, the key point of this selection is to understand solitude as a primary discipline in the spiritual life. Kempis writes, "The person who wants to arrive at interiority and spirituality has to leave the crowd behind and spend some time with Jesus." But why, why are experiences of solitude so foundational to building a spiritual life? First and foremost because in times of solitude we take the world off our shoulders and suspend our need to manage and control everyone and everything. One person with great relief, said to me, "I hereby resign as CEO of the universe." Solitude, you see, gives us perspective about our place in God's great kingdom of love. For example, in our first experiences of solitude we will be astonished (and humbled) to realize that the world—even our family and neighbors and coworkers—are able to get along quite well without us.

Solitude, you see, gives us the space to look carefully and prayerfully at all the hair-trigger responses we have for doing and saying exactly the opposite of how Jesus taught us to live. I am thinking of things like our spontaneous anger whenever others voice opinions different from ours, our instant fear whenever our position is threatened, our verbal manipulation aimed at getting others to think and do as we want. And once we see these hair-trigger responses to life's situations we can then prayerfully discover and enter into new, more Christlike responses. This, and much more, is the fruit of solitude.

RICHARD J. FOSTER

GOING DEEPER

THOMAS À KEMPIS, _The Imitation of Christ_, edited by William C. Creasy (Notre Dame, IN: Ave Maria, 1989). The introduction to the book tells the reader much about the life of Kempis, the birth of the book, the history of the manuscripts, and just how one goes about translating a classic into English. The translation itself has been done with an eye for the needs of the modern reader.

Devotion Moderna: Basic Writings, translated with an introduction by John Van Engen, preface by Heiko A. Oberman (New York: Paulist, 1988). This places Kempis in the spiritual world of the Netherlands in the fifteenth century, with selections from such other writers as Geert Grote, John Brinckerinck, Salome Sticken, and Gerard Zerbolt of Zutphen.

John Main

(1926–1982)

Dom John Main understood well the value of both silence and solitude. Born in London to a family of Irish descent, he served in British intelligence during World War II and later was stationed in Malaya with the British Colonial Service.

Always drawn to religion and the spiritual life, Main rediscovered meditation while living in the Far East. He returned to lecture in International Law at Trinity College, Dublin, and afterward (1957) entered the Benedictine order at Ealing Abbey in London.

Influenced by the fifth-century writings of John Cassian, Main learned the ancient Christian discipline of the prayer of silence. He began teaching the ways of silence, solitude, and prayer to a wide variety of audiences in many parts of the world. He founded the Benedictine Priory of Montreal and established a world-wide spiritual family linked through the practice of meditation.

In the following selection, an essay taken from his book *Moments of Christ: The Path of Meditation*, Father John is not just teaching us a style of praying. Neither does he advise either solitude or silence just for its own sake. Silence is a path into the reality of the universe, where God is in charge and we are not, where we can be flooded by God's love. Notice also how his understanding of this way of being flows out of scriptural understandings, such as those of St. Paul.

MOMENTS OF CHRIST: THE PATH OF MEDITATION

The Meaning of Silence

There is a great feeling among our contemporaries, I think, of the need, perhaps even the extremely urgent need, to recover the spiritual dimension in our lives. There is a feeling that unless we do recover that spiritual dimension we are going to lose our grip on life altogether. In meeting that feeling we must be perfectly clear that a commitment to spiritual values is by no means a rejection of the ordinary things of life. Indeed the exact opposite is true. Commitment to the spiritual reality is simply commitment to reality and it is the way to really appreciate the wonder of all life. It is the way to come to understand the extraordinary fact of the mystery of life itself, the inner hidden secret of life that gives it its real excitement.

Entering on the spiritual path is coming to appreciate our life as a voyage of discovery. It is certainly my experience that, if you set out on the path of meditation with this commitment to enter deeply into your own interior hidden life, then every day for you will become a revelation of new dimensions to that life and a deeper understanding of it.

A journey into profound silence

Now to tread the spiritual path we must learn to be silent. What is required of us is a journey into profound silence. Part of the problem of the weakening of religion in our times is that religion uses words for its prayers and rituals, but those words have to be charged with meaning and they must be charged with sufficient meaning to move our hearts, to set us out in new directions and to change our lives. They can only be charged with this degree of meaning if they spring from spirit, and spirit requires silence. We all need to use words, but to use them with power we all need to be silent. We all need religion, we all need the Spirit. Meditation is the way to silence because it is the way of silence. . . .

Now we don't need to be too abstract about this. We all know that we can often come to know another person most profoundly in silence. To be silent with another person is a deep expression of trust and confidence and it is only when we are unconfident that we feel compelled to talk. To be silent with another person is truly to *be* with that other person. Nothing is so powerful in building mutual confidence between people than a silence which is easeful and creative. Nothing reveals inauthenticity more dramatically than silence that is not creative but fearful.

Letting silence emerge

I think what all of us have to learn is that we do not have to create silence. The silence is there within us. What we have to do is to enter into it, to become silent, to become the silence. The purpose of meditation and the challenge of meditation is to allow ourselves to become silent enough to allow this interior silence to emerge. Silence is the language of the Spirit.

These words of St. Paul writing to the Ephesians, are charged with the power of silence.

> With this in mind, then, I kneel in prayer to the Father, from whom every family in heaven and on earth takes its name, that out of the treasures of his glory he may grant you strength and power through his Spirit in your inner being, that through faith Christ may dwell in your hearts in love (Eph. 3:14–16).

The words we use in trying to communicate the Christian message in the Christian experience have to be charged with strength and power, but they can only be charged with strength and power if they spring from the silence of the Spirit in our inner being. . . . Leaving behind all other words, ideas, imaginations and fantasies is learning to enter into the presence of the Spirit who dwells in your inner heart, who dwells there in love. The Spirit of God dwells in our hearts in silence, and it is in humility and in faith that we must enter into that silent presence. St. Paul ends that passage in Ephesians with the words, "So may you attain to fullness of being, the fullness of God himself." That is our destiny.

BIBLE SELECTION
Ephesians 3:14–21

For this reason I bow my knees before the Father from whom every family in heaven and on earth takes its name. I pray that, according to the riches of his glory, he may grant that you may be strengthened in your inner being with power through his Spirit, and that Christ may dwell in your hearts through faith, as you are being rooted and grounded in love. I pray that you may have the power to comprehend, with all the saints, what is the breadth and length and height and depth, and to know the love of Christ that surpasses knowledge, so that you may be filled with the fullness of God.

Now to him who by the power at work within us is able to accomplish abundantly far more than all we can ask or imagine, to him be glory in the church and in Christ Jesus to all generations, forever and ever. Amen.

DISCUSSION QUESTIONS

The following can be used for discussion within a small group, or used for journal reflections by individuals:

1. Have I tried a disciplined time of silence as a way of listening to God and to my own heart? What obstacles do I sense to the use of silence or solitude as a discipline?
2. How can I restructure my daily routine to practice silence at some time of the day or week?

SUGGESTED EXERCISES

The following exercises can be done by individuals, shared between spiritual friends, or used in the context of a small group. Choose one or more of the following:

1. Plan an experience of solitude that includes some formal use of silence. Perhaps this could be in a retreat center near you, or even in an unexpected locale, like an urban park in the center of a noisy metropolis. It is important to keep a journal record about an experience of solitude; also, it is well, at some later time, to reflect on the benefits of such an experience.
2. Design a group experience that includes a time of solitude followed by a time of sharing the experience gained. The group might agree that each individual practices some silence or solitude during the week, then reflects upon the experience at the next meeting. Or the group time may be divided in half: during the first half, individuals move into solitude within the space where the meeting is being held (plans must be made for this meeting space); during the second half of the meeting, the group reflects on the difficulties and blessings of practicing solitude and prayerful silence.

REFLECTIONS

Solitude is never complete without silence. Silence is solitude's necessary and natural companion. Dom John Main writes, "Now to tread the spiritual path we must learn to be silent. What is required of us is a journey into profound silence." Why is silence so helpful? It is not just that we use words to control and manage others and need to be free from such soul-destroying habits, though this is true enough. It is that we use words constantly to adjust our public image. You see, we fear so deeply what others think of us. If I have done some wrong thing, or even some good thing that I think you might misunderstand, and I learn that you know about it I am going to be very tempted to speak up and straighten you out on that matter. Now, silence is one of the deepest disciplines of the spiritual life simply because it puts the stopper on all that self-justification.

Through the discipline of silence, then, we are learning to place our reputation in God's hands. We no longer need to be sure everyone understands us or thinks well of us. We let go of even needing to know what they think of us. We are silent.

Interestingly, we come to value words more in times of silence. This is because we are no longer cheapening words by overuse. We are still, and in the stillness we are creating an open, empty space where God can draw near. And in this stillness we just may hear God's voice in his wondrous, terrible, loving, all-embracing silence.

RICHARD J. FOSTER

GOING DEEPER

JOHN MAIN, *Word Made Flesh* (New York: Continuum, 1998). In this short work Main illuminates "the consciousness of Jesus" and shows us how spiritual disciplines help us to have the mind of Christ.

JOHN MAIN, *The Heart of Creation* (New York: Continuum, 1998). This brief work of instructions and counsels describes "the art of unlearning" so that we can draw closer to God.

JOHN MAIN, *Word into Silence* (New York: Crossroad, 1998). Talks first given in Britain, then circulated worldwide. Do note the one entitled "John Cassian," in which Main describes how Cassian discovered "purity of heart" and what he called the "way of poverty" from teachers in the North African desert.

JOHN MAIN, *Moments of Christ: The Path of Meditation* (New York: Continuum, 1998). "The Meaning of Silence" is only one of the thirty-five brief chapters in this book.

Paul Tournier

(1898–1986)

———

Paul Tournier was a deeply religious Christian doctor and counselor who lived and worked in Geneva, Switzerland. He helped many believers by putting the insights of psychology and psychiatry into Christian perspective.

At one point in his career, Tournier told his wife that he wanted to leave the practice of medicine and become an evangelist. But she was opposed to it!

Listening and openness to compromise provided him with the answer that benefited so many: he would combine his spiritual insights with his knowledge of psychoanalysis.

His many books—among them *The Adventure of Living* and *The Meaning of Persons*—integrated the psychological and the spiritual and were widely popular.

In the following selection, taken from a 1984 interview, notice Tournier's practical approach to silent meditation. He likes to meditate with a pencil in his hand because it keeps him from woolgathering!

He mentions his own clumsiness about the use of silence, instead of pretending that he is the world's greatest authority. He says also that silence is not an end in itself, but a means, a way, of coming closer to God.

Listen to Tournier as he speaks from the treasure trove of fifty years of spiritual discipline.

A LISTENING EAR: REFLECTIONS ON CHRISTIAN CARING

The Power of Listening, the Power of Silence

Doctors are among the busiest people in our day. It is significant, therefore, that it is a doctor who emphasizes for us the importance of silence, of meditation. You have practiced meditation constantly for the last fifty years. Why?

Modern people lack silence. They no longer lead their own lives; they are dragged along by events. It is a race against the clock. I think that what so many people come to see me for is to find a quiet, peaceful person who knows how to listen and who isn't thinking all the time about what he has to do next. If your life is chock-full already, there won't be room for anything else. Even God can't get anything else in. So it becomes essential to cut something out. I'm putting it as simply as I can.

Can one define silence?

It is extremely difficult. For me, above all it is a waiting. I wait for God to stimulate my thoughts sufficiently to renew me, to make me creative instead of being what St. Paul calls a tinkling cymbal. It's the cornerstone of my life. It is an attempt at seeing people and their problems from God's point of view, insofar as that is possible.

What was your first experience of meditation?

Trying to listen to God for a whole hour and hearing nothing at all!

Others would have been put off. You weren't?

It put me on my mettle! Was I really not capable of doing something so simple? What had interested me was the idea of listening in to God. That goes beyond silence. Silence is no longer an end, but a means. The most precious thing of all is the possibility of being, through the words in my mind or through my inborn unconscious faculties, the recipient of thoughts that come from God.

After that first failure, or that first challenge, did you persevere?

Often after that my meditations seemed pretty unproductive. There comes into one's mind the thought of some step to take, perhaps a letter to write. We have to realize that we always resist doing quite simple things that we know we ought to do. If we can manage to understand the reason for this resistance we are on the way to self-discovery. That's what makes meditation precious.

There's a resemblance here to psychoanalysis. Who was it who established the value of silence?

Freud. He revealed its enormous power. Under psychoanalysis, there is a moment when the subject feels silence weighing on him terribly. He longs for the doctor to say something to him. Silence has the power to force you to dig deep inside yourself. It was a phenomenon well known to Jesus, who would go off to spend a whole night in the desert. St. Paul was aware of it, and all the mystics as well. It involves a restructuring of the person, which leads to the discovery of underlying motives.

Can silence be an important element in the life of a nonbeliever?

Of course. Silence has a psychological aspect. For me it means listening to God, but for others it may represent a way of deepening self-knowledge.

I have often had occasion to share silence with others. I can say in general that it is the less sophisticated person who understands best. A rustic who decides to listen in to God can in five minutes make you a list of all his problems, which a professor of philosophy would be incapable of doing. Children understand straightaway, too. The naked truth comes out. We are dealing with simple matters, and modern people have lost their understanding of such things.

So that intellectualism can, in a way, be a hindrance?

Yes, indeed. In medical practice too it is the intellectual who is the most difficult to treat. Not for nothing did Jesus say that we must become like little children. On the other hand, an intellectual who undergoes a profound spiritual experience has much that he or she can offer.

You said in a recent lecture that meditation had helped you to discover "the immensity of the personal problems" that almost everyone has to face. How did you come to this perception?

People confide their problems to us in accordance with our readiness to listen. It is a barometer. The ability to offer oneself depends to a great extent on this discipline of meditation in which we bring our human relationships before God in order to smooth the way.

You spoke just now of meditation practiced in the company of others. Is there not a danger there of imposing your thoughts on others?

The more I am persuaded of the importance of seeking God's will for oneself, the more skeptical I become about the possibility of saying what is his will for others. That is the source of all kinds of intolerance and abuse. People who claim to know what is God's will try to impose it upon others with the arrogance which comes from the conviction that they are the repositories of divine truth. I avoid that at all costs. I can never know what is God's will for someone else. Even in psychoanalysis doctors generally prefer that their patients should make their own discoveries. If doctors start making suggestions of their own, they almost always go astray.

If it is wrong to tell others what they ought to do, do you still think that one can help them to overcome their mental blockages?

It is only insofar as I can overcome my own reluctance to recognize the truth about myself, that I can help others to overcome their own resistance.

I ought to say a little about the role of silence in the marriage relationship. For my wife and me it was essential. It is in silence that one thinks of the things that are not easy to say to each other, and which one is afraid may be misunderstood or arouse criticism. In silence, these restraints lose their force. Without these periods of silence we tend to confess only the favorable things and not the things we are ashamed of. For us, meditation became the road to really knowing each other. Many couples who think they are talking openly to one another about everything are just deluding themselves. You can even say prayers and sing hymns together and still have mental reservations and no true openness towards one another. In meditation there takes place a reciprocal interpenetration which cannot be achieved by any other means.

The morning quiet time seems so difficult at first. Can one get used to it so that it comes naturally?

Quite often I have persevered with it just in order to stick to a resolution I have made. Obviously there are times when you are more or less forcing yourself to do it for the sake of your own self-esteem. You get through periods of spiritual drought that way. And then the thing becomes real again; you get a fresh start, as it were, and you don't any longer have to rely on the motivation of vanity.

We know you don't like laying down rules, but can you give some indication of what a typical meditation might consist of?

I practice written meditation. It may not suit everybody. There are some who say that having a pencil in their hand is enough to prevent them meditating, because they feel that it makes it too mechanical. But it suits me very well, because I used to have a tendency to daydream in my meditation. The act of writing prevents me from slipping into wool gathering. Aimless musing may be agreeable, but it has nothing to do with the realities of life. Another thing is that writing things down is like knocking nails in to make them firmer. It commits us more.

Do you consciously direct your thoughts?

As little as possible. God's way of thinking is different from ours. And the whole point is that we should take the great leap from our own thoughts to those of God.

One last point. How are we to discern God's will amongst the clutter of our own imaginings?

The most important thing is patience. If I may recount a personal experience, I must tell you that I once almost gave up medicine in order to become an evangelist. The idea tempted me, but my wife was not in agreement. You can see that it is not easy to be sure what is God's will. We spent some months in great perplexity, and I was even in despair at times, until I became convinced that I ought not to leave medicine, but instead introduce into medicine the experience I had had. Suddenly it all became clear: it was not a compromise, but a synthesis. That was what made it creative. It was not that the view of the one or the other had triumphed, but that a third way, a most productive one, had been found. I am happy to speak of this, because it illustrates both the importance of trying to let God guide us, and the difficulties that that involves. Patience is vital. Generally when God's will is made manifest, it is obvious and everyone recognizes it. Unfortunately, however, that is infrequent. One would like it to happen more often. But then, that would make us arrogant. . . .

BIBLE SELECTION
Psalm 40:1–8

I waited patiently for the LORD;
    he inclined to me and heard my cry.
He drew me up from the desolate pit,
    out of the miry bog,
and set my feet upon a rock,
    making my steps secure.
He put a new song in my mouth,
    a song of praise to our God.
Many will see and fear,
    and put their trust in the LORD.

Happy are those who make
    the LORD their trust,

who do not turn to the proud,
    to those who go astray after false gods.
You have multiplied, O LORD my God,
    your wondrous deeds and your thoughts toward us;
    none can compare with you.
Were I to proclaim and tell of them,
    they would be more than can be counted.

Sacrifice and offering you do not desire,
    but you have given me an open ear.
Burnt offering and sin offering
    you have not required.
Then I said, "Here I am;
    in the scroll of the book it is written of me.
I delight to do your will, O my God;
    your law is within my heart."

DISCUSSION QUESTIONS

The following can be used for discussion within a small group, or used for journal reflections by individuals:

1. What disappointments have I had in practicing spiritual disciplines? Do any funny stories come to mind?
2. How have I experienced that "God's way of thinking is different from ours"? What scriptural parallels come to mind?

SUGGESTED EXERCISES

The following exercises can be done by individuals, shared between spiritual friends, or used in the context of a small group. Choose one or more of the following:

1. This week set aside a time to listen to God and write down what you hear God saying to you.
2. Exercise the discipline of silence with someone close to you, a spouse or a coworker or another family member with whom you must spend a lot of time. Agree to be silent together for a time, listening to what God wants to say about your relationship.

REFLECTIONS

I met Paul Tournier only once. I was at the beginning of my career path; he at the end of his. I learned only at the very last moment that he would be coming to the meetings where I was scheduled to speak. I tried to get the director to have him speak rather than me. In vain. Now, you might well imagine (as I did at the time) what kind of "wisdom" was upon my head in those days so long ago. But I spoke as required, and I must tell you that Tournier was very kind and affirming to me; and he did indeed speak to us toward the end of the conference—powerful, life-giving words.

Tournier, by his own admission, was a withdrawn and private person. And yet through his practice of listening to God he learned to become no longer "monsieur le docteur" in white coat and stethoscope but a fellow human being facing life problems like our own. In one of his writings he tells of a startling result of this listening to God and sharing with others. Listen.

"One time God directed me to share with a patient something that to me seemed so trivial—indeed faintly embarrassing—that only years of learning to trust Him made me do it. This particular man had been coming to see me for weeks without ever getting down to what was really bothering him. One morning he asked me, 'How do you use the quiet time you speak of in your books?'

"Suspecting that he was not really interested but just seeking again to avoid some subject that frightened him, I said, 'Let's not talk about it. Let's try it.'

"We closed our eyes, and I prayed earnestly that he might have a real experience with God. How faith building it would be if He would give us both some inspiring message! But instead of inspiration all I seemed able to think about was the bills that were due this month. I've got to sit down tonight, I thought, and go over the household accounts with my wife. This would never do! I should have been setting an example of prayer, not fretting over money!

"Then came the unmistakable directive: Confess to this man what you've been thinking about. Well, I wrestled as I always do, but I finally got it out. He looked startled. 'That is my problem!' he cried. 'I must lie to my wife about money every day because I have a secret life. How did you know?'

"With the truth at last out in the open, we were able to face his problems together. But it might not have happened if I had tried to hide behind the facade of 'spiritual' mentor. . . . For I have found that it is not when we are most lofty minded but when we are most human that we come closest to God. It is a truth He must reteach me every day."

Me too.

RICHARD J. FOSTER

GOING DEEPER

PAUL TOURNIER, *A Listening Ear: Reflections on Christian Caring* (Minneapolis, MN: Augsburg, 1984). This book gathers random talks and interviews, including Tournier's address to the World Council of Churches in 1978.

PAUL TOURNIER, *The Adventure of Living* (New York: Harper & Row, 1965). In this widely popular volume, Tournier explores both positives and negatives associated with the human yearning for adventure. His chapter on "Meditation" is also very much about guidance: learning to recognize and accept the thoughts and inspirations that come to us from God when we are still and attentive (and sometimes when we aren't).

PAUL TOURNIER, *Guilt and Grace* (San Francisco: Harper & Row, 1983). A simple and clear discussion of human guilt feelings and freedom in Christ, this book draws on Tournier's extensive knowledge gained in psychiatric practice.

PAUL TOURNIER, *The Whole Person in a Broken World* (New York: Harper & Row, 1964). An important work on the inner conflict felt by contemporary people; an articulate statement of the task for the Christian church in addressing such needs.

PAUL TOURNIER, *The Meaning of Persons* (New York: Harper, 1957). In this fine work Tournier develops a picture of the life quest in terms of his own personal story. It seems to apply to everyone in a most particular way.

Submission

—

John Milton

(1609–1674)

———

John Milton is considered one of the great writers of the English language. His passion was to become an epic poet in the service of God. "My father destined me from a child to the pursuits of literature," he wrote, "and my appetite for knowledge was so voracious that, from twelve years of age, I hardly ever left my studies, or went to bed before midnight."

He devoured the ancient writers, in Latin, Greek, and Hebrew, became deeply conversant with the Holy Scriptures, received two degrees at Cambridge University, and planned eventually to write several major religious epics.

Milton was drawn into the religious and political controversies of his time, and in 1649 he received an appointment to Oliver Cromwell's government. Plunged into political life, he became a persuasive orator and politician but was forced to put off his writing. Soon his eyesight began to fail; by the age of forty-three he was totally blind.

In spite of this handicap, Milton wrote two great epics, *Paradise Lost* and *Paradise Regained*, as well as a moving drama, *Samson Agonistes*.

The two short poems that follow show the depth of Milton's spiritual life. Each one describes a crisis of faith in which he feels trapped by circumstances but gains the grace to trust God's will.

In the first, written soon after he left Cambridge University, Milton complains that he has turned twenty-three without having accomplished anything. His life feels empty and inconclusive. Midway through the poem, he grasps the importance of submission: God's will, not his own, will ensure the right outcome.

In the second poem, written late in life, Milton's obstacle is the blindness, which, he fears, has left his great talent "useless." Again, as in youth, Milton submits to God's will for him, aligning himself with the submission of the angels to the will of God: "they also serve who only stand and wait."

On Reading Milton's Poems

A good way to appreciate Milton's words fully is to read these short works out loud. In a group, you may want to choose one person who especially likes to read aloud. Or you may break the poems (each fourteen lines) into shorter sections, taking turns. Use thought breaks in doing this, following Milton's sentence structure, rather than just stopping at the end of a line.

Before reading the poems, mark the unfamiliar usages like "hath" and "endueth," and make sure that you know what the modern word or meaning would be. When you read the poem aloud, do so confidently, and you will find that the old-fashioned words begin to feel comfortable and familiar.

Identify with Milton as you read. How does it feel to have your whole life dream apparently taken away from you? What kind of trust does it take to accept God's will when you must work against severe and disabling handicaps?

As each poem turns away from complaint and toward a positive statement of faith, rejoice with Milton as he surrenders to the will of God.

IN MY GREAT TASK-MASTER'S EYE

On His Having Arrived at the Age of Twenty-three

How soon hath time the subtle thief of youth,
    Stolen on his wing my three and twentieth year!
    My hasting days fly on with full career,
    But my late spring no bud or blossom showeth.
Perhaps my semblance might deceive the truth,
    That I to manhood am arrived so near,
    And inward ripeness doth much less appear,
    That some more timely-happy spirits endueth.
Yet be it less or more, or soon or slow,
    It shall be still in strictest measure even,
    To that same lot, however mean or high,
Toward which time leads me, and the will of heaven;
    All is, if I have grace to use it so,
    As ever in my great task-master's eye.

On His Blindness

When I consider how my light is spent,
    Ere half my days, in this dark world and wide,
    And that one talent which is death to hide,
    Lodged with me useless, though my soul more bent
To serve therewith my maker, and present
    My true account, lest he returning chide,

"Doth God exact day-labor, light denied,"
   I fondly ask; But patience to prevent
That murmur, soon replies, "God doth not need
   Either man's work or his own gifts, who best
   Bear his mild yoke, they serve him best, his state
Is kingly. Thousands at his bidding speed
   And post o'er land and ocean without rest:
   They also serve who only stand and wait."

BIBLE SELECTION
Psalm 130

Out of the depths I cry to you, O LORD.
   Lord, hear my voice!
Let your ears be attentive
   to the voice of my supplications!

If you, O LORD, should mark iniquities,
   Lord, who could stand?
But there is forgiveness with you,
   so that you may be revered.

I wait for the LORD, my soul waits,
   and in his word I hope;
my soul waits for the LORD
   more than those who watch for the morning,
   more than those who watch for the morning.

O Israel, hope in the LORD!
   For with the LORD there is steadfast love,
   and with him is great power to redeem.
It is he who will redeem Israel
   from all its iniquities.

DISCUSSION QUESTIONS

The following can be used for discussion within a small group, or used for journal reflections by individuals:

1. Was there a time in my life when I was resentful against my own life circumstances and may have questioned God's providence? How did I deal with that? Were there certain thoughts and experiences that helped me submit to God's leading at last?
2. Which of Milton's expressions relate especially to trusting God's Providence? How do I relate to these?

SUGGESTED EXERCISES

The following exercises can be done by individuals, shared between spiritual friends, or used in the context of a small group. Choose one or more of the following:

1. To the extent that you feel comfortable doing so, share a personal experience of graced submission with a group, or confide it to your journal.
2. Tell stories from your own experience that illustrate Milton's point, "They also serve who only stand and wait."
3. Consider the positives and negatives of the idea of God as "the great taskmaster." What expectations does God appear to present to us for our life's work? Is there a grand design that we can glimpse, based on our own gifts and talents? How do we learn to wait upon the Lord in the development of a large-scale life project?
4. Some gifted individuals, like John Milton, have triumphed over great physical handicaps to accomplish great creative and spiritual tasks. How can we learn from their experience?

REFLECTIONS

It is certainly unusual for someone at twenty-three years of age to have such keen insight into himself. Outwardly Milton has attained manhood but inwardly he is keenly aware of how far he has to go: "inward ripeness doth much less appear." But inward maturity is his goal as he is ever under "my great task-master's eye." May we all have such a worthy goal and see ourselves ever under the eye of God, working, if you will, to the audience of One.

It amazes me that the most famous line in all of Milton's writings grew out of his struggle with impending blindness. Milton so desperately wanted to do something great for God, but blindness threatened to destroy it all. But then, in the very struggle Milton learns that God does not need his work nor his gifts. We, you see, do not have to prove our worth—God does not value us by our output but simply because we are. And so it is a "mild yoke" he gives us for "they also serve who only stand and wait."

RICHARD J. FOSTER

GOING DEEPER

EMILIE GRIFFIN, "John Milton: Sing Heavenly Muse," in *Reality and the Vision*, edited by Philip Yancey (Dallas, TX: Word, 1990), pp. 102–10. In this essay Griffin explains her personal attraction to Milton and her ways of identifying with his religious zeal, his style of self-examination, and his ways of service to God, in spite of a gap of several hundred years.

MICHAEL ERNEST TRAVERS, *The Devotional Experience in the Poetry of John Milton* (Lewiston, ME, and Queenston, ON: Edwin Mellen, 1988). This formal scholarly study takes Milton's own ideas on Christian devotion and uses them as a point of departure for a review of Milton's major works, in which our love of God and God's love for us are expressed in a variety of ways.

A. N. WILSON, *The Life of John Milton* (Oxford, UK: Oxford University Press, 1983). Wilson, an English novelist, pundit, and biographer, writes in a biting, controversial style. Some of his comments are clearly meant to annoy: "It needs an act of supreme historical imagination to be able to recapture an atmosphere in which Anglican bishops might be taken seriously." But once you know what you are in for, the advantage of Wilson's account is that its gossipy tone makes Milton's story vivid and accessible. This is a good popular life of Milton, more literary and political than spiritual in tone.

Thomas R. Kelly

(1893–1941)

———

Thomas Raymond Kelly was born into a devout Quaker farm family living near Chillicothe, Ohio. His father died when he was quite small, and young Kelly grew up helping his mother, grandmother, and sister with the farm operations. In 1903 the family moved to Wilmington, Ohio, which gave Kelly a chance to attend high school and Wilmington College, a small Quaker school. From there Kelly earned a scholarship to Haverford College, where a significant pilgrimage began.

Originally attracted to the sciences, Kelly now found himself drawn to philosophy and religion. Under the teaching of Rufus Jones, Kelly encountered a different kind of Quakerism than he had known in the Midwest, one that focused on the mystical life. Soon he came to believe that this mystical Quaker life was closer to the original vision of George Fox. Yet the mystical experience eluded him.

Through many years of teaching and study, Kelly, who became a Ph.D. candidate at Harvard working under the world-renowned British mathematician and philosopher Alfred North Whitehead, labored for recognition. He was torn by differences in Quakerism, suffered ill health, and was pained by the repeated refusals of Harvard to allow him to complete the Ph.D.

Finally, out of this crucible of failure and pain, a new Thomas Kelly arose, one who genuinely floated in the grace of God with a simple and childlike obedience and trust. This renewed Thomas Kelly is the one whose teaching and example have gained wide attention. Yet all of Kelly's works represent a reaching for the same simple and pure devotional understanding.

In the following selection, which is taken from his masterwork, *A Testament of Devotion*, notice that he suggests some will be swept into holy obedience and some will have to wrestle for it. Also take note of the beautiful language he uses to describe this spiritual gift.

A TESTAMENT OF DEVOTION

The Shepherd in Search of Lost Obedience

Out in front of us is the drama of men and of nations, seething, struggling, laboring, dying. Upon this tragic drama in these days our eyes are all set in anxious watchfulness and in prayer. But within the silences of the souls of men an eternal drama is ever being enacted, in these days as well as in others. And on the outcome of this inner drama rests, ultimately, the outer pageant of history. . . . It is the drama of the lost sheep wandering in the wilderness, restless and lonely, feebly searching, while over the hills comes the wiser Shepherd. For His is a shepherd's heart, and He is restless until He holds His sheep in His arms. . . .

It is to one strand in this inner drama, one scene, where the Shepherd has found His sheep, that I would direct you. It is the life of absolute and complete and holy obedience to the voice of the Shepherd. But ever throughout the account the accent will be laid upon God, God the initiator, God the aggressor, God the seeker, God the stirrer into life, God the ground of our obedience, God the giver of the power to become children of God. . . .

The tender persuading love at the center

In considering one gateway into this life of holy obedience, let us dare to venture together into the inner sanctuary of the soul, where God meets man in awful immediacy. . . .

It is an overwhelming experience to fall into the hands of the living God, to be invaded to the depths of one's being by His presence, to be, without warning, wholly uprooted from all earth-born securities and assurances, and to be blown by a tempest of unbelievable power which leaves one's old proud self utterly, utterly defenseless, until one cries, "All Thy waves and thy billows are gone over me" (Ps. 42:7). Then is the soul swept into a Loving Center of ineffable sweetness, where calm and unspeakable peace and ravishing joy steal over one. And one knows now why Pascal wrote, in the center of his greatest moment, the single word, "Fire." There stands the world of struggling, sinful, earth-blinded men and nations, of plants and animals and wheeling stars of heaven, all new, all lapped in the tender, persuading Love at the Center. There stand the saints of the ages, their hearts open to view, and lo, their hearts are our heart and their hearts are the heart of the Eternal One. In awful solemnity the Holy One is over all and in all, exquisitely loving, infinitely patient, tenderly smiling. Marks of glory are upon all things, and the marks are cruciform and blood-stained. And one sighs, like the convinced Thomas of old, "My Lord and my God" (John 20:28). Dare one lift one's eyes and look? Nay, whither can one look and not see Him? For field and stream and teeming streets are full of Him. Yet as Moses knew, no man can look on God and live—live as his old self. Death comes, blessed death, death of one's alienating will. And one knows what Paul meant when he wrote, "The life which I now live in the flesh I live by the faith of the Son of God" (Gal. 2:20).

Emerging into obedience

One emerges from such soul-shaking, Love-invaded times into more normal states of consciousness. But one knows ever after that the Eternal Lover of the world, the Hound of Heaven, is utterly, utterly real, and that life must henceforth be forever determined by that Real. Like Saint Augustine one asks not for greater certainty of God but only for more steadfastness in Him. There, beyond, in Him is the true Center, and we are reduced, as it were, to nothing, for He is all. . . .

Self is emptied into God, and God in-fills it. In glad, amazed humility we cast on Him our little lives in trusting obedience, in erect, serene, and smiling joy. And we say, with a writer of Psalms, "Lo, I come: in the book of the law it is written of me, I delight to do Thy will, O my God" (40:7–8). For nothing else in all of heaven or earth counts so much as His will, His slightest wish, His faintest breathing. And holy obedience sets in, sensitive as a shadow, obedient as a shadow, selfless as a shadow. . . . Gladly, urgently, promptly one leaps to do His bidding, ready to run and not be weary and to walk and not faint.

Passive or active?

Do not mistake me. Our interest just now is in the life of complete obedience to God, not in amazing revelations of His glory graciously granted only to some. Yet the amazing experiences of the mystics leave a permanent residue, a God-subdued, a God-possessed will. States of consciousness are fluctuating. The vision fades. But holy and listening and alert obedience remains, as the core and kernel of a God-intoxicated life, as the abiding pattern of sober, workaday living. And some are led into the state of complete obedience by this well-nigh passive route, wherein God alone seems to be the actor and we seem to be wholly acted upon. And our wills are melted and dissolved and made pliant, being firmly fixed in Him, and He wills in us.

But in contrast to this passive route to complete obedience most people must follow what Jean-Nicholas Grou calls the active way, wherein we must struggle and, like Jacob of old, wrestle with the angel until the morning dawns, the active way wherein the will must be subjected bit by bit, piecemeal and progressively, to the divine Will.

The flaming vision

But the first step to . . . obedience . . . is the flaming vision of the wonder of such a life, a vision which comes occasionally to us all, through biographies of the saints, through the journals of Fox and early Friends, through a life lived before our eyes, through a haunting verse of the Psalms—"Whom have I in heaven but Thee? And there is none upon earth that I desire beside Thee" (Ps. 73:25)—through meditation upon the amazing life and death of Jesus, through a flash of illumination or, in Fox's language, a great opening. . . . There is an infinite fountain of lifting power, pressing within us, luring us by dazzling visions, and we can only say, The creative God comes into our souls. An increment of infinity is about us. Holy is imagination, the gateway of Reality into our hearts. The Hound of Heaven is on our track, the God of Love is wooing us to His Holy life.

Begin where you are

Once having the vision, the second step to holy obedience is this: Begin where you are. Obey now. Use what little obedience you are capable of, even if it be like a grain of mustard seed. Begin where you are. Live this present moment, this present hour as you now sit in your seats, in utter, utter submission and openness toward Him. Listen outwardly to these words, but within, behind the scenes, in the deeper levels of your lives where you are all alone with God the Loving Eternal One, keep up a silent prayer. "Open Thou my life. Guide my thoughts where I dare not let them go. But Thou darest. Thy will be done." Walk on the streets and chat with your friends, offering yourselves in continuous obedience. I find this internal continuous prayer life absolutely essential. It can be carried on day and night, in the thick of business, in home and school. Such prayer of submission can be so simple. It is well to use a single sentence, repeated over and over and over again, such as this: "Be Thou my will. Be Thou my will," or "I open all before Thee. I open all before Thee," or "See earth through heaven. See earth through heaven." This hidden prayer life can pass, in time, beyond words and phrases into mere ejaculations, "My God, my God, my Holy One, my Love," or into the adoration of the Upanishad, "O Wonderful, O Wonderful, O Wonderful." Words may cease and one stands and walks and sits and lies in wordless attitudes of adoration and submission and rejoicing and exultation and glory.

Begin again and relax

And the third step in holy obedience, or a counsel, is this: if you slip and stumble and forget God for an hour, and assert your old proud self, and rely upon your own clever wisdom, don't spend too much time in anguished regrets and self-accusations but begin again, just where you are.

Yet a fourth consideration in holy obedience is this: Don't grit your teeth and clench your fists and say, "I will! I will!" Relax. Take hands off. Submit yourself to God. Learn to live in the passive voice—a hard saying for Americans—and let life be willed through you. For "I will" spells not obedience.

BIBLE SELECTIONS
Psalm 23

The LORD is my shepherd, I shall not want.
  He makes me lie down in green pastures;
he leads me beside still waters;
  he restores my soul.
He leads me in right paths
  for his name's sake.

Even though I walk through the darkest valley,
  I fear no evil;
for you are with me;
  your rod and your staff—
  they comfort me.

You prepare a table before me
  in the presence of my enemies;
you anoint my head with oil;
  my cup overflows.
Surely goodness and mercy shall follow me
  all the days of my life,
and I shall dwell in the house of the LORD
  my whole life long.

DISCUSSION QUESTIONS

The following can be used for discussion within a small group, or used for journal reflections by individuals:

1. Do I think Thomas Kelly seems to be reaching for an impossible ideal? Or is his notion of "holy obedience" available to all of us? Why?

2. How do I feel about the word "mystical"? Do I think it puts me closer to God, or farther away? Explain.

3. How can I come into holy obedience?

SUGGESTED EXERCISES

The following exercises can be done by individuals, shared between spiritual friends, or used in the context of a small group. Choose one or more of the following:

1. Have your group pray in Quaker style. Gather the group in a circle. Begin in silence. Allow each person to speak as moved by the Spirit, but do not feel that people must take turns. Allow the Spirit to move, and allow God to be awakened in hearts. Allow long silences to fall, and do not expect much speech or chatter. Surrender to God's leading. Let the group session end by having each person leave when she or he thinks it is time.

2. Try the preceding exercise by yourself, with your spouse, or with another friend.

REFLECTIONS

Virtually all of Kelly's published writings, apart from his Ph.D. dissertation, come from the last three years of his life. I have read a good number of his unpublished sermons and lectures from before this period, and while they are far above the average in insight and scholarship, they simply do not rise to the same level of breathtaking radiance as those last three years. Why is this? What happened in 1937–38 to cause the speeches and essays of his final years to erupt with such fire and heartsearing passion? What made him so utterly "blinded by the splendor of God"? What would cause him to write, "The fires of the love of God, of our love toward God, and of His love toward us, are very hot"? Did God visit him in some kind of special epiphany of glory? Quite the contrary. The abrupt and glorious change in Kelly arose out of two powerful experiences: the one a crushing personal defeat, the other a fiery baptism into the suffering of humanity.

By 1924 Kelly had earned a Ph.D. in philosophy from Hartford Theological Seminary, and by 1936 he was teaching at the prestigious Haverford College. Even so, he longed for the scholarly recognition of a Harvard Ph.D., and so he pursued this second doctorate at great personal cost, both financially and physically. Finally, he completed all of his doctoral requirements except for the final oral exams. But in the fall of 1937 on the day Kelly went in for his orals he had one of his occasional and dreadful "woozy spells," and his mind went complete blank. He failed his orals miserably and was rejected for the Ph.D. with no opportunity of reconsideration. The rejection was catastrophic. Kelly sunk into deep depression. And yet, out of the ashes of this dashed dream of academic acclaim arose the phoenix of a new, captivating vision of "the God-intoxicated life." In April 1938 he wrote to Rufus Jones, "The reality of Presence has been very great at times recently. One knows at first hand what the old inquiry meant, 'Has Truth been advancing among you?'"

The second experience came in the summer of 1938 when Kelly went to Hitler's Germany, an experience in which his soul was immeasurably deepened by seeing and sharing in the suffering of the German people. "I have never had such a soul-overturning . . . period as this," he wrote. "It is not merely heroism, it is depth of con-secration, simplicity of faith, beauty in the midst of poverty or suffering, that shames us. I have met some giant souls. . . . One can't be the same again." Upon returning to Haverford he kept repeating to Douglas Steere, "It is wonderful. I have been liter-ally melted down by the love of God." Later he told several close students of a partic-ular experience in the great cathedral at Cologne where, on his knees, he seemed to feel God laying upon his heart the whole congealed suffering of humanity—a bur-den too terrible to be borne—and yet somehow bearable with God's help.

These two experiences help us understand the enormous power that flowed from Kelly's writing and speaking in the three remaining years of his earthly pilgrimage.

RICHARD J. FOSTER

GOING DEEPER

THOMAS R. KELLY, *A Testament of Devotion,* with an introduction by Richard J. Foster (San Francisco: HarperSanFrancisco, 1996). One of the few classics of devotion to emerge out of the twentieth century. Republished in this edition in its entirety, it contains an excellent "Biographical Memoir" by Douglas Steere. A must read.

THOMAS R. KELLY, *The Eternal Promise* (Richmond, IN: Friends United Press, 1988). These essays and talks come from the same period of Kelly's life as *Testament,* and they radiate the same glow from the fire burning in his heart. This edition also contains an excellent introduction by Howard R. Macy.

THOMAS R. KELLY, *Reality of the Spiritual World* (Wallingford, PA: Pendle Hill, 1976). This is a forty-seven-page pamphlet of four talks Kelly gave during the winter of 1940–41. Soon after he died suddenly of a heart attack on January 17, 1941.

Quaker Religious Thought, Vol. 27, No. 3, July 1995. This quarterly journal did an entire issue on Thomas Kelly, with essays by T. Canby Jones, E. Glenn Hinson, Elaine M. Prevallet, Howard R. Macy, and Richard M. Kelly. It is a fine collection for those who are interested in more about the man behind such powerful spiritual writings. It can be ordered from *Quaker Religious Thought*, Friends Homes at Guilford, No. 1201; 925 New Garden Road, Greensboro, NC 27410. Ask for Journal No. 85.

Richard of St. Victor

(?–1173)

———

Richard of St. Victor is considered a major spiritual writer of the twelfth century. Hailed by Dante in *The Divine Comedy* as being "in contemplation more than human," he was also praised by St. Bonaventure as being on a par with the ancient fathers.

A native of Scotland, Richard entered the monastic community of St. Victor in Paris sometime in the 1150s. During his lifetime new religious orders and religious reforms were springing up, emphasizing the contemplative life. Richard was among the first to write a work of systematic instruction in the practice of disciplined prayer and contemplation.

Along with other gifted writers of his time, Richard helped to formulate the distinctive aspects of medieval spirituality: inwardness, the role of the affections, emphasis on experience, definite patterns of contemplation, and the importance of the individual. His approach was deeply biblical. He also wrote extensively on the Trinity.

In the following selection, Chapter 15 from his work *The Mystical Ark*, notice how vividly Richard describes the experience of loving God as an intimate nuptial encounter. He is using the erotic language that is part of the great mystical tradition. A man of vowed and chaste celibacy, he nevertheless feels comfortable with this intimate love language and is not even slightly awkward about it.

THE MYSTICAL ARK

Wait and Wait Again

That it is hard and difficult for any perfect soul to gather itself completely within itself and to rest in longing only for the Godhead

A very small, brief delay—I shall not say of a year, nor shall I say of a month or a day—is troublesome enough to the longing of one who is impatient. Indeed, hope which is put off grieves the soul. And so the beloved of a true friend and the friend of a true beloved . . . always ought to be prompt and prepared to receive without any insult of a delay the friend who knocks and to run with all due speed to meet the one who calls.

However, we know that a singular love does not accept a partner nor does it admit a companion. See to it that the very time He begins to knock at the door is not the first time that you begin to want to throw out the crowds of those who make noise.

Dispersing the crowd

Moreover, when such a crowd is found with you at that time, what will you say? I say, what will you say, except, "Wait and wait again"? Waiting and waiting again for throwing out the crowd of strangers, for throwing out your household. All thoughts, empty as well as noxious, which do not serve for our benefit must be judged to be strangers.

In truth, we possess them like domestic servants or slaves, whom we involve for our use or benefit. But because a singular love loves solitude and seeks for a solitary place, it behooves us to throw out the entire crowd of such a sort, not only of thoughts but also even of affections, so that we may be at liberty to cling more freely and more joyfully to the embraces of our beloved one.

How great, I ask, is the delay in such waiting? How often must one repeat: "Wait and wait again, a moment here and a moment there"? A moment in one place, a moment in another. A moment in the garden, a moment in the hall, a moment in the chamber until at last finally after much waiting and great weariness He enters the bedchamber and occupies the most intimate and secret place.

A moment in the garden while the whole crowd of those making a disturbance is dispersed. A moment in the hall while the chamber is decorated. A moment in the chamber while the bridal bed is prepared.

Our beloved arrives

And the Beloved is forced to wait a moment and a moment in all of these places: a moment here and a moment there. He is heard from the garden. He is seen in the hall. He is kissed affectionately in the chamber. He is embraced in the bedchamber. He is heard by memory; seen by understanding; kissed warmly by affection; embraced by applause. He is heard by recollection; seen by wonder; kissed warmly by love; embraced by delight.

Or if this pleases you better, He is heard by a showing; seen by contemplation; kissed warmly by devotion; drawn close for the infusion of His sweetness. He is heard by a showing when the whole tumult of those who make noise is quieted down and His voice only is heard as it grows stronger.

At last that whole crowd of those who make a disturbance is dispersed and He alone remains with her alone and she alone looks at Him alone by contemplation. He is seen by contemplation when on account of the sight of an unexpected vision and wonder at the beauty of it, the soul gradually glows, burns more and more, and finally at last catches fire completely until it is thoroughly reformed to true purity and internal beauty.

And that chamber of internal habitation is superbly adorned everywhere with purple garments, linen the color of hyacinth, and twice-dyed scarlet, until finally at some time after the chamber has been adorned and the beloved has been led in, when boldness now increases and longing distresses, when she is no longer able to restrain herself, she suddenly rushes into a kiss and with pressing lips fixes a kiss of intimate devotion.

By devotion He is kissed often and in many ways while in the meantime the bedchamber is prepared, until the innermost recess of the soul is composed in supreme peace and tranquillity and finally, when the Beloved is brought between the breasts, she melts completely in desire for Him with a kind of ineffable infusion of divine sweetness and that spirit which clings to the Lord is made one spirit.

No longer wait and wait again
Concerning the things that happen later, I think that after having known by experience so much sweetness and such inward pleasantness, the soul can no longer contrive any delay nor further weary the Beloved with any waiting while He is knocking.

In this respect the soul will no longer say, "Wait and wait again," especially when to her every delay is excessively long and waiting seems burdensome. From now on I think she will gladly watch with the patriarch Abraham or even with the prophet Elijah at the entrance of her habitation so that she may always be prepared for receiving her Beloved.

At this time, I think, our beaten work begins to make a great deal of progress and to approach consummation since our cherubim now begin to spread out their wings widely and to suspend themselves at every hour for flying, as it were.

BIBLE SELECTION
Song of Solomon 3:1–5

Upon my bed at night
    I sought him whom my soul loves;
I sought him, but found him not;
    I called him, but he gave no answer.
"I will rise now and go about the city,
    in the streets and in the squares;

I will seek him whom my soul loves."
  I sought him, but found him not.
The sentinels found me,
  as they went about in the city.
"Have you seen him whom my soul loves?"
Scarcely had I passed them,
  when I found him whom my soul loves.
I held him, and would not let him go
  until I brought him into my mother's house,
  and into the chamber of her that conceived me.
I adjure you, O daughters of Jerusalem,
  by the gazelles or the wild does:
do not stir up or awaken love
  until it is ready!

DISCUSSION QUESTIONS

The following can be used for discussion within a small group, or used for journal reflections by individuals:

1. How can we deal with any embarrassment we may feel about Richard of St. Victor's love language? Or biblical love language?
2. What spiritual benefits may result from thinking of God as a sweetheart or spouse?

SUGGESTED EXERCISES

The following exercises can be done by individuals, shared between spiritual friends, or used in the context of a small group. Choose one or more of the following:

1. Discuss "waiting" as a way of practicing the discipline of submission.
2. List the ways that you or the people in the group feel that they fall short in spiritual life. This can include prayer, especially contemplative prayer, or any other way of practicing the spiritual disciplines. Can these feelings of inadequacy contribute to the way we practice submission? Or do they get in the way?
3. Tell funny stories about your observations on impatience. How do people look when they get cranky and impatient? Have we ourselves sometimes

looked the same way? Are there some ways the discipline of submission can help us?

REFLECTIONS

Once we get accustomed to the use of erotic language to describe the divine-human encounter, Richard of St. Victor has much to teach us. The very first image we see in this selection is the waiting. It really is a haunting image of God, the divine Suitor, standing out on the front step; patiently knocking on the door of our heart; waiting, waiting, waiting for us to chase out the crowd in order for the proper privacy between lovers. But it is also an image of our waiting; waiting on God to be sure, but also waiting upon ourselves, <u>waiting until we are ready for the time of intimate mystical encounter.</u>

Next we see the image of the crowd. The crowd includes our thoughts, "empty as well as noxious, which do not serve for our benefit," and our affections which divide our loyalties and keep us from single-hearted devotion to "our beloved one." This image provides us with ample fodder for reflecting upon all our thoughts and affections that may be crowding God out, keeping him at a distance, hindering the intimacy of lovers.

The third image is of the senses to describe the progression into intimacy between the soul and God: hearing, seeing, kissing, embracing. But how is this actually done since the physical senses are only an outward image of an inward and spiritual grace?

The hearing of God, Richard explains, <u>comes by memory</u> or "a showing." That is to say we remember past encounters or we receive an immediate revelation of God's love and presence. It might come through reading Scripture or an awareness of God as we walk through a beautiful wood or by a heaven-sent vision or dream. This is the hearing.

Seeing God, according to Richard, comes by contemplation. <u>Contemplation is the swinging of our heart like a magnet to the pole star of the Spirit.</u> It is the gaze of the soul upon the God who loves us. This is the seeing.

Kissing God, says Richard, occurs by our devotion. Devotion in the old writers speaks of <u>our intention</u>, the direction of our will, our singleness of purpose, our obedience in all things.

Finally there is the "ineffable infusion of divine sweetness." Richard is speaking here of the climax of intimacy, but his analogy is beginning to break down at this point. In human sexuality the climax is a mutually active encounter, but here God is the one bringing the spiritual infusion; <u>we only receive and rejoice in his loving</u>

care. *This is why Richard's language here becomes less precise. We are standing under the great mystery of the action of divine love upon us, and the words to describe what is happening fail us. Adoration alone is appropriate.*

RICHARD J. FOSTER

GOING DEEPER

RICHARD OF ST. VICTOR, *The Twelve Patriarchs; The Mystical Ark; Book Three of the Trinity,* translated and introduced by Grover A. Zinn (New York: Paulist, 1979); a volume in *The Classics of Western Spirituality* series. This fine collection includes all of Richard's principal writings. The editor, Grover A. Zinn, a native of Arkansas who writes and teaches in the United States, has done much of his scholarly work on Richard of St. Victor in Glasgow, Scotland (where he served as assistant minister in the Barony Church), and at Oxford University in England. Besides providing an excellent introduction, Zinn also has provided new translations of the texts. The preface is by French scholar Jean Chatillon, who has devoted a lifetime of study to the Abbey of St. Victor and some of its leading figures.

Alan Paton

(1903–1988)

———

Alan Stewart Paton was educated at the University of Natal (South Africa) and was national president of the South African Liberal Party until it was declared illegal in 1968. In that same year Paton, a white Anglican clergyman who had been an outspoken opponent of apartheid, wrote *Instrument of Thy Peace*, a book of twenty-one short meditations based on the familiar prayer attributed to St. Francis of Assisi. This prayer, the spirituality of Francis, and biblical reflection had been deeply formative to Paton.

Alan Paton is even better known for his novel *Cry, the Beloved Country,* also a protest against the unjust social structures of apartheid. Its central figure is a black clergyman, the Reverend Stephen Kumalo, who sets off from his impoverished homeland at Ndotsheni, Natal, for Johannesburg in search of his sister Gertrude and his son Absalom. There he learns that Gertrude has adopted a life of prostitution and his son has murdered the son of a white farmer, James Jarvis. Despite Kumalo's efforts, his son is condemned to die. Kumalo returns home with Gertrude's son and Absalom's pregnant wife. The novel ends with a reconciliation between Kumalo and Jarvis, in which Jarvis resolves to rise above his son's death by helping poor blacks. Published in 1948, the novel continues to be widely read; it is a moving plea for racial understanding.

In the following brief selections, we see Paton writing out of his own struggle for acceptance of God's will. Notice in the following selection that his debt is not only to Francis of Assisi but also to such people as Dag Hammarskjöld (secretary-general of the United Nations at the time) and Sir Alexander Paterson, men who came out of a European and English context with a strong moral conviction. Yet Paton is not working with messages of violent resistance; instead, he is speaking in a language of forgiveness and love.

INSTRUMENT OF THY PEACE

God's Instrument

Lord, make me an instrument of Thy peace. Prayer of St. Francis

We pray for many things, for loved ones, for one sick, for one dying, for health, for much-needed money, for success in examinations, for our country, for the peace of the world. We pray for forgiveness of sins, for conquest of one particular sin that defeats us, for help in some situation that frightens or threatens us. We pray especially hard—most of us—when our own safety or security is threatened.

I myself have done this, but now I wish to place on record that I am in unrepayable debt to Francis of Assisi, for when I pray his prayer, or even remember it, my melancholy is dispelled, my self-pity comes to an end, my faith is restored, because of this majestic conception of what the work of a disciple should be.

So majestic is this conception that one dare no longer be sorry for oneself. This world ceases to be one's enemy and becomes the place where one lives and works and serves. Life is no longer nasty, mean, brutish, and short, but becomes the time that one needs to make it less nasty and mean, not only for others, but indeed also for oneself.

We are brought back instantaneously to the reality of our faith, that we are not passive recipients but active instruments. The right relationship between man and God is instantly restored.

Francis of Assisi no doubt often prayed for something for himself, or for the order he had founded, or for the chapel and huts at Porziuncula. But in his prayer he asks nothing for himself, or perhaps he asks everything, and that is that his whole life, all his gifts, his physical strength, shall be an instrument in God's hand.

And I say to myself, this is the only way in which a Christian can encounter hatred, injury, despair, and sadness, and that is by throwing off his helplessness and allowing himself to be made the bearer of love, the pardoner, the bringer of hope, the comforter of those that grieve. And I believe that if you allow yourself to be so made, you will be so.

I think as I write this of a man who is leaving prison to return to the world. During these years he has paid more attention to religion than ever before in his life. As he leaves, the prison chaplain assures him that the past is done, the past is forgiven. But when he returns to the world, he finds that the world has not forgiven, that it has not forgotten his past. So hope changes to despair, faith to doubt. It seems that God has not forgiven him after all.

It is here that a great duty falls upon us all, to be the bearers of God's forgiveness, to be the instrument of his love, to be active in compassion. This man's return to the world is made tragic because *we were not there*. God moves in his own mysterious ways, but a great deal of the time he moves through us. And it is because we are not there that so many do not believe in God's love.

JESUS: He came to the disciples and found them asleep; and he said to Peter, "What! Could none of you stay awake with me one hour?"

JESUS: You are salt to the world. And if salt becomes tasteless, how is its saltness to be restored?

DAG HAMMARSKJÖLD (to himself on the eve of a meeting of the Security Council): Your responsibility is indeed terrifying. If you fail, it is God, thanks to your having betrayed Him, who will fail mankind. You fancy you can be responsible *to* God; can you carry the responsibility *for* God?

> O Lord, help us to be masters of ourselves, that we may be servants of others. Sir Alexander Patterson (who devoted his life and great talents to the reform of British prisons and institutions for delinquent boys and girls)

> O Lord, open my eyes that I may see the need of others, open my ears that I may hear their cries, open my heart so that they need not be without succour, let me be not afraid to defend the weak because of the anger of the strong, nor afraid to defend the poor because of the anger of the rich. Show me where love and hope and faith are needed, and use me to bring them to those places. And so open my eyes and my ears that I may this coming day be able to do some work of peace for Thee.

> No one is too weak, too vile, too unimportant, to be God's instrument.

And Moses said unto God, Who am I that I should go unto Pharaoh, and that I should bring forth the children of Israel out of Egypt?

And the Lord said unto Moses, Certainly I will be with thee; and this shall be a token unto thee, that I have sent thee: When thou hast brought forth the people out of Egypt, ye shall serve God upon this mountain.

And Moses said unto the Lord, O my Lord, I am not eloquent, neither heretofore, nor since thou hast spoken unto thy servant: but I am slow of speech, and of a slow tongue.

And the Lord said unto him, Who hath made man's mouth? or who maketh the dumb, or deaf, or the seeing, or the blind? have not I, the Lord? Now therefore go, and I will be with thy mouth, and teach thee, what thou shalt say. (Exod. 3; 4; KJV)

No Christian should ever think or say that he is not fit to be God's instrument, for that in fact is what it means to be a Christian. We may be humble about many things, but we may never decline to be used. John the Baptist told the people by the river Jordan, "I baptize you with water, for repentance, but the one who comes after me is mightier than I, and I am not fit to take off his shoes." Then Jesus himself came to be baptized by him, and John tried to dissuade him, saying to him, "Do you come to me? I need rather to be baptized by you." Jesus replied, "Let it be so for the present; we do well to conform in this way with all that God requires." So John baptized him whose shoes he was not fit to take off.

The gospel is full of reassurances to us, some of them startling. You are salt to the world! You are light to all the world! Even the hairs of your head have all been counted! These words were exciting to those who heard them. Things might be dark but they were to be the light of the world. They were given a new sense of their value as persons. Especially was this true of women. One can hardly describe the joy of the first disciples, who were given by Jesus such a sense of their significance in the world. This same sense of significance has been given again and again to other people by disciples of Jesus. Of these none was greater than Francis of Assisi. He might well have prayed:

To those who have lost their way, let me restore it to them.
To those who are aimless, let me bring purpose.
To those who do not know who they are, let me teach them that they are the children of God and can be used as His instruments in the never-ending work of healing and redemption.

There are therefore two things for us to do. The first is never to doubt that God can use us if we are willing to be used, no matter what our weaknesses. The second is to see that God can use any other person who is willing to be used, whatever his weaknesses, and if need be, to assure him of this truth.

One day as St. Francis was returning from his prayers in the wood, Brother Masseo met him, and wishing to test how humble he was, asked in a mocking manner, saying, "Why after thee? Why after thee? Why after thee?" St. Francis replied, "What is it thou wouldst say?" And Brother Masseo answered, "Say, why is it that all the world comes after thee, and everybody desires to see thee, and to hear thee, and to obey thee? Thou art not a man either comely of person, or of noble birth, or of great knowledge; whence then comes it that all the world runs after thee?"

Hearing this, St. Francis, filled with joy in his spirit, raised his face towards heaven, and remained for a great while with his mind lifted up to God; then returning to himself, he knelt down, and gave praise and thanks to God; and then, with great fervour of spirit, turning to Brother Masseo, he said, "Wouldst know why after me? Wouldst know why after me? Why all the world runs after me? This comes to me, because the eyes of the Most High God, which behold in all places both the evil and the good, even those most holy eyes have not seen amongst sinners one more vile, nor more insufficient, nor a greater sinner than I, and therefore to do that wonderful work which He intends to do, He hath not found on earth a viler creature than I; and for this cause He elected me to confound the nobility, and the grandeur, and the strength, and beauty, and wisdom of the world, that all men may know that all virtue and all goodness are of Him, and not of the creature, and that none should glory in his presence; but that he who glories should glory in the Lord, to whom is all honour and glory in eternity!"

Then Brother Masseo, at this humble and fervent reply, feared within himself, and knew certainly that St. Francis was grounded in humility.

The Little Flowers of St. Francis of Assisi

Lord, make me willing to be used by Thee. May my knowledge of my unworthiness never make me resist being used by Thee. May the need of others always be remembered by me, so that I may ever be willing to be used by Thee.

And open my eyes and my heart that I may this coming day be able to do some work of peace for Thee.

BIBLE SELECTION
Matthew 5:13–16

"You are the salt of the earth; but if salt has lost its taste, how can its saltiness be restored? It is no longer good for anything, but is thrown out and trampled under foot.

"You are the light of the world. A city built on a hill cannot be hid. No one after lighting a lamp puts it under the bushel basket, but on a lampstand, and it gives light to all in the house. In the same way, let your light shine before others, so that they may see your good works and give glory to your Father in heaven."

DISCUSSION QUESTIONS

The following can be used for discussion within a small group, or used for journal reflections by individuals:

1. How can I put the sayings "salt of the earth" and "light of the world" in concrete terms? Are there individuals or movements that readily come to mind?
2. "Submission" and "active social protest" seem to be opposed to each other. Are there ways they can fit together?

SUGGESTED EXERCISES

The following exercises can be done by individuals, shared between spiritual friends, or used in the context of a small group. Choose one or more of the following:

1. Have the group take a look at the ministry of Jesus in terms of three different dimensions: activism, submission, and forgiveness. Identify moments in Jesus' ministry when he seems to exemplify one or another of these three modes of God-centered living.
2. Identify ministries and movements personally known to you in which racial injustice or social injustice of another kind is being actively resisted. Have you ever felt called to join such a movement? If you have not done so, do you think you might do so in the future?

REFLECTIONS

The dominant image in this selection by Paton is of us as "instruments" for God's use. Of course Paton, and St. Francis before him, are merely following the lead of the Apostle Paul who gave this image classic expression. The relevant passage is Romans 6:13: "No longer present your members to sin as instruments of wickedness, but present yourselves to God as those who have been brought from death to life, and present your members to God as instruments of righteousness." The "members" Paul is referring to here is simply our bodies; our hands, our feet, our eyes, our tongue. These literal, physical parts of our person are to be submitted to God as instruments for his use, much like the surgical tools are submitted to the surgeon for his good purposes.

To be an instrument of righteousness is challenging indeed. And such a challenge is made all the more pointed as Paton faced the horrors of South Africa's apartheid. Such a context gives added power and poignancy to his call for us to be "the bearer of love, the pardoner, the bringer of hope, the comforter of those that grieve. . . . It is here that a great duty falls upon us all, to be the bearers of God's forgiveness, to be the instrument of his love, to be active in compassion." Challenging words indeed spoken as they were in the midst of apartheid's cruelty.

Isn't it interesting that St. Francis was such a formative figure for Paton? Somehow this simple monk of Assisi has been able to reach across continents and centuries and touch all who have ears to hear and eyes to see. This is especially true in situations of unbearable evil as Paton himself faced. We could all hope to have such an impact for good, even if our circle of influence is exceedingly small.

RICHARD J. FOSTER

GOING DEEPER

ALAN PATON, *Instrument of Thy Peace* (New York: Ballantine, revised edition, 1982). This book of twenty-one short meditations based on the familiar prayer attributed to St. Francis of Assisi also draws on biblical sources and contemporary experience.

ALAN PATON, *Cry, the Beloved Country* (New York: Scribner, 1950). This novel has gone through many editions, and even though apartheid no longer prevails in South Africa, it remains a moving plea for racial understanding.

Service

Hadewijch of Antwerp

(13th Century)

———

There were many pious women in the thirteenth century named Hadewijch. But this one is known (though the particulars of her life are not fully known) for her enduring spiritual writings. She was not a nun but a Beguine—that is, a devout woman who chose to lead a life of poverty and contemplation without taking vows as a nun. Her familiarity with the language of chivalry and courtly love suggests that she was a member of the upper class.

This is typical of the Beguines, who came from privileged families but rejected the life of the castle—and the life of the cloister—in favor of nonvowed religious life, which included manual work, study, teaching, and the recitation of the Hours (that is to say, set times of prayer, based on the Psalms, according to a recognized pattern used in religious communities throughout Europe).

Hadewijch was unquestionably a mystic, probably the founder of a Beguine group, and certainly the director of one, with a number of younger Beguines under her care (women whom she believed were called to be contemplatives, but often in need of correction or instruction). Her writings reflect the spiritual direction she gave them and her concern for their maturing spiritual lives.

Later on in life she was excluded from her community, for reasons that may have something to do with her very high standards for spirituality. Also, her growing reputation as a spiritual teacher may have aroused jealousies.

In the selection that follows, which is taken from her collected letters, notice the emphasis that Hadewijch continually places upon God's love for us and our love for God as the source of our desire to serve. She compares our relationship to God to our attitude toward a beloved person. This fundamental sense of intimacy and closeness governs the whole of the spiritual life.

At the same time that she encourages this passionate spiritual intensity, she is also offering counsels of detachment. "Be on your guard, therefore, and let nothing disturb your peace." No doubt this is because she is counseling women less experienced than herself in spiritual life. However, her advice is very appropriate for us. "All you do or omit should be for the honor of Love."

Notice, also, how her spiritual counsel flows out of and is deeply connected to Scripture, which she seems to cite at every turn. "Take upon you Love's interests," she counsels us, "as one who wishes to be ever in her [that is, Love's] noble service."

It is clear that for Hadewijch, God is Love, and genuine, godly Love should govern us and inspire us to serve God and others.

COLLECTED LETTERS

Give All for All

Consider now all the things you have failed in, either by self-will or by unnecessary sadness.

It is true, as I well know: A person often grows sad when he is without his Beloved and cannot tell whether he is approaching him or withdrawing from him; and this is sincere. But anyone who is truly faithful will know that the goodness of his Beloved is greater than his own failures. One must not be sorrowful because of suffering or sigh after repose, but give all for all and entirely renounce repose. Rejoice continually in the hope of winning love; for if you desire perfect love for God, you must not desire in return any repose whatever except Love.

Do all for the honor of God

Be on your guard, therefore, and let nothing disturb your peace. Do good under all circumstances, but with no care for any profit, or any blessedness, or any damnation, or any salvation, or any martyrdom; but all you do or omit should be for the honor of Love. If you behave like this, you will soon rise up again. And let people take you for a fool; there is much truth in that. Be docile and prompt toward all who have need of you, and satisfy everyone as far as you can manage it without debasing yourself. Be joyful with those who rejoice, and weep with those who weep (Rom. 12:13). Be good toward those who have need of you, devoted toward the sick, generous with the poor, and recollected in spirit beyond the reach of all creatures.

And even if you do the best you can in all things, your human nature must often fall short; so entrust yourself to God's goodness, for his goodness is greater than your failures. And always practice true virtues, with confidence, and be diligent and constant in always following unconditionally our Lord's guiding and his dearest will wherever you can discern it, taking trouble and doing your utmost to examine your thoughts strictly, in order to know yourself in all things.

Put God's work first

And live for God in such a way, this I implore you, that you be not wanting in the great works to which he has called you. Never neglect them for any less important work, this I implore and counsel you. For you have great motives impelling you to take trouble in God's service. He has protected you from all trouble, if you yourself will but take heed; so that your way is smoothed by grace, if you will but recognize it. And all things considered, you have suffered too little to grow up, as in justice you owed it to God to do—although, now and then, you willingly comply in this. . . .

Although, too, you sometimes feel such affliction in your heart that it seems to you you are forsaken by God, do not be discouraged by it. For verily I say to you: Whatever misery we endure with good will and for God is pleasing to God in every respect. . . .

Serve nobly

You are still young, and you must grow a good deal, and it is much better for you, if you wish to walk the way of Love, that you seek difficulty and that you suffer for the honor of Love, rather than wish to feel love. But take upon you Love's interests, as one who wishes to be ever in her noble service. Have no care, therefore, for honor or shame; fear neither the torments of earth nor those of hell, if by them you could prevail on Love, in order to serve this Love worthily. Her noble service consists in the care you take to recite your Hours and to keep your Rule, without wishing or receiving pleasure in any of your service. . . .

Serve nobly, wish for nothing else, and fear nothing else: and let Love freely take care of herself! For Love rewards to the full, even though she often comes late. Let no doubt or disappointment ever turn you away from performing acts of virtue; let no ill success cause you to fear that you yourself will not come to conformity with God. You must not doubt this, and you must not believe in men on earth, saints, or angels, even if they work wonders (Gal. 1:8); for you were called early, and your heart feels, at least sometimes, that you are chosen, and that God has begun to sustain your soul in abandonment. . . .

Abandon yourself to God

If, in fine, you wish to have what is yours (1 Cor. 3:22), give yourself completely in abandonment to God, to become what he is. For the honor of Love, renounce yourself as far as you can, to be purely obedient in all that belongs to your greatest perfection, both in doing and in omitting. To this end you must remain humble, and unexalted by all the works you can accomplish, but wise with generous and perfect charity to sustain all things in heaven and on earth, as befits true charity, according to their order. Thus you may become perfect and possess what is yours!—if you wish. . . .

BIBLE SELECTION
1 John 4:7–21

Beloved, let us love one another, because love is from God; everyone who loves is born of God and knows God. Whoever does not love does not know God, for God is love. God's love was revealed among us in this way: God sent his only Son into the world so that we might live through him. In this is love, not that we loved God but that he loved us and sent his Son to be the atoning sacrifice for our sins. Beloved, since God loved us so much, we also ought to love one another. No one has ever seen God; if we love one another, God lives in us, and his love is perfected in us.

By this we know that we abide in him and he in us, because he has given us of his Spirit. And we have seen and do testify that the Father has sent his Son as the Savior of the world. God abides in those who confess that Jesus is the Son of God, and they abide in God. We have known and believe the love that God has for us.

God is love, and those who abide in love abide in God, and God abides in them. Love has been perfected among us in this: that we may have boldness on the day of judgment, because as he is, so are we in this world. There is no fear in love, but perfect love casts out fear; for fear has to do with punishment, and whoever fears has not reached perfection in love. We love because he first loved us. Those who say, "I love God," and hate their brothers or sisters, are liars; for those who do not love a brother or sister, whom they have seen, cannot love God whom they have not seen. The commandment we have from him is this: those who love God must love their brothers and sisters also.

DISCUSSION QUESTIONS

The following can be used for discussion within a small group, or used for journal reflections by individuals:

1. In what ways may our acts of service become lukewarm or routine?
2. What can help us to gain an enthusiastic, noble-minded attitude like that Hadewijch describes?
3. How can I experience love that overflows into service?

SUGGESTED EXERCISES

The following exercises can be done by individuals, shared between spiritual friends, or used in the context of a small group. Choose one or more of the following:

1. This week, do something romantic about your faith commitment. Go and visit a sick or aged person who needs your companionship. Sign up to work in a soup kitchen. Volunteer to be on a hardworking church committee. As you do this, tell God that what you are doing is your Valentine, and hear God thanking you in love language.

2. In your group, tell love stories. If you know some Christian love stories, about people who served God lovingly and well, tell them to each other. But you might also want to consider your favorite human love stories, stories of love between men and women, between parents and children, between friends. Reflect on what these human love stories show us about our love relationship with God.

3. In a group, or privately, list the names of your favorite love songs. Note how some of them seem to have a spiritual, rather than just a secular, meaning.

REFLECTIONS

Hadewijch's discussion of divine Love takes us up into dizzy heights to which we who live at the beginning of the twenty-first century are unaccustomed. Oh, we are used to talking about love here and there, seeing it perhaps in this action of thoughtfulness or that deed of compassion. But for her, Love is the beginning and the end, the height and the depth of all life. We know love as an idea, a thought, perhaps an action. But for her, Love covers all; all longing, all honor, all desire, all hope—all in all. We see love as soft and pliable. For Hadewijch, Love simply IS— the reality out of which we are to live and through which we serve others.

Hadewijch is talking to us about the Love of God, I know, but I have to admit I wasn't too excited about this reading. It is a reading easy to dismiss as too nice, too romantic, too utopian perhaps. That is what I was about to do—dismiss it—but then I focused on the Scripture reading for this section. Wham! I mean if ever a writing takes us up into the dizzy heights of divine Love it is 1 John 4. I had to slow down and reevaluate Hadewijch again. In the end I decided that while I may visit 1 John 4 now and again, Hadewijch of Antwerp lives there.

RICHARD J. FOSTER

GOING DEEPER

Hadewijch: The Complete Works, translated and introduced by Mother Columba Hart, O.S.B., with a preface by Paul Mommaers, S.J. (New York: Paulist, 1980); a volume in *The Classics of Western Spirituality* series. This handsome volume provides in-depth biographical treatment of Hadewijch, explains her teaching and instruction on spiritual life, and includes letters, poems in stanzas, poems in couplets, and Hadewijch's visions. The notes, bibliography, and indexes are excellent.

ELIZABETH DREYER, "Hadewijch of Antwerp," in *Passionate Women: Two Medieval Mystics* (New York: Paulist Press, 1989), pp. 43–71. The Madeleva Lecture in Spirituality for 1989, given by Dreyer, a professor of ecclesiastical history, deals with the theme of spiritual passion. Hildegard of Bingen is the other medieval mystic who is treated here.

Meister Eckhart

(1260–1328)

Meister Eckhart was more than likely named John but has been invariably called Meister Eckhart. He entered the Dominican order near the German town of Erfurt in Germany, in 1277 was a student of arts at Paris, and by 1280 began studying philosophy at Cologne.

In 1293–94 he wrote a commentary on the *Sentences* of Peter Lombard, as a Bachelor of Theology in Paris. While there, one of his teachers was probably Albert the Great, who also taught Thomas Aquinas and who made an effort to defend Aquinas against a massive effort by fellow theologians to discredit Thomas's work.

In 1294, Eckhart became prior of the Dominicans at Erfurt and vicar of the vicariate of Thuringia. In 1302 he graduated as Master of Theology in Paris, and in 1303 he lectured there as regent master. From 1303 to 1311 he served as provincial of the Dominican province of Saxony, returning to Paris from 1311 to 1313 for a second regency in theology.

For the next decade Eckhart was Professor of Theology at Strasbourg, probably at the Dominican house of studies. Active as a preacher and spiritual director, he gained a high reputation with Dominican and Cistercian nuns, Beguines, and others.

Although he must have enjoyed the good opinion of his fellow Dominicans (judging by the positions of authority he held), trouble arose in 1326. Serious questions were raised about his teachings; formal challenges were brought by theological inquisitors at Cologne.

Eckhart defended himself vigorously, charging that the inquisitors were not competent to judge his work and also claiming an exemption as a mendicant friar. (In fact, many of these inquisitors did not actually read Eckhart's work but relied on summaries.)

After the judgment went against him in Cologne, Eckhart traveled to Avignon where he hoped to make a direct appeal to the Holy See, but he died before the matter was resolved.

The case, which rested on certain statements quoted from Eckhart's sermons, resulted in the condemnation of only some of his statements. Others were said to be permissible if properly explained. In fact, it is now thought that the entire case against him was politically motivated.

Because of these controversies, Eckhart's work was seldom copied or consulted at first. But in the fourteenth, fifteenth, and sixteenth centuries, his ideas influenced such figures as John Tauler, Henry Suso, and John Ruusbroec, a selection of whose work appears in the section entitled "Guidance."

Today Eckhart is widely read and appreciated, not so much for his theological opinions as for his vision of God. The selection that follows is from Sermon 34. In it, notice how he develops the two characters of Martha and Mary. Martha is the older, mature sister who is protective and concerned for Mary's well-being. Mary is the younger one who loves Jesus but hasn't yet learned mature responsibility. Although Eckhart is a teacher of the spiritual life, he apparently wants prayer to lead to a life of mature service!

SERMON 34

When Our Work Becomes a Spiritual Work Working in the World

> Jesus went into a certain city, and a certain woman named Martha received him. (Luke 10:38)

Three things caused Mary to sit at our Lord's feet. The first was that God's goodness had embraced her soul. The second was a great, unspeakable longing: she yearned without knowing what it was she yearned after, and she desired without knowing what she desired! The third was the sweet consolation and bliss that she derived from the eternal words that came from Christ's mouth.

Three things also caused Martha to run about and serve her dear Christ. The first was maturity of age and a depth of her being, which was thoroughly trained to the most external matters. For this reason, she believed that no one was so well suited for activity as herself. The second was a wise prudence that knew how to achieve external acts to the highest degree that love demands. The third was the high dignity of her dear guest.

The masters of the spiritual life say that God is ready for every person's spiritual and physical satisfaction to the utmost degree that that person desires. . . .

Martha is mature, Mary immature

Now Martha says, "Lord, tell her to help me." Martha did not say this out of anger. She spoke rather out of a loving kindness because she was hard pressed. We must indeed call it a loving kindness or a lovable form of teasing. How was this? Pay attention! . . . Martha knew Mary better than Mary knew Martha, for Martha had already lived quite a long time. Living affords the most noble kind of knowl-edge. . . . Living causes pleasure and light to be better known . . .

This was how it was with Martha. Therefore she said, "Lord, tell her to help me." It was as if she meant: "My sister thinks that she *can* already do what she *wishes* so long as she is only seated beneath your consolation. Let her know now if this is so, and tell her to get up and go away from you!" Next, it was tender love although Martha said it after due reflection. Mary was so filled with longing that she yearned without knowing why . . . Then Christ replied . . . "Martha, Martha, you are concerned, you are upset about many things. One thing is necessary!" . . .

This was how things were with our dear Martha. Therefore he said to her: "*One thing* is necessary, not *two things*. I and you, embraced *once* by the eternal light—that is *one thing*." . . . Light and spirit are *one thing* in the embrace of the eternal light.

The circle of eternity

Pay attention to what the "circle of eternity" is. The soul has three ways to God. One of them is to seek God in all creatures through multiple "pursuits" and through burning love. This is what King David meant when he said: "In all things I have found rest" (Eccl. 24:11).

The second way is a wayless way that is free and yet bound. On it we are raised up and carried without will and without form above ourselves and all things . . . This is what Christ meant when he said: "You are a happy man, Peter! Flesh and blood do not enlighten you. . . . "

The third way is indeed called a "way," yet it means being "at home": seeing God directly in his own being. Our dear Christ says, "I am the Way, the Truth, the Life" (John 14:6).

Listen then to this wonder! How wonderful it is to be both outside and inside, to seize and to be seized, to see and at the same time to be what is seen, to hold and to be held—*that* is the goal where the spirit remains at rest, united with our dear eternity. . . .

Mary was still learning

Martha was so real that her works did not hinder her. Her activity and works brought her to eternal happiness. This happiness was indeed somewhat indirect, but a noble nature, constant industry, and virtue . . . are very helpful in this connection. Mary also had to become such a Martha before she could become the mature Mary. For when she sat at our Lord's feet, she was still not the true Mary. . . .

Only after the disciples received the Holy Spirit did they begin to carry out acts of virtue. For this reason, when Mary was sitting at our Lord's feet, she was still learning. Then she was admitted into the school and learned how to live. . . .

May God help us to follow him sincerely in the practice of the true virtues! Amen.

BIBLE SELECTION
Luke 10:38–42

Now as they went on their way, he entered a certain village, where a woman named Martha welcomed him into her home. She had a sister named Mary, who sat at the Lord's feet and listened to what he was saying. But Martha was distracted by her many tasks; so she came to him and asked, "Lord, do you not care that my sister has left me to do all the work by myself? Tell her to help me." But the Lord answered her, "Martha, Martha, you are worried and distracted by many things; there is need of only one thing. Mary has chosen the better part, which will not be taken away from her."

DISCUSSION QUESTIONS

The following can be used for discussion within a small group, or used for journal reflections by individuals:

1. Am I surprised that Meister Eckhart holds Martha up as a spiritual example instead of Mary? What is the "one needful thing," and how does he manage to make it belong to Martha as well as to Mary?
2. What can I learn from Martha about maturity in the Christian life?

SUGGESTED EXERCISES

The following exercises can be done by individuals, shared between spiritual friends, or used in the context of a small group. Choose one or more of the following:

1. Martha and Mary illustrate different aspects of Christian life: service and spirituality. Discuss how these two aspects are interlinked and how they influence each other.

2. Identify some important ministries of service in Christian history. Were these prayer-driven? Discuss.

3. Be "Martha" for a day or an evening. Do the dinner or the housework so that others can be at ease. How does it feel? How can this practice of serving others bring us closer to God?

REFLECTIONS

The lesson Eckhart seeks to instill within us is this: remember, always remember that Mary and Martha were sisters. That is to say, service and spirituality go hand in hand, the active life and the contemplative life should never be separated.

It is a hard lesson for us to learn. We seem constantly to swing from one extreme of the pendulum to the other. First we are out working and serving, doing and accomplishing. But, sooner or later, exhaustion of body and barrenness of soul can no longer be ignored. And so we drop everything and withdraw into a tight circle of self-care and self-interest.

What we need to see is the way the Mary and Martha impulses within us are to function in symbiosis. We first need the "one necessary thing" that Jesus spoke of. Eckhart describes this one necessary thing as "I and you, embraced once by the eternal light—that is one thing. . . . Light and spirit are one thing in the embrace of the eternal light." His somewhat obtuse language means simply that we first enter a loving, ongoing, ever-growing relationship with God. Another way to put it is that we learn to become a branch, gaining our life sustenance from Christ, the vine.

Once this reality has worked its way deep within us then, out of the abundance of this life, we serve others, freely and joyfully. Even the clarity about which services to undertake and the means for accomplishing them flow out of the "one necessary thing." This is why Eckhart could hold Martha up as an example for us of "the practice of the true virtues." She had, according to Eckhart's understanding of the story, the one necessary thing that Mary was in the process of entering into. We may want to differ with Eckhart's interpretation of the spiritual maturity of Martha, but we can all appreciate and learn from his central point, namely, that spirituality and service are inseparable twins.

RICHARD J. FOSTER

GOING DEEPER

Meister Eckhart: The Essential Sermons, Commentaries, Treatises, and Defense, edited by Edmund Colledge and Bernard McGinn (New York: Paulist, 1981); a volume in *The Classics of Western Spirituality* series. This volume provides a fine introduction to Meister Eckhart and includes his own defense of his life's work.

Meister Eckhart: Teacher and Preacher, edited by Bernard McGinn (New York: Paulist, 1986); a volume in *The Classics of Western Spirituality* series. This is a scholarly but very readable collection that includes Eckhart's commentary on Exodus, selections from his commentary on the book of Wisdom, from his sermons and lectures on Ecclesiasticus, and from the commentary on John. It also includes quite a number of his Latin and German sermons in translation.

Breakthrough: Meister Eckhart's Creation Spirituality in New Translation, with introductions and commentaries by Matthew Fox (Garden City, NY: Doubleday/Image, 1980). These days, Matthew Fox is himself under a cloud, but his translation of a number of Eckhart's sermons continues to sparkle.

Dorothy Day

(1897–1980)

———

Dorothy Day's life is one of apostolic service. She is principally remembered for her love of the poor and her willingness to go to prison for the gospel's sake. But her Christianity was deeply formed by prayer and study of the Gospels.

While most people remember her for her vigorous social protest, hers was no splinter-group advocacy. She wanted Christianity whole and entire: its devotions, its depth of prayer and spirituality, its love of humanity, its celebration of creative and created things.

Born in Brooklyn, raised in Chicago, Dorothy Day met the sights and smells of urban poverty close-up. She resolved to do something with her life—to be a writer and a socialist—in order to change things for the better.

In adulthood, while working as a journalist in New York City, Day moved from atheistic socialism to Christian belief, shocking her friends by embracing Roman Catholic faith. As cofounder (with Peter Maurin) of the Catholic Worker movement, she took her stand on the Lower East Side of Manhattan, offering hospitality to the poor and outreach to New York City's millions through the one-penny newspaper the *Catholic Worker*.

Soon the Catholic Worker movement had spread throughout the United States. Day's writing was a considerable form of Christian service as well as her hands-on work with the poor on her doorstep. "In order to have a Christian social order we must first have Christians," she wrote.

In cofounding the Catholic Worker movement she wanted, like Francis of Assisi, to call the whole people of God to renewal and reform, to renew the Church with the Gospel. But most of all she felt, and said in the *Catholic Worker*, "It is time to take the lid off the well of truth from which the mystics and saints drew" (January 1972, p. 1).

Notice, in the reading that follows, which is taken from her autobiography, *The Long Loneliness*, how Day's ideas of service flow from attentiveness to Christ's word and his example of Christian service. (The "Peter" referred to is Peter Maurin, her longtime collaborator.)

THE LONG LONELINESS

Hospitality to the Poor

Our Detroit house of hospitality for women is named for St. Martha. We are always taking care of migrant families in that house, southern families who are lured to the North because they hear of the high wages paid. It is a house of eight large rooms, and each of the bedrooms has housed a family with children, but the congestion has meant that the husbands had to go to the men's house of hospitality named for St. Francis. Sometimes the families overflow into a front parlor and living room downstairs. The colored take care of the white children, and the white the colored, while the parents hunt for homes and jobs. Such an extreme of destitution makes all men brothers.

Yes, we have lived with the poor, with the workers, and we know them not just from the streets, or in mass meetings, but from years of living in the slums, in tenements, in our hospices in Washington, Baltimore, Philadelphia, Harrisburg, Pittsburgh, New York, Rochester, Boston, Worcester, Buffalo, Troy, Detroit, Cleveland, Toledo, Akron, St. Louis, Chicago, Milwaukee, Minneapolis, Seattle, San Francisco, Los Angeles, Oakland, even down into Houma, Louisiana, where Father Jerome Drolet worked with Negroes and whites, with shrimp shellers, fishermen, longshoremen, and seamen.

Just as the Church has gone out through its missionaries into the most obscure towns and villages, we have gone too. Sometimes our contacts have been through the Church and sometimes through readers of our paper, through union organizers or those who needed to be organized.

We have lived with the unemployed, the sick, the unemployables. The contrast between the worker who is organized and has his union, the fellowship of his own trade to give him strength, and those who have no organization and come in to us on a breadline is pitiable.

A heartbreaking situation

They are stripped, then, not only of all earthly goods, but of spiritual goods, their sense of human dignity. When they are forced into line at municipal lodging houses, in clinics, in our houses of hospitality, they are then the truly destitute. Over and over again in our work, many young men and women who come as volunteers have not been able to endure it and have gone away. To think that we are forced by our own lack of room, our lack of funds, to perpetuate this shame, is heartbreaking.

"Is this what you meant by houses of hospitality," I asked Peter.

"At least it will arouse the conscience," he said.

Many left the work because they could see no use in this gesture of feeding the poor, and because of their own shame. But enduring this shame is part of our penance.

All men are brothers

"All men are brothers." How often we hear this refrain, the rallying call that strikes a response in every human heart. These are the words of Christ, "Call no man master, for ye are all brothers." It is a revolutionary call which has even been put to music. The last movement of Beethoven's Ninth Symphony has that great refrain—"All men are brothers." Going to the people is the purest and best act in Christian tradition and revolutionary tradition and is the beginning of world brotherhood.

Never to be severed from the people, to set out always from the point of view of serving the people, not serving the interests of a small group or oneself. . . . It is almost another way of saying that we must and will find Christ in each and every man, when we look on them as brothers.

BIBLE SELECTION
Matthew 25:31–46

"When the Son of Man comes in his glory, and all the angels with him, then he will sit on the throne of his glory. All the nations will be gathered before him, and he will separate people one from another as a shepherd separates the sheep from the goats, and he will put the sheep at his right hand and the goats at the left. Then the king will say to those at his right hand, 'Come, you that are blessed by my Father, inherit the kingdom prepared for you from the foundation of the world; for I was hungry and you gave me food, I was thirsty and you gave me something to drink, I was a stranger and you welcomed me, was naked and you gave me clothing, I was sick and you took care of me, I was in prison and you visited me.' Then the righteous will answer him, 'Lord, when was it that we saw you hungry and gave you food, or thirsty and gave you something to drink? And when was it that we saw you a stranger and welcomed you, or naked and gave you clothing? And when was it that we saw you sick or in prison and visited you?' And the king will answer them, 'Truly I tell you, just as you did it to one of the least of these who are members of my family, you did it to me.' Then he will say to those at his left hand, 'You that are accursed, depart from me into the eternal fire prepared for the devil and his angels; for I was hungry and you gave me no food, I was thirsty and you gave me nothing to drink, I was a stranger and you did not welcome me, naked and you did not give me clothing, sick and in prison and you did not visit me.' Then they also will answer, 'Lord, when was it that we saw you hungry or thirsty or a stranger or naked or sick or in prison, and did not take care of you?' Then he will answer them, 'Truly I tell you, just as you did not do it to one of the least of these, you did not do it to me.' And these will go away into eternal punishment, but the righteous into eternal life."

DISCUSSION QUESTIONS

The following can be used for discussion within a small group, or used for journal reflections by individuals:

1. What forms of service to others do I engage in on a daily basis? (Do not hesitate, in this evaluation, from mentioning any paid service you render, as well as unpaid service.)
2. In what ways may my personal history be leading me to specific forms of Christian service?
3. How can I balance service with other dimensions of Christian life?

SUGGESTED EXERCISES

The following exercises can be done by individuals, shared between spiritual friends, or used in the context of a small group. Choose one or more of the following:

1. This week, investigate ministries of Christian service in your community. Evaluate them with a view to volunteering for one or more.
2. Ask others you know (or members of your group) to evaluate your "track record" of Christian service.
3. Visit a soup kitchen or a homeless shelter in your community. Volunteer to work there for a time if that is appropriate. Record in your journal about the effects of the visit on you.

REFLECTIONS

Reading Dorothy Day heals me. Not because she speaks comfort and counsel, sweetness and light. Far from it. Dorothy Day rebukes me, always she rebukes me, but that is what is so very healing. When I begin trusting in influence and privileged position she rebukes me. When I start caring more about the number of shopping days until Christmas than I care about the poor she rebukes me. When I begin to love status more than I love justice and shalom she rebukes me. When I start to set aside the concerns of social justice in favor of evangelism she rebukes me. And that rebuke—that stinging rebuke—is what is so very healing.

The decisive event in Dorothy Day's "call" to work among the poor is a moving story. At the height of the Great Depression she was in Washington, DC, reporting on a "hunger strike" being staged by a small army of desperately impoverished demonstrators. Deeply saddened at the brutal treatment of these demonstrators and angered at the conditions that made them so vulnerable, Dorothy went to the National Shrine of the Immaculate Conception at Catholic University to pray. The upper church was still under construction, so she went into the crypt beneath, with its low vaulted ceilings and dark chapels lit by the flickering of vigil candles. "There," she wrote, "I offered up a special prayer, a prayer which came with tears and with anguish, that some way would open up for me to use what talents I possessed for my fellow workers, for the poor." Returning to her New York apartment, she found a stranger waiting to meet her. "I am Peter Maurin," he said in a thick French accent. "George Shuster, editor of The Commonweal, *told me to look you up. Also, a red-headed Irish Communist in Union Square told me to see you. He says we think alike." This was the beginning of a lifelong collaboration that proved to be the vivid answer to Dorothy's desperate prayer.*

RICHARD J. FOSTER

GOING DEEPER

DOROTHY DAY, *The Long Loneliness: The Autobiography of Dorothy Day* (Chicago: Thomas More, 1989 [1952]). In this candid personal story, Day leads the reader from her early childhood and youth, through coming to faith and the Catholic Worker movement, convincing us that "heaven is a banquet and life is a banquet too."

DOROTHY DAY, *Loaves and Fishes*, with an introduction by Robert Coles (Maryknoll, NY: Orbis Books, 1997). Originally published in 1963. Contains the inspiring story of the Catholic Worker movement.

Dorothy Day: Selected Writings, edited by Robert Ellsberg (Maryknoll, NY: Orbis Books, 1983). A selection of short pieces spanning more than fifty years. Samplings from all her books are included, as well as pieces from the *Catholic Worker*.

WILLIAM D. MILLER, *Dorothy Day: A Biography* (San Francisco: Harper & Row, 1982). Miller, a lifelong friend and sympathizer, has written a very full treatment of Day's life, drawing on a great deal of previously unpublished material.

Karl Rahner

(1904–1984)

———

Karl Rahner, a major Christian theologian of the twentieth century, was one of the chief architects of the Second Vatican Council.

He entered the Society of Jesus in 1922, was ordained in 1932, and after a time of study under Martin Heidegger earned his doctorate in 1936.

During World War II he taught and did pastoral work in Vienna. After the war ended he held professorships of Dogmatic Theology at the Universities of Innsbruck, Munich, and Münster.

He was a prolific writer and editor. His *Theological Investigations* includes some fourteen volumes, and he wrote more than 3,000 published articles.

Rahner's thought (and participation) influenced much of the language and content of the documents of Vatican II. His vision was world embracing and provided theological support for openness and dialogue between Catholics and other Christians, as well as a recognition of God's love for all humankind.

When Rahner's work first broke on the scene, he was at first admired for his modernity and progressiveness. Now it can be seen how firmly he is standing in a long theological tradition.

Karl Rahner was also a man of intense spirituality. Looking over the tremendous productivity of his life, it is easy to see him as one who practices the discipline of service.

In the following selection, however, which comes from his book *Encounters with Silence*, notice how that life of diligent service looks to him: it is a matter of daily routine, one that is not so grand and mighty, but a matter of "countless trivialities . . . empty talk . . . pointless activity . . . idle curiosity." Because Karl Rahner is honest with God and honest with us, we may be able to identify our daily routines with his.

ENCOUNTERS WITH SILENCE

God of My Daily Routine

I should like to bring the routine of my daily life before You, O Lord, to discuss the long days and tedious hours that are filled with everything else but You.

Look at this routine, O God of Mildness. Look upon us men, who are practically nothing else but routine. In Your loving mercy, look at my soul, a road crowded by a dense and endless column of bedraggled refugees, a bomb-pocked highway on which countless trivialities, much empty talk and pointless activity, idle curiosity and ludicrous pretensions of importance all roll forward in a never-ending stream.

When it stands before You and Your infallible Truthfulness, doesn't my soul look just like a market place where the second-hand dealers from all corners of the globe have assembled to sell the shabby riches of this world? Isn't it just like a noisy bazaar, where I and the rest of mankind display our cheap trinkets to the restless, milling crowds?

The warehouse of my soul

Many years ago, when I was a schoolboy distinguished by the name of "philosopher," I learned that the soul is somehow everything. O God, how the meaning of that lofty-sounding phrase has changed! How different it sounds to me now, when my soul has become a huge warehouse where day after day the trucks unload their crates without any plan or discrimination, to be piled helterskelter in every available corner and cranny, until it is crammed full from top to bottom with the trite, the commonplace, the insignificant, the routine.

What will become of me, dear God, if my life goes on like this? What will happen to me when all the crates are suddenly swept out of the warehouse? How will I feel at the hour of my death? Then there will be no more "daily routine"; then I shall suddenly be abandoned by all the things that now fill up my days here on earth.

What final yield?

And what will I myself be at that hour, when I am only myself and nothing else? My whole life long I have been nothing but the ordinary routine, all business and activity, a desert filled with empty sound and meaningless fury. But when the heavy weight of death one day presses down upon my life and squeezes the true and lasting content out of all those many days and long years, what will be the final yield?

Maybe at that last reckoning, at the time of the great disillusionment that will take the place of the great illusion of my tritely spent earthly life, maybe then, O God, if you have been merciful to me, the genuine yield of my ungenuine life will be only a few blessed moments, made luminous and living by Your grace. Maybe then I shall see the few precious instants when the grace of Your Love has succeeded in stealing into an obscure corner of my life, in between the countless bales of second-hand goods that fill up my everyday routine.

Escaping from my exile

How can I redeem this wretched humdrum? How can I turn myself toward the one thing necessary, toward You? How can I escape from the prison of this routine? Haven't You Yourself committed me to it? And didn't I find myself already in exile, from the very first moment I began to realize that my true life must be directed toward You? Wasn't I already deeply entangled in the pettiness of everyday cares, when it first dawned on me that I must not allow myself to be suffocated under the weight of earthly routine?

Aren't You my Creator? Haven't You made me a human being? And what is man but a being that is not sufficient to itself, a being who sees his own insufficiency, so that he longs naturally and necessarily for Your Infinity? What is man but the being who must follow the urge to run toward Your distant stars, who must keep up his chase until he has covered all the highways and byways of this world, only in the end to see your stars still coursing their serenely ordered way—and as far away as ever?

What would lift me?

Even if I should try to escape from my routine by becoming a Carthusian, so that I'd have nothing more to do but spend my days in silent adoration of Your holy presence, would that solve my problem? Would that really lift me out of my rut?

I'm afraid not, since not even the sacred actions I now perform are free from the corrosive dust of this spirit of routine. When I think of all the hours I have spent at Your holy altar, or reciting Your Church's official prayer in my Breviary, then it becomes clear to me that I myself am responsible for making my life so humdrum. It's not the affairs of the world that make my days dull and insignificant; I myself have dug the rut. Through my own attitude I can transform the holiest events into the grey tedium of dull routine. My days don't make *me* dull—it's the other way around.

The path to you

That's why I now see clearly that, if there is any path at all on which I can approach You, it must lead through the very middle of my ordinary daily life. If I should try to flee to You by any other way, I'd actually be leaving myself behind, and that, aside from being quite impossible, would accomplish nothing at all.

But is there a path through my daily life that leads to You? Doesn't this road take me ever farther away from You? Doesn't it immerse me all the more deeply in the empty noise of worldly activity, where You, God of Quiet, do not dwell?

I realize that we gradually get tired of the feverish activity that seems so important to a young mind and heart. I know that the *taedium vitae*, of which the moral philosophers speak, and the feeling of satiety with life, which Your Scripture reports as the final earthly experience of Your patriarchs, will also become more and more my own lot. My daily routine will automatically turn into the great melancholy of life, thus indirectly leading me to You, the infinite counterpart of this earthly emptiness.

But I don't have to be a Christian to know that—don't the pagans experience it too? Is this the way my everyday life is supposed to lead to You? Do I come into Your presence just because this life has revealed its true face to me, finally admitting that all is vanity, all is misery?

Isn't that the road to despair rather than the way to You? Isn't it the crowning victory for routine, when a man's burned-out heart no longer finds the least bit of joy in things that formerly gave him relief, when even the simple things of his ordinary life, which he used to be able to call upon to help him over the periods of boredom and emptiness, have now become tasteless to him?

Pleasures and disappointments

Is a tired and disillusioned heart any closer to You than a young and happy one? Where can we ever hope to find You, if neither our simple joys nor ordinary sorrows succeed in revealing You to us? Indeed our day-to-day pleasures seem somehow especially designed to make us forget about You, and with our daily disappointments it's no better: they make our hearts so sick and bitter that we seem to lose any talent we ever had for discovering You.

O God, it seems we can lose sight of You in anything we do. Not even prayer, or the Holy Sacrifice, or the quiet of the cloister, not even the great disillusion with life itself can fully safeguard us from this danger. And thus it's clear that even these sacred, non-routine things belong ultimately to our routine. It's evident that routine is not just a part of my life, not even just the greatest part, but the whole. *Every* day is "everyday." Everything I do is routine, because everything can rob me of the one and only thing I really need, which is You, my God.

Finding you in everything

But on the other hand, if it's true that I can lose You in everything, it must also be true that I can find You in everything. If You have given me no single place to which I can flee and be sure of finding You, if anything I do can mean the loss of You, then I must be able to find You in every place, in each and every thing I do. Otherwise I couldn't find You at all, and this cannot be, since I can't possibly exist without You. Thus I must seek You in all things. If every day is "everyday," then every day is *Your* day, and every hour is the hour of Your grace.

Everything is "everyday" and your day together. And thus, my God, I again understand something I have always known. A truth has again come to life in my heart, which my reason has already often told me—and of what value is a truth of reason when it is not also the life of the heart?

God comes to us continually

Again and again I must take out the old notebook in which I copied that short but vital passage from Ruysbroeck many years ago. I must reread it, so that my heart can regrasp it. I always find consolation in rediscovering how this truly pious man felt about his own life. And the fact that I still love these words after so many years of routine living is to me a sacred pledge that You will one day bless *my* ordinary actions too.

God comes to us continually, both directly and indirectly. He demands of us both work and pleasure, and wills that each should not be hindered, but rather strengthened, by the other. Thus the interior man possesses his life in both these ways, in activity and in rest. And he is whole and undivided in each of them, for he is entirely in God when he joyfully rests, and he is entirely in himself when he actively loves.

The interior man is constantly being challenged and admonished by God to renew both his rest and his work. Thus he finds justice; thus he makes his way to God with sincere love and everlasting works. He enters into God by means of the pleasure-giving tendency to eternal rest. And while he abides in God, still he goes out to all creatures in an all-embracing love, in virtue and justice. And that is the highest stage of the interior life.

Those who do not possess both rest and work in one and the same exercise, have not yet attained this kind of justice. No just man can be hindered in his interior recollection, for he recollects himself as much in pleasure as in activity. He is like a double mirror, reflecting images on both sides. In the higher part of his spirit he receives God together with all His gifts; in the lower he takes in corporeal images through his senses. . . .

Both everyday and your day

I must learn to have both "everyday" and Your day in the same exercise. In devoting myself to the works of the world, I must learn to give myself to You, to possess You, the One and Only Thing, in everything. But how? Only through You, O God. Only through Your help can I be an "interior" man in the midst of my many and varied daily tasks. Only through You can I continue to be in myself with You, when I go out of myself to be with the things of the world.

It's not anxiety or non-being, not even death that can rescue me from being lost to the things of the world. Not the modern philosophers, but only Your love can save me, the love of You, who are the goal and attraction of all things. Only You are fulfilment and satiety, You who are sufficient even unto Yourself. It is only the love of You, my Infinite God, which pierces the very heart of all things, at the same time transcending them all and leaping upward into the endless reaches of Your Being, catching up all the lost things of earth and transforming them into a hymn of praise to Your Infinity.

Homecoming to you

Before You, all multiplicity becomes one; in You, all that has been scattered is reunited; in Your Love all that has been merely external is made again true and genuine. In Your Love all the diffusion of the day's chores comes home again to the evening of Your unity, which is eternal life.

This love, which can allow my daily routine to remain routine and still transform it into a homecoming to You, this love only You can give. So what should I say to You now, as I come to lay my everyday routine before You? There is only one thing I can beg for, and that is Your most ordinary and most exalted gift, the grace of Your Love.

Touch my heart with this grace, O Lord. When I reach out in joy or in sorrow for the things of this world, grant that through them I may know and love You, their Maker and final home. You who are Love itself, give me the grace of love, give me Yourself, so that all my days may finally empty into the one day of Your eternal Life.

BIBLE SELECTION
Psalm 127:1–2

Unless the LORD builds the house
   those who build it labor in vain.
Unless the LORD guards the city,
   the guard keeps watch in vain.
It is in vain that you rise up early
   and go late to rest,
eating the bread of anxious toil;
   for he gives sleep to his beloved.

DISCUSSION QUESTIONS

The following can be used for discussion within a small group, or used for journal reflections by individuals:

1. Are there some ways that my life feels scattered? What causes for this do I see?
2. In what ways can I cope with a sense of daily routine? How does this relate to the discipline of service?

SUGGESTED EXERCISES

The following exercises can be done by individuals, shared between spiritual friends, or used in the context of a small group. Choose one or more of the following:

1. Make a list of the most unremarkable, ordinary, boring things that happened today. Was this unremarkable day rather typical of your daily routine? Compare notes, and laugh about it.
2. Bring calendars and appointment books (or a page copied from your calendar) to the next group meeting. Do the pages seem overcrowded? Are there any empty spaces for thought and reflection? Consider how these may be accomplished.
3. Offer your daily routine to God. You may do this by praying over your daily appointment book or calendar (as a sign of your daily routine) or in any other way.
4. Write a description of the big-picture life task that you are reaching for. Is this a way of practicing the discipline of service?

REFLECTIONS

Karl Rahner's questions and doubts and pleas speak directly to my condition and the condition of so many I know. I love his utter honesty and his refusal to let himself off the hook. How easy it would be to rationalize, "I'm serving the church, I'm serving others, what more can be required of me?" But no, Karl Rahner recognized that so much of what took up his days was of little eternal value, and he turns to ask of himself: when he faces his last day, the day when there are no more routines, "what will be the final yield?"

In this selection Karl Rahner is engaging in the classical Christian discipline of examen, a discipline perfectly summed up in the prayer of the psalmist, "Search me, O God, and know my heart; try me and know my thoughts. See if there is any wicked way in me, and lead me in the way everlasting"(Ps. 139:23–24).

It is a sadness today that many people can go to our churches week after week for years without a single experience of examen. *Just about the last vestige of* examen *today is in the liturgical season of Lent. But there need to be many times and many ways in which we invite God's scrutiny of love. Karl Rahner's writings here give us a shining example of one way to do this. We too can write out our prayers of* examen, *our prayers of questioning and wondering, even if we have no plans for their publication.*

What I especially like about this selection is the way in which God gently leads Karl Rahner to a resolution of his dilemma without in the least absolving him of responsibility for his daily activities. Without stepping back from recognizing that so much of daily life is "a desert filled with empty sound and meaningless fury" Rahner comes to see this very activity as the place where he will meet God and where he will build a history with God. "If You have given me no single place to which I can flee and be sure of finding You, if anything I do can mean the loss of You, then I must be able to find You in every place, in each and every thing I do." What he is teaching us here is that God meets us right where we are, and only where we are, because that is the only place we are! It is a good teaching for us to hear, we for whom so much of our days are also "crammed full from top to bottom with the trite, the commonplace, the insignificant, the routine."

RICHARD J. FOSTER

GOING DEEPER

KARL RAHNER, *Encounters with Silence* (London: Sands, 1960). A book of brief and penetrating personal meditations. They are encouraging for the very reason that in them this theologian of remarkable achievement allows himself to be open and vulnerable.

KARL RAHNER, *Prayers for a Lifetime* (New York: Crossroad, 1984). This is a comprehensive collection of the prayers of Karl Rahner, including those from *Encounters with Silence* as well as other collections of his prayers. Some are newly translated from the German and previously unpublished. They touch on many themes, including peace, justice, love of neighbor, and the life of grace. Grace was, of course, a central theme in Karl Rahner's theological work.

KARL RAHNER, *Words of Faith* (New York: Crossroad, 1987). These are short, prayerful writings drawn from many different sources in Karl Rahner's work, all suitable for reflection and meditation.

Corporate Disciplines

CONFESSION

WORSHIP

GUIDANCE

CELEBRATION

Confession

———

Hildegard of Bingen

(1098–1179)

From her earliest childhood, Hildegard of Bingen had visions of God. But for decades she kept them secret. Finally, her prophetic gift, sanctioned by her archbishop and the pope himself, gained wide influence.

Hildegard was born in Germany, near the cathedral city of Mainz, tenth child of wealthy and noble parents. They followed the tithing custom of noble families by placing Hildegard in religious life.

When Hildegard was eight, she was put in the care of Jutta von Spanheim, an anchoress (religious recluse) attached to the Benedictine monastery of Disibodenberg. Under Jutta's care, Hildegard's education did not compare with that of the monks. However, with the monk Volmar as her confessor and tutor, she learned Scripture, the early fathers, and some medieval authors. As Hildegard's influence grew, Volmar became her secretary, assistant, and confidant.

When Jutta died (1136) Hildegard was elected abbess of the anchorhold, by now a small convent. She managed the affairs of the group for decades without disclosing her frequent religious visions. Finally, Hildegard received a vision directly calling her into prophetic work. But even so, and despite Volmar's urging, Hildegard was afraid to put her experience in writing. She worked for ten years on her first book. She avoided the word "I" and became "a feather on the breath of God."

In 1146–47 she consulted Bernard of Clairvaux about whether she should speak openly or remain silent; Bernard advised her to speak. Formal investigations were made at the behest of the Archbishop of Mainz. Confident of her gifts, he sent some of her writings to Pope Eugenius III. He approved her prophetic ministry.

Then, during the Synod of Trier in 1147–48, Pope Eugenius read her writings aloud to the assembled bishops. Hildegard's prophetic gifts became known far and wide, attracting many new postulants to her small convent.

Soon she announced that God had instructed her in a vision to start an independent convent on the Rupertsberg, a mountain near Bingen. Objections were raised. The Disibodenberg monks and Hildegard's own community were opposed. But with help from the Archbishop of Mainz, she bought property, had a convent built, and gained legal separation from the monks.

By 1165, Hildegard started a second convent in Eibingen on the other side of the Rhine. She continued as an able administrator and writer. Through extensive correspondence she influenced the great and near great, intervening with Emperor Frederick I (Barbarossa) who was attempting to challenge the papacy.

As her work gained influence, she did several extensive preaching tours. In one of these, at Cologne, she opposed the teaching of the Cathars. She wrote three major spiritual books as well as a natural history, a medical book, and two biographies of saints. She also composed seventy-seven liturgical songs. Paintings, done under her direction, illustrate the various written accounts of her visions. In spite of controversies, opposition, and ill health, Hildegard continued active until her death at eighty-one.

Hildegard wrote many letters to clergy and members of religious communities, but she was also concerned with laypeople. In the selection that follows, "Letter 36," which appears in *Book of Divine Works,* a collection of her writings, she writes as though God were speaking and directs her thoughts to the spiritual growth of Christian laypeople.

BOOK OF DIVINE WORKS

Letter to Christian Laypeople

All of you people who were born and cleansed through God's wisdom, hear what I, the radiant light and Creator of all of you, have to say to you. You were planted in My heart at daybreak on the first day of creation. When I created the first human being, I made him a touchstone of what the Devil mocked. In other words, I gave him the commandment the Devil through his evil nature had disregarded. But evil does not correspond to My nature, for I am the good in all its fullness, power, and penetrating clarity.

Why do you forget?
But you, O people, do not know what you say. The crafty traitor has sneaked up behind you so that he can teach you the opposite of what I command. When I gave you the commandment, I did not prescribe that you carry on indecently with adultery, murder, theft, and imprisonment. It was also not My intention that you throw someone in prison whom you did not create. Rather I commanded that you should increase through having offspring in the lawful institution of marriage and not in mere lust. I also specified that you should possess the Earth by building it up through your work, with fruit and wine and everything needful for life. And this is why you must adhere to my commandment and not discard it. For I specified that you love your children in an environment of lawful love and

not in the poisonous atmosphere of adultery. But you act as though you are at liberty to do whatever you want and to carry out whatever evil purpose you can complete. But why do you cast off the cohesive structure of law by saying: "The regulation that we restrain ourselves and exercise discipline—as though we were angels—does not apply to us. For life in the world does not allow us to be heavenly. Then, too, our children and our farmlands, our sheep and our cattle and all the rest of our livestock and all our possessions make this kind of attitude impossible." It is God who has given us all of these things. Why do you forget the One who has created you and given you everything? When God gives you what is necessary, God does it in such a way that sometimes allows you certain things and sometimes does not.

You are like my servants

But you say: "It is not our job to live a good, disciplined life. That is the business of priests and those who are in religious communities." Since you are not concerned about these things, there is something which is important for you to hear: More than all these clergy, you are bound as God has commanded, to live in that way which was declared to you. For those who live in the religious state do not carry those legal responsibilities incumbent on you. And thus they are free, because the binding character of the commandment, that was established in a special way for you, is not applicable to them. But they embrace Me with the kiss of love when for My sake they leave the world and by climbing the mountain of holiness become My beloved children. But through the binding character of the Law which is especially placed on you, you are like My servants. Thus you must understand Me and obey your law, so that when the Lord comes your conscience cannot accuse you of having thrown off God's commands. For the guiltless Lamb of God embraced you with great love when because of your sins God allowed the Divine Son to be placed in the winepress of the Cross.

Remember your loving Creator

O beloved sons and daughters, remember your loving Creator who redeemed you from all the wounds of your burdens and cleansed you in the blood of the beloved Son from the worst of all sins, murder. Woe to this evil that Cain committed through his shameful rage, the companion of death. For that same end adheres to you as well, that the disintegration of your bodies is accompanied by great pain. That was Abel's experience in his sufferings when his bodily life ended in pain through that first murder, because his brother Cain in that sinful fratricide forced Abel's soul, before its time, to forsake the tent of its body.

Now may there be salvation and redemption in the blood of My beloved Son for all those who because of their sins have decided to run on the path of true repentance.

BIBLE SELECTION
Romans 13:11–14

Besides this, you know what time it is, how it is now the moment for you to wake from sleep. For salvation is nearer to us now than when we became believers; the night is far gone, the day is near. Let us then lay aside the works of darkness and put on the armor of light; let us live honorably as in the day, not in reveling and drunkenness, not in debauchery and licentiousness, not in quarreling and jealousy. Instead, put on the Lord Jesus Christ, and make no provision for the flesh, to gratify its desires.

DISCUSSION QUESTIONS

The following can be used for discussion within a small group, or used for journal reflections by individuals:

1. In what ways do the standards of the time in which I live, casual attitudes about sexual practice, and the like, influence me without my fully realizing it?
2. When my conscience is not clear on such matters, what steps should I take?

SUGGESTED EXERCISES

The following exercises can be done by individuals, shared between spiritual friends, or used in the context of a small group. Choose one or more of the following:

1. Exercise the discipline of confession within your group as follows. Break the group into twos or, at the most, threes. Allow people to practice the discipline of confession by confiding certain failings to each other. Don't feel constrained to mention anything major in a group setting; but if you find you have something major on your mind, arrange to see your pastor or another counselor about it.
2. Recall and recount incidents in which, after confessing or acknowledging a fault, individuals were much renewed and encouraged in Christian life.

3. Confide your besetting sin, in written form, to your journal. Pray for clarity about why this continues to trouble you. Ask for the grace to be relieved of this burden.

REFLECTIONS

In this selection Hildegard is attacking our perennial tendency to think in sacred/secular dichotomies. Remember she is writing directly to those in "secular" employment, and she takes on the two major objections we have about developing a spiritual life.

The first objection: "life in the world does not allow us to be heavenly." Let me try to state this objection in more contemporary categories just so we can see how much we identify with the concern. Business is business. We live in the rough and tumble of power lunches and tough negotiations and backroom deals. All religious talk about loving enemies and turning the other cheek is simply not realistic in our world. The language of the marketplace is the language of position, advantage, and leverage.

And the second objection: "our children and our farmlands, our sheep and our cattle and all the rest of our livestock and all our possessions make this kind of attitude impossible." Again, a more contemporary expression might help us understand and identify with the concern. Time is precious. With ballet lessons and soccer practice and dentist appointments there simply is no space nor energy to think about a spiritual life. I work and my husband works; we come home exhausted to a house full of dirty dishes and demanding kids. How can we be expected to develop a spiritual life in the midst of all these pressures?

And what is Hildegard's answer? Simply this: obey the commandments. Now, at first blush this seems like a rather hard-hearted answer to these substantial dilemmas, but a little reflection reveals how very wise her counsel is. First, notice that she does not place a long list of religious practices upon people. In fact, she appears to agree that the disciplines of life for those who are in the "religious communities" are not what is expected of them. They are simply and surely to obey the commandments.

What are these commandments? The commandments for life, the commandments for a civil society, the commandments for a healthy marriage and family life. Take the ten commandments, for example. These are commandments for the rule of law for a civil society. Notice here how she especially stresses the prohibition against murder. This was no joke or exaggeration; in that day killing someone was a very live option. So too today; just think of the killings from domestic altercations and road rage and business disputes. Then there are the commandments for the household; love and honor and mutual subordination out of reverence for Christ. These are the things that make a family work. So, you see, by stressing the commandments Hildegard is merely turning people back to their living and showing them how it can be done well and how they can discover God in it.

RICHARD J. FOSTER

GOING DEEPER

RENATE CRAINE, *Hildegard: Prophet of the Cosmic Christ* (New York: Crossroad, 1997). This is a fine introduction to the life and work of Hildegard, providing a narrative and interpretation of her many ideas and actions, using many excerpts from her writing. A number of black-and-white illustrations are included of the "illuminations" of her books. Also there is a good chronology of her life and an extensive bibliography of her works and scholarly works about her.

Hildegard of Bingen's Book of Divine Works, with Letters and Songs, edited and introduced by Matthew Fox (Santa Fe, NM: Bear & Company, 1987). This volume includes selections from *The Book of Divine Works,* forty-two of Hildegard's letters to various notables, and twelve of her sacred songs.

Dorothy L. Sayers

(1893–1957)

———

Dorothy Leigh Sayers is an imaginative and witty writer and scholar who mastered many literary forms. She is known for her fiction, drama, literary criticism, and theological books and essays.

The only child of an Anglican clergyman and his wife, Sayers was a precocious child who learned Latin at home before she went to school. She distinguished herself at Somerville College, Oxford, where she earned both the B.A. and the M.A., specializing in Medieval French.

Then followed a bout of youthful adventure as an advertising copywriter in London, where her comic advertising campaigns (especially "The Mustard Club" campaign for Colman's mustard) set a bright new style in the field.

Sayers next wrote a detective fiction series, featuring an upper-class amateur detective, Lord Peter Wimsey, and his Oxford-educated associate, Harriet Vane. *Gaudy Night* celebrates Oxford University. *The Nine Tailors* and *Murder Must Advertise* are considered among her best. Sayers helped found the Detection Club, a circle of detection writers with G. K. Chesterton as its first president.

Her religious writing included *The Mind of the Maker*, a treatise on the nature of God based on her own observations about the way writers invent character and story. She also wrote a radio play sequence about Jesus called *The Man Born to Be King* and the festival play *The Emperor Constantine*, about the coming of Christianity to the later Roman Empire. Her cathedral play *The Zeal of Thy House* dealt with ambition and pride.

Sayers was vigorous and imaginative in her resistance to the drift toward modernity in the Church and society.

Later in life she plunged into reading Dante's *The Divine Comedy* in Italian with no prior instruction in the language; it was typical of the way she assaulted the higher realms of knowledge. She then began an English verse translation of the poem in *terza rima*, which remained unfinished at her death.

Sayers was married in 1926 to O. A. Fleming, a journalist and former military man.

Notice how, in the selection that follows, which is taken from "Creed or Chaos?" which appears in a book of essays with the same title, Sayers takes the Christian view that society is sinful. She does this, it seems, to encourage us, to save us from the common supposition that idealistic schemes of social reform will make everything all right. Sayers is speaking out of her own experience. She herself has wrestled with her own sinfulness and knows that the individual's sinfulness is multiplied many times over in the social order. At the same time, take note that she is quite clear about the importance of grace.

CREED OR CHAOS?

Sinfulness in Society

A word or two about the Christian doctrine of society. . . . It rests on the doctrine of what God is and what man is. . . . This is, or should be, obvious. The one point to which I should like to draw attention is the Christian doctrine of the moral law. The attempt to abolish wars and wickedness by the moral law is doomed to failure because of the fact of sinfulness. Law, like every other product of human activity, shares the integral human imperfection; it is, in the old Calvinistic phrase, "of the nature of sin." That is to say, all legality, if erected into an absolute value, contains within itself the seeds of judgment and catastrophe. The law is necessary, but only, as it were, as a protective fence against the forces of evil, behind which the divine activity of grace may do its redeeming work.

We can, for example, never make a positive peace or a positive righteousness by enactments against offenders; law is always prohibitive, negative, and corrupted by the interior contradictions of man's divided nature; it belongs to the category of judgment. That is why an intelligent understanding about sin is necessary to preserve the world from putting an unjustified confidence in the efficacy of the moral law taken by itself. It will never drive out Beelzebub; it cannot because it is only human and not divine.

Nevertheless, the law must be rightly understood, or it is not possible to make the world understand the meaning of grace. There is only one real law—the law of the universe; it may be fulfilled either by way of judgment or by the way of grace, but it *must* be fulfilled one way or the other. If men will not understand the meaning of judgment, they will never come to understand the meaning of grace. "If they hear not Moses or the prophets, neither will they be persuaded, though one rose from the dead" (Luke 16:31).

BIBLE SELECTION
Matthew 13:24–30

[Jesus] put before them another parable: "The kingdom of heaven may be compared to someone who sowed good seed in his field; but while everybody was asleep, an enemy came and sowed weeds among the wheat, and then went away. So when the plants came up and bore grain, then the weeds appeared as well. And the slaves of the householder came and said to him, 'Master, did you not sow good seed in your field? Where, then, did these weeds come from?' He answered, 'An enemy has done this.' The slaves said to him, 'Then do you want us to go and gather them?' But he replied, 'No; for in gathering the weeds you would uproot the wheat along with them. Let both of them grow together until the harvest; and at harvest time I will tell the reapers, Collect the weeds first and bind them in bundles to be burned, but gather the wheat into my barn.'"

DISCUSSION QUESTIONS

The following can be used for discussion within a small group, or used for journal reflections by individuals:

1. What flaws in society particularly trouble me? How can I connect these flaws to my own sense of sinfulness?
2. What realistic expectations do I have for social reform?
3. About social change, am I: exasperated? discouraged? hopeful? motivated? Why?

SUGGESTED EXERCISES

The following exercises can be done by individuals, shared between spiritual friends, or used in the context of a small group. Choose one or more of the following:

1. Have group members make a list of the worst sins and offenses in society, and reflect on these. Have these problems existed over time? Or are they attached to recent historical developments? How can it help us to confess or acknowledge these tendencies in our own life and society? Take grace into account.

2. Mention examples of Christian social reform that have made an impact in particular situations, such as the United States civil rights movement or the Truth and Reconciliation Commission in South Africa. How should we react to these developments?

REFLECTIONS

In this selection Sayers is reminding us of three things: the reality of sin, the limitation of moral law, and the potential of grace.

Sayers believes in sin. After two world wars and a whole catalog of atrocities since, we should too. I am, however, constantly amazed at the power of human denial at this point. Perhaps folk long so desperately for the innocence and purity that existed before the fall and for which we are created. Perhaps it is the modern infatuation with Pollyanna utopias. Perhaps it is human arrogance. Perhaps it is all of these, and more. Whatever it is, we do well to be reminded by Sayers of the reality of sin: personal, social, institutional.

Now, apart from grace we'd better thank God for moral law, which, with appropriate cultural distinctions, is universal among all civilizations, and without which civilizations simply could not exist. Moral law has the negative function in society of restraining evil, no more. Sayers here reminds us of this inherent limitation on moral law. We should not try to make moral law do something it was never intended to do. Moral law cannot make for righteous individuals and societies. Human beings—and society is merely collective human beings—have such a bent toward evil that they will always find ways to circumvent law. Always. This is why we need grace.

Sayers here only hints at the potential of grace. Of course, behind her brief hints stands the entire Christian message of redemption. How thankful we are that moral law is not the whole story. God, out of unrestrained love, sent his only Son as the propitiation for our sins so that we may have life through him. This is the glory of the exchanged life. Christ lives within us with such transforming power (all of this, of course is dependent upon our turning and seeking and receiving and that continually) that we go beyond the demands of moral law and into the potentialities of grace: love, joy, peace, patience, kindness, generosity, faithfulness, gentleness, and self-control. Against such there is no law.

RICHARD J. FOSTER

GOING DEEPER

DOROTHY L. SAYERS, *The Mind of the Maker* (Westport, CT: Greenwood, 1970 [1941]). A collection of essays, including "The Laws of Nature and Opinion," "Maker of All Things—Maker of Ill Things," and "The Worth of the Work."

DOROTHY L. SAYERS, *Creed or Chaos?* (Manchester, NH: Sophia Institute Press, 1995 [1949]). The title essay, delivered at Derby, England, even as German bombs were falling on London, contains the famous sentence "When we abandon the creed, we court disaster." Other essays in the book include "The Dogma Is the Drama" and "Why Work?"

DOROTHY L. SAYERS, *The Whimsical Christian, 18 Essays by the Creator of Lord Peter Wimsey*, with a foreword by William Griffin (New York: Macmillan, 1978). Eighteen essays previously published as *Christian Letters to a Post-Christian World*. One particularly striking essay is entitled "The Dogma Is the Drama."

JAMES BRABAZON, *Dorothy L. Sayers: A Biography* (New York: Charles Scribner's Sons, 1981). This biography has an extra note of authority because Brabazon actually knew Sayers personally. The foreword is by P. D. James, distinguished writer of detective fiction.

BARBARA REYNOLDS, *The Passionate Intellect: Dorothy L. Sayers' Encounter with Dante* (Kent, OH: Kent State University Press, 1989). Reynolds is a major Dante scholar who worked with Sayers. She completed the third book of Sayers's translation of Dante's *Divine Comedy* after Sayers died.

Leo Tolstoy

(1828–1910)

———

Leo Tolstoy is ranked as a great writer and thinker, especially honored for his two influential novels, *War and Peace* and *Anna Karenina*. All his writing has a strong moral dimension.

He was born into a privileged Russian landowning family in Tula province, some one hundred miles south of Moscow. Tolstoy was a child when his parents died. Relatives raised him; he was educated by private tutors and briefly attended Kazan University.

He intended to manage his estate and pursue education on his own but was soon swept into the social whirl of Moscow and St. Petersburg. In the 1850s, influenced by his brother Nikolay, he became a soldier and served on the Danube front in the Crimean War, in the Siege of Sevastopol.

During this period he began to write a memoir called *Childhood*, short stories, sketches of wartime experience, and military life. In 1856 he left the army and was lionized by literary groups in St. Petersburg but soon fled from what he considered trivial celebrity.

Tolstoy's deep affinity for peasants led him to establish a school on his estate; he traveled throughout Europe to learn the latest educational theories. In 1862 he married Sonya (Sofya) Andreyevna Bers, a woman of wide intellectual interests. It was for some years a very happy match, and they had thirteen children.

Tolstoy's masterpieces *War and Peace* and *Anna Karenina* required tremendous commitment and energy. Both are strongly moral works, but *Anna Karenina*, the darker of the two, about the destructive force of an adulterous love affair, almost brought Tolstoy himself to suicide. His spiritual crisis in 1879 was resolved by turning to Jesus Christ, inspired by the strong faith of the peasants among whom he lived.

After his conversion, Tolstoy became still more preoccupied with moral questions. Now a successful author and a well-to-do landholder, Tolstoy attempted to live as a simple peasant and give possessions away. His wife disagreed, and conflicts over money and ownership estranged them in their last years.

In the following selection, taken from *The Lion and the Honeycomb*, a collection of his religious essays, Tolstoy not only deplores the addictive practices of drinking, smoking, and using opium, but he also contends that such practices prevent us from listening to our consciences. His principal concern is that conscience can and should guide us into virtuous paths.

THE LION AND THE HONEYCOMB

Why Do Men Stupefy Themselves?

For man is both a spiritual and an animal being. One can move a man either by influencing his animal being or by influencing his spiritual essence. In the same way one can change the time on a clock either by moving the hands or by moving the main wheel. And just as it is better to change the time by moving the inner mechanism, so it is better to move a man—whether oneself or another person— by influencing his consciousness.

And just as one must take special care of the part of the clock which most easily moves the inner mechanism, so one must take special care of the clarity and purity of the consciousness which moves a man. All this is indisputable and everyone knows it; what we must consider, however, is man's need to deceive himself.

What people most want is not that their consciousness should work correctly; it is that their actions should appear to them to be just. It is for this end that they use substances which disturb the correct working of their consciousness.

How conscience is best

People smoke and drink not out of boredom or in order to cheer themselves up, not simply because they like it, but in order to suppress their conscience. If that is true, then the consequences must be awful indeed. Imagine a building constructed by people who, instead of using a rule and a square to get the walls perpendicular and the corners rectangular, used a soft rule which adapted to the irregularities in the wall and a square which bent to fit any angle, acute or obtuse!

But this is just what happens in life when we intoxicate ourselves. Life does not accord with our conscience, so we bend our conscience to fit life. This happens in the life of individuals, and in the life of humanity as a whole—composed as it is of separate individuals.

The clouding of the conscience

In order to grasp the full significance of this clouding of consciousness, let everyone carefully bring to mind the state of their soul at each period of their life. Everyone will find that at each period of his life he was confronted by several moral dilemmas, and that his well-being depended on the correct resolution of these dilemmas. The resolution of such dilemmas requires a degree of attention which constitutes true labour. In any labour, especially at the beginning, there comes a time when the work seems painfully difficult, and our human weakness prompts us to abandon it. Physical labour seems painful at the beginning; intellectual labour all the more so. As Lessing says, people have a tendency to stop thinking when it first becomes difficult; and it is at that point, I would add, that thinking becomes fruitful. A man senses that the resolution of the questions before him demands labour—often painful labour—and he wants to evade this. If he had no means of stupefying himself, he would be unable to drive the questions out of his consciousness, and he would be forced, against his will, to resolve them. Instead of this, however, he has found means to drive the questions away as soon as they arise. As soon as the questions demanding resolution begin to torment him, he resorts to these means and so avoids the anxiety they evoke. His consciousness ceases to demand a resolution, and the unresolved questions remain unresolved until the next moment of clarity. But at this next moment of clarity he does exactly the same; often he remains entire months, years or even his whole life, confronted by the same moral questions, failing to take even one step towards their resolution. And yet it is the resolution of moral questions that constitutes the movement of life.

Blunting the blade of thought

It is almost as though a man who wanted to see to the bottom of some muddy water in order to lay his hands on a precious pearl, but who wanted not to have to enter the water, were to stir up the water on purpose as soon as it began to settle and clear. Often a man stupefies himself all through his life, staying with the same obscure, self-contradictory view of the world to which he is accustomed, pushing at every moment of dawning clarity against the same wall as he did ten or twenty years before, unable to break through the wall because he has consciously blunted the blade of thought which alone could penetrate it.

Let every man think of himself at a time when he was drinking or smoking, and let everyone do the same with his experience of others, and he will see a constant line distinguishing those who indulge in stupefying substances from those who do not. The more a man stupefies himself, the more fixed he is in his morals.

BIBLE SELECTION
Luke 15:11–13, 17, 18–19, 22, 24, 25, 28–29, 31–32

Then Jesus said, "There was a man who had two sons. The younger of them said to his father, 'Father, give me the share of the property that will belong to me.' So he divided his property between them. A few days later the younger son gathered all that he had and traveled to a distant country, and there he squandered his property in dissolute living. . . . But when he came to himself he said . . . 'I will get up and go to my father, and I will say to him, "Father, I have sinned against heaven and before you; I am no longer worthy to be called your son."' . . . But the father said, 'Quickly, bring out a robe—the best one—and put it on him . . . and get the fatted calf' . . . and they began to celebrate. . . . Now his elder son . . . became angry and refused to go in. His father came out and began to plead with him. But he answered his father, 'Listen! For all these years I have been working like a slave for you, and I have never disobeyed your command; yet you have never even given me a young goat so that I might celebrate with my friends. . . .' Then the father said to him, 'Son, you are always with me, and all that is mine is yours. But we had to celebrate and rejoice, because this brother of yours was dead and has come to life; he was lost and has been found.'"

DISCUSSION QUESTIONS

The following can be used for discussion within a small group, or used for journal reflections by individuals:

1. Are there substances that I have abused? Even if I have not experienced chemical dependency, am I aware of the risks of overattachment to certain kinds of pleasures?
2. Is it also possible to overdo the practice of virtue? Should I be cautious about trying to compete with others, or put others in the shadow, where virtuous behavior is concerned?

SUGGESTED EXERCISES

The following exercises can be done by individuals, shared between spiritual friends, or used in the context of a small group. Choose one or more of the following:

1. Think of a time in your life when "living in the fast lane" may have estranged you from Jesus Christ. How were you able to resolve that? Write in your journal about this, or share it with the group.

2. Discuss the attitude of the older brother in the story of the Prodigal Son as he realized he made a mistake. Have you had a similar situation in your life? If so, how did you respond?

REFLECTIONS

I am not fully happy with Tolstoy's notion of conscience as a moral guide since it is, in my estimation, the weaker of the moral faculties. And it is especially problematic in our day in which modern relativism has turned conscience into virtually anything we want it to mean. But then maybe this very relativism is the modern "stupefying substance" in the moral life. Tolstoy in his day worried about tobacco, alcohol, and opium, and I certainly do not want to downplay their destructive effects. But perhaps today we especially need to concern ourselves with the way certain ideas suppress the conscience and dull the consciousness. The idea I am particularly referring to is the notion of the complete relativism of conscience: i.e., your values and behaviors are right for you, my values and behaviors are right for me. Behind this, of course, is the relativism of truth and the complete autonomy of the individual as the source of ultimate authority. These are powerful ideas that can do exactly what Tolstoy feared from substance abuse, they "blunt the blade of thought."

We today work very hard to protect ourselves against any moral reality. Philosopher Dallas Willard has written about the modern predicament: "there now is no recognized moral knowledge upon which projects of fostering moral development could be based." We simply have no moral knowledge today upon which a student could be graded in a state university class. Why is this? Because in the current world of accepted knowledge we cannot even know the truth of a moral theory or principle. Moral truths about right and wrong, according to the accepted dogma of our day, are simply outside the realm of "knowledge."

Under these assumptions "virtue," in the old sense of something we can agree upon as a right and good way to live, is simply meaningless. And if virtue be meaningless can conscience be far behind? This is the power of the idea of moral relativism.

Tolstoy himself struggled with these matters earlier in his life. In A Confession he describes how his elite circle of Russian intellectuals was captured by the idea that "only two things are real: particles and progress." This nineteenth-century relativistic notion that life is nothing more than the accidental amalgamation of particles that is being carried on in an evolutionary spiral upward sounds awfully contemporary, doesn't it? (Little, you see, has changed in a century of thinking on this matter.) But Tolstoy was turned in another direction—a Christward direction—as he observed the peasants among whom he lived. He saw how they, in the most miserable of conditions, found life deeply meaningful, even glorious. Their lives—living testimonies to a God who loved and cared for them—pulled him out of the relativism of his intellectual friends and into the light of Christian devotion. As a result right living took on substance and urgency for Tolstoy, and he wanted nothing to impair his thinking as clearly as possible about the virtuous life. So too for us.

RICHARD J. FOSTER

GOING DEEPER

The Lion and the Honeycomb: The Religious Writings of Tolstoy, edited by A. N. Wilson (San Francisco: Harper & Row, 1987). Wilson deeply admires Tolstoy, though he himself is somewhat uncertain about Christianity. Even so, Tolstoy's texts here speak for themselves.

You may also want to discover Tolstoy as a novelist by reading *War and Peace* and *Anna Karenina*. With a keen moral sense, Tolstoy shows people either in touch with God through their consciences or in rebellion against God. A number of film and television adaptations of both novels have been made. Viewing them may also be of value.

Adolfo Quezada

(1940–)

Adolfo Quezada is a licensed professional counselor in Tucson, Arizona. Born in Salt Lake City, Utah, he was raised in Arizona and educated at the University of Arizona, where he earned a B.A. in political science and two M.A. degrees, in journalism and in counseling.

Quezada's extensive counseling practice, known as "Equanimity Center," offers various programs and seminars to help people get through difficult times; depression, anxiety, grief and trauma, among others. He also leads prayer retreats.

Quezada is married and the father of four children. One was killed at the age of seventeen. He also has four grandchildren.

He has written a number of books directed toward themes of faith in difficult times. Among these are *Wholeness: The Legacy of Jesus, Walking with God, Through the Darkness,* and the book from which the following selection is taken, *Loving Yourself for God's Sake.*

As you read, observe how supportive Quezada is. He wants to assure you of God's loving support on every step of your journey. When you can't believe in yourself, or forgive yourself for what you have done, God can.

Quezada's role is to be the one who reminds you convincingly of God's unflagging support and love. Listen to him. Also take note of the clarity that comes out of experienced counseling. He wants you to acknowledge wrongdoing but never to exaggerate it or wallow in a sense of guilt.

LOVING YOURSELF FOR GOD'S SAKE

Reconcile Your Past

Set your guilt before you. Be specific about the wrongs you charge against yourself. You have hurt others, you have committed acts that infringed on the rights of others. You have neglected to do the loving thing toward others. Now you can do something about it, but it is not enough to feel guilt or sorrow. Make restitution as best you can in ways that bring healing and restore harmony to your life and the lives of those you have hurt. Let go of whatever you have done. . . .

Let go of memories that tie you to a darkened past. Release thoughts of yesterday that fill you with sadness, guilt, or shame. Allow the forgiving spirit of love to cleanse your mind and set you free. Release yourself from the bondage of your own judgment. Love yourself without condition. Love yourself through the walls of defensiveness and the darkness of your deeds. Love yourself beyond whatever you deserve for such is the love of God. . . .

Love breaks the chains
Love breaks the chains that hold you to the past; it allows for growth, change, and new life. When you accept God's love, you also accept God's forgiveness. As you love yourself, you also forgive as you are forgiven and you love even more. . . .

When you forgive, you also regain your own soul.

The memories of your childhood can be painful and crippling, influencing your present. They come back and haunt you when you least expect it. You hear the voices and see the faces of those times. The circumstances of life robbed much of your childhood. That child, neglected and repressed, grew up too fast. There were too many responsibilities, too many fires to put out. . . . You were expected to know what to do to be perfect. . . .

Whether they intend to or not, parents are capable of hurting their children and interfering with their self love. God is not. The love of God is forever true. You will never feel rejection from God. . . .

The love that you allow washes away all that encumbers your life. You will remember how it was, but these memories will be just memories. No longer will they rule your thoughts, emotions, and behavior. Love for yourself melts away the chains that bind you to the past and sets you free for the now.

Discard unrealistic expectations
Life has beginnings and endings, deaths and resurrections. . . . In your life there may be unfulfilled yearnings. Your peace will depend on the acceptance of these unfulfillments.

Reconsider your expectations. Examine the demands you make on yourself. Are they realistic? What do you base them on? Does the pressure to meet these demands take away the centerdness you need to live in peace? Are these demands your own or do they come from others in spoken and unspoken messages? . . .

Discard the unrealistic expectations and appreciate what is actual in your life instead of constantly looking at what ought to be. Work from reality and release the tension that comes from discontentment. . . .

God helps you to let go of unfulfilled dreams and expectations. God helps you dream new dreams and hope new hopes. Let go of control. Surrender it to the love and mercy of God. . . .

Let God control

The more control you try to grasp, the less you have; the more control you surrender to God, the more under control your life becomes. Surrendering control doesn't mean you have become passive or fatalistic. It does mean you trust that God has given you the physical, emotional, and spiritual tools necessary to negotiate life. To surrender control to God releases the tension within that keeps you from responding to life with all your capacity. When you stop pushing and pulling to have things your way, you are more apt to see things God's way.

As you focus love on God and on yourself, you detach from your obsession with control and perfection. You learn to relax and play as a child and protect yourself from harm. You see things from a spiritual point of view. You set aside anxiety, experience emotions fully, and express them effectively. You leave guilt and shame behind, embrace hope, and build on the foundation of good.

BIBLE SELECTION
1 John 3:18–22

Little children, let us love, not in word or speech, but in truth and action. And by this we will know that we are from the truth and we will reassure our hearts before him whenever our hearts condemn us; for God is greater than our hearts, and he knows everything. Beloved, if our hearts do not condemn us, we have boldness before God; and we receive from him whatever we ask, because we obey his commandments and do what pleases him.

DISCUSSION QUESTIONS

The following can be used for discussion within a small group, or used for journal reflections by individuals:

1. What are some ways I avoid admitting my failings?
2. Are there ways that—after I admit my faults—I can relax and let them go? What steps can I take to keep from reliving over and over the wrongs I have done?

SUGGESTED EXERCISES

The following exercises can be done by individuals, shared between spiritual friends, or used in the context of a small group. Choose one or more of the following:

1. Specifically recall an incident in your early life that made you feel inferior or inadequate. Write in your journal about it, or confide it to another person. Let go of it.
2. Make a list of things that remind you of the generous and unconditional love of God. Examples might be sunshine, springtime, orchards ripe with fruit, letters from friends, birthday celebrations.

REFLECTIONS

Quezada is helping us move beyond the crushing condemnation of heart that John highlights for us in the Scripture reading. John writes, "Beloved, if our hearts do not condemn us . . ." but I find that many people do have hearts that condemn them. Now, let me be just as plain as I possibly can about this condemnation of heart: What is it? It is simply the feeling that I am not right, and there are three things, at least, that the heart uses to condemn us.

First, there is condemnation of heart for who we are. I mean very simply the fact that we are a man or a woman. Or that we have a certain kind of body; we feel we are too tall or too short, or that we are too fat or too thin, or that we have big ears or freckles or a big nose. Just think of the condemnation that people labor under just because of who they are. And the world is full of people who have something to sell or something to get out of others who will condemn them and who will build up associations in their minds to get them to condemn themselves. We are condemned because of the way we dress. We are condemned because of the way we smell. We are condemned because we have too much hair. We are condemned because we do not have enough hair. Now, how do we get out of that? We don't. It is an essential feature of a fallen world that it is filled with condemnation. We do not have to look very deeply behind that to see a fundamental strategy of the enemy of our souls to get us to believe that God is not good. We are who we are, and who we are is not right, and so how can God be good?

Second, there is condemnation of heart for where we are. It is a rare thing today to find people who feel completely right and good about where they live, or the job that they hold, or the family they are in. There is so much shame in families, for example: husbands ashamed of wives, and wives ashamed of husbands; parents ashamed of children, and children ashamed of parents. I wish it were not so. I wish I could tell you that it is only an illusion. But it is not. Condemnation for all of these places where people are.

Third, there is condemnation of heart for what we do. Now, right here we just have to say that a lot of the condemnation is completely justified. But, of course, if we are wanting to condemn someone and we are looking for a basis upon which to condemn them, we can find it in all of these areas, can't we? Condemnation for what we do and for what we do not do, and one of the reasons it is so hard for us to witness to those who are near to us is that they know what we do and we feel condemned. There is condemnation for sin, wrongdoing, and that is true guilt and Jesus came that the matter of sin could be dealt with. But there is also condemnation for things that are not sins, just mistakes. A failure in business, for example. Or a wrong decision about a job to take, or a place to live, or a purchase to make. And all this condemnation just leaps up, and the effect of that is to make people completely without strength, completely without hope, completely without faith in God beyond the bare minimum of believing that he will take them to heaven when they die.

But here is the good news that is stated so beautifully right in the Scripture reading: "we will reassure our hearts before him whenever our hearts condemn us; for God is greater than our hearts." If we find that we have a condemning heart we can know that God is greater than our heart. Remember that significant statement of Jesus, "God did not send the Son into the world to condemn the world" (John 3:17). And as we learn to trust God more than we trust our condemning hearts we can, as Quezada says, "relax and play as a child . . . leave guilt and shame behind, embrace hope, and build on the foundation of good."

RICHARD J. FOSTER

GOING DEEPER

ADOLFO QUEZADA, *Loving Yourself for God's Sake* (Magnolia, NY: Resurrection, 1997). This brief book of meditations is rich with wise spiritual counsel.

ADOLFO QUEZADA, *Heart Peace: Embracing Life's Adversities* (Magnolia, NY: Resurrection, 1999). In this book of spiritual advice, Quezada offers suggestions about ways to deal with trials, crises, and the unexpected. He helps us with our insecurities and anxieties and to give way to God's love.

Worship

———

Evelyn Underhill

(1875–1941)

Evelyn Underhill (Mrs. Hubert Stuart Moore) is an invaluable twentieth-century guide to the devotional life. She wrote several major studies on mystical life and, late in her life, an important work on worship. A devout Anglican, she was one of the earliest laywomen to gain a wide reputation as a retreat leader and spiritual director.

The only daughter of a distinguished but agnostic British family, Underhill attended King's College, London. As an adult she experienced a sudden religious conversion and was drawn toward Roman Catholicism but ultimately remained within the Anglican Church.

Her spiritual struggles led to the publication in 1911 of *Mysticism: A Study in the Nature and Development of Man's Spiritual Consciousness*. This comprehensive study established her as a foremost authority on the subject. She also wrote poetry, fiction, and smaller works blending scholarship and devotion.

Her second major work, *Worship* (1936), showed broad understanding of the nature and forms of Christian worship. Her spiritual director and friend was the renowned Baron Friedriech von Hügel, himself a well-known scholar of the spiritual life. She was the first woman to be invited to give a series of theological lectures at Oxford University (1921), and she was made a fellow of Kings College, Cambridge University, in 1928. She received the degree of Doctor of Divinity from Aberdeen University in 1938.

In her latter years she continued to write and conduct retreats; some of her addresses were published. In the first years of World War II before her death she became an ardent pacifist.

In the selection that follows, notice the wisdom and the joy with which Underhill describes the worshiping life. She writes out of the fullness of a lifetime of authentic Christian practice.

WORSHIP

We Are Called to Worship

There remains the question of the effect upon man himself of this deep action of the soul. Why are we called [to worship] and pressed to it? Is it, ultimately, for our sake? How does it enter into the creative plan?

First, perhaps, we are called to worship because this is the only safe, humble, and creaturely way in which men can be led to acknowledge and receive the influence of an objective Reality. The tendency of all worship to decline from adoration to demand, and from the supernatural to the ethical, shows how strong a pull is needed to neutralize the anthropocentric trend of the human mind; its intense preoccupation with the world of succession, and its own here-and-now desires and needs. . . . It is the mood of deep admiration, the meek acknowledgment of mystery, the humble and adoring gaze . . .

Leading away from self

Worship, then, is an avenue which leads the creature out from his inveterate self-occupation to a knowledge of God, and ultimately to that union with God which is the beatitude of the soul; though we are never to enter on it for this, or any other reason which is tainted by self-regard. We see in its first beginnings man's emerging recognition of the Living Will which is the cause of all his living; and the gradual deepening and widening of this recognition, in diverse ways and manners, till at last all ways and manners are swallowed up in a self-giving love. By this door and this alone, humanity enters into that great life of the spiritual universe which consists in the ceaseless proclamation of the Glory of God.

Worship is creative and redemptive

Thus worship purifies, enlightens, and at last transforms, every life submitted to its influence: and this not merely in the ethical or devotional sense. It does all this, because it wakes up and liberates that "seed" of supernatural life, in virtue of which we are spiritual beings, capable of responding to that God Who is Spirit; and which indeed gives to humanity a certain mysterious kinship with Him. Worship is therefore in the deepest sense creative and redemptive. Keeping us in constant remembrance of the Unchanging and the Holy, it cleanses us of subjectivism, releases us from "use and wont" and makes us realists. God's invitation to it and man's response, however limited, crude or mistaken this response may be, are the appointed means whereby we move towards our true destiny. . . .

The transfigured soul

Each separate soul thus transfigured by the spirit of selfless adoration advances that transfiguration of the whole universe which is the Coming of the Kingdom of God. . . . It is well to remind ourselves that worship, though the whole man of sense and spirit, feeling, thought, and will, is and must be truly concerned in it, is above all the work of that mysterious "ground" of our being, that sacred hearth of personality, where the created spirit of man adheres to the increate Spirit of God.

BIBLE SELECTION
Mark 9:2–9

Six days later, Jesus took with him Peter and James and John, and led them up a high mountain apart, by themselves. And he was transfigured before them, and his clothes became dazzling white, such as no one on earth could bleach them. And there appeared to them Elijah with Moses, who were talking with Jesus. Then Peter said to Jesus, "Rabbi, it is good for us to be here; let us make three dwellings, one for you, one for Moses, and one for Elijah." He did not know what to say, for they were terrified. Then a cloud overshadowed them, and from the cloud there came a voice, "This is my Son, the Beloved; listen to him!" Suddenly when they looked around, they saw no one with them any more, but only Jesus.

As they were coming down the mountain, he ordered them to tell no one about what they had seen, until after the Son of Man had risen from the dead.

DISCUSSION QUESTIONS

The following can be used for discussion within a small group, or used for journal reflections by individuals:

1. What obstacles may sometimes hold me back from full assent to the experience of worship?
2. How can I enter more freely into the transfigured life as exemplified by Moses, Elijah, and Jesus himself?

SUGGESTED EXERCISES

The following exercises can be done by individuals, shared between spiritual friends, or used in the context of a small group. Choose one or more of the following:

1. Enter a sacred space, one that has particular meaning for you, one that may call you into a worship experience through stillness, light filtering through stained-glass windows, beautiful ornamentation, or simplicity. Worship God uninterruptedly there for a time.
2. Describe to others in your group (or confide to your journal or to a trusted friend) a worship experience that meant a great deal to you.
3. Design a worship time, either by yourself or with others, that can recapture some of your best worshiping experiences. Then do it!

REFLECTIONS

I have a love/hate relationship with Evelyn Underhill. She always wins me over in the end, but it takes a while because, frankly, I struggle with her writings. It doesn't matter which of her books I am reading, I inevitably pick an intellectual fight with her. I may object to her logic or line of argument, or to her obtuse, cerebral way of analyzing some issue, or perhaps it is her frustrating flights into mystical devotion that I can never quite follow. Whatever, I always start out by arguing with her.

But then she will make some astonishing statement, and it seems like all heaven opens up. Sometimes she has said no more than a phrase, but somehow it "speaks truth to power," and I realize that I am in the presence of someone who truly knows God and I must yield to her greater authority.

Two phrases struck me in this way from the selection here. The first came when she spoke of union with God as the "beatitude of the soul." When I read this my soul exclaimed its Amen; this indeed is my destiny, what I am created for, who I am meant to be. But immediately my guard went up again for the language of "union" always leaves me dangling. To be sure, Underhill here is saying nothing new—many before her have used the same language. And, please understand, they do not mean union in the eastern Hindu sense of "merging with the Cosmic Consciousness," for Underhill and all the classic Christian writers had a clear understanding of God's transcendence. Still, even as I say my YES to "union with God" as the "beatitude of the soul," I struggle with what it means in any practical sense.

Because of my quandary over the first phrase the second one immediately took on added significance. It was the very simple statement that worship is "the appointed means whereby we move towards our true destiny." Underhill's use of the term "appointed means" is important. Classical Christian writers have made much of the notion of the "means of grace" for the formation of the soul under God, and Underhill is tapping into that stream of thought. She had said earlier that "worship purifies, enlightens, and at last transforms, every life submitted to its influence." Yes, indeed, and the act of worship as an appointed means of grace is one way I can offer myself to God as a living sacrifice, which, as Paul tells us, is the only reasonable thing to do (Rom. 12:1–3). This helps me a great deal. Worship is something I can do and in doing it I have assurance that it is moving me more and more toward my "true destiny." And the matter of union with God? I shall leave that in God's hands.

RICHARD J. FOSTER

GOING DEEPER

EVELYN UNDERHILL, *Worship* (Guildford, UK: Eagle, 1992). One of Underhill's major works, this is a scholarly and exhaustive study of the meaning of worship.

EVELYN UNDERHILL, *Practical Mysticism* (New York: E. P. Dutton & Co., Inc., 1943); originally published in 1914. Underhill extends an appealing invitation to contemplative life as an everyday affair, using popular language and vivid illustrations.

EVELYN UNDERHILL, *The Spiritual Life: Four Broadcast Talks* (New York: Harper & Row, 1937). For many people this slender volume has served as an authoritative guide to spiritual formation.

EVELYN UNDERHILL, *Mysticism: A Study of the Nature and Development of Man's Spiritual Consciousness* (London: Methuen, 1922). This work established her as a major scholar of spiritual practice.

The Letters of Evelyn Underhill, edited and with an introduction by Charles Williams (Westminster, MD: Christian Classics, 1989 [1943]). This delightful collection introduces us to Underhill in a very personal way.

Charles Wesley

(1707–1788)

Charles Wesley, along with his brother John, helped found the Methodist Church, one of the most dynamic spiritual movements in the eighteenth century. Charles was indispensable to the early growth of Methodism, which began as a renewal within the Church of England and only later became a separate denomination.

Born in Lincolnshire, he attended Westminster School and Christ Church College, Oxford, where he translated many Greek and Latin classics into English verse.

Charles experienced a spiritual awakening in the winter of 1728–29 and as a result became a founding member of what was called derisively "the Holy Club." In fact plenty of derision went around in those days; they (by now John had joined with his brother Charles) were also called "Bible moths" for the way they fed on the Bible as moths on cloth, and "methodists" for their strict methods of study, fasting, communion, and prayer.

In 1735 Charles took Anglican holy orders in order to help his brother John with a mission to Georgia in the new world. It was an unmitigated disaster due in large part to a failed romance John had with Sophia Hopkey—which is a whole story in itself. Both Charles and John returned to England overcome by spiritual despair and physical exhaustion.

Finally in May of 1738 through the ministry of the Moravian Brethren Charles found "peace with God." Three days later John had his famous Aldersgate experience where he felt "my heart strangely warmed." At last the two Wesleys were together, prepared to lead the great Methodist revival that revolutionized English society. Charles was an eloquent preacher, but it was his hymn writing for which we remember him. In reality his hymns—and he wrote more than 8,000— became a powerful means of evangelism for the growing Methodist movement.

In 1749 Charles married Sarah Gwynne. Out of eight children three survived, two sons and a daughter. Both of the sons, Charles II and Samuel, followed in their father's footsteps, and Samuel was the most prolific in musical composition, fashioning much of his work after J. S. Bach.

In later life Charles had something of a falling-out with John over two matters in particular. Charles disapproved of John's decision to ordain ministers, and he prevented John's marriage to Grace Murray. Still he left the Methodist Church and many others beyond it with a wealth of hymns and songs that have endured through the ages as timeless treasures.

Among Charles Wesley's best-known hymns are "Love Divine, All Loves Excelling," "Hark the Herald Angels Sing," "Christ the Lord is Ris'n Today," and "Jesus, Lover of My Soul." Then there is perhaps the most famous Charles Wesley hymn, "O For a Thousand Tongues to Sing," which is the text for our reading selection.

While many know "O For a Thousand Tongues to Sing," few know more than five or six of the up to eighteen stanzas. (Stanzas varied somewhat, and an exact number is difficult to determine.) It was written in 1739, one year after Charles Wesley's "second birth," and was as he says, "For the anniversary day of one's conversion."

It is a powerful exercise to sing through all the stanzas of "O For a Thousand Tongues to Sing," following its progression and logic and noting how the verses you are familiar with fit into the whole. Prayerfully reading and meditating upon specific stanzas are also of substantial benefit to the soul.

O FOR A THOUSAND TONGUES TO SING

Glory to God, and praise and love
be ever, ever given,
by saints below and saints above,
the church in earth and heaven.

On this glad day the glorious Sun
of Righteousness arose;
on my benighted soul he shone
and filled it with repose.

Sudden expired the legal strife,
"twas then I ceased to grieve;
my second, real, living life
I then began to live.

Then with my heart I first believed,
believed with faith divine,
power with the Holy Ghost received
to call the Savior mine.

I felt my Lord's atoning blood
close to my soul applied;
me, me he loved, the Son of God,
for me, for me he died!

I found and owned his promise true,
ascertained of my part,
my pardon passed in heaven I knew
when written on my heart.

O for a thousand tongues to sing
my great Redeemer's praise!
The glories of my God and King,
the triumphs of his grace.

My gracious Master and my God,
assist me to proclaim,
to spread through all the earth abroad
the honors of thy name.

Jesus! The name that charms our fears,
that bids our sorrows cease;
'tis music in the sinner's ears,
'tis life, and health, and peace!

He breaks the power of canceled sin,
he sets the prisoner free;
his blood can make the foulest clean;
his blood availed for me.

He speaks, and listening to his voice
new life the dead receive;
the mournful, broken hearts rejoice,
the humble poor believe.

Hear him, ye deaf, his praise, ye dumb,
your loosened tongues employ;
ye blind, behold your Savior come,
and leap, ye lame, for joy.

Look unto him, ye nations, own
your God, ye fallen race!
Look, and be saved through faith alone,
be justified by grace!

See all your sins on Jesus laid;
the Lamb of God was slain,
his soul was once an offering made
for every soul of man.

Harlots and publicans and thieves,
in holy triumph join!
Saved is the sinner that believes
from crimes as great as mine.

Murderers and all ye hellish crew,
ye sons of lust and pride,
believe the Savior died for you;
for me the Savior died.

With me, your chief, you then shall know,
shall feel your sins forgiven;
anticipate your heaven below,
and own that love is heaven.

BIBLE SELECTION
Psalm 150

Praise the LORD!
Praise God in his sanctuary;
    praise him in his mighty firmament!
Praise him for his mighty deeds;
    praise him according to his
        surpassing greatness!

Praise him with trumpet sound;
    praise him with lute and harp!
Praise him with tambourine and dance;

praise him with strings and pipe!
Praise him with clanging cymbals;
    praise him with loud clashing cymbals!
Let everything that breathes praise the LORD!
    Praise the LORD!

DISCUSSION QUESTIONS

The following can be used for discussion within a small group, or used for journal reflections by individuals:

1. How can I enhance the experience of worship for others?
2. In what ways can I guard against diminishing the worship experience for others? How can I avoid needless criticism and complaint?

SUGGESTED EXERCISES

The following exercises can be done by individuals, shared between spiritual friends, or used in the context of a small group. Choose one or more of the following:

1. Plan a Charles Wesley hymn-sing in your group. If someone can accompany this on the piano, well and good. But since many of Charles Wesley's hymns are so familiar, it's likely they can be sung without accompaniment.
2. Make note of the names of your favorite hymns (no matter who wrote them). Reflect on what it is that makes a particular hymn dear to you. Exchange these hymn titles and the stories that accompany them in your group, or confide them to your journal.
3. Listen, in a worshiping frame of mind, to a recording of great traditional hymns.

REFLECTIONS

I love this Charles Wesley hymn. I love the verses we sing often. I love the verses we never sing. I love the whole of it. I love its strength and power. I love its graced theology. I love that Charles wrote it to celebrate the one-year anniversary of his commitment to Christ.

Two stanzas deserve special comment; one which is sung frequently though seldom fully understood, and the other sung not at all though I wish it were.

The familiar stanza I am referring to is this: "He breaks the power of canceled sin, / he sets the prisoner free; / his blood can make the foulest clean; / his blood availed for me." Wesley understood the matters of the heart so clearly. He knew that it was possible for sin to be canceled out, that is, forgiven, but that it could still have power over a person. He had addressed the matter of forgiveness as canceling out sin in the third stanza when he wrote, "Sudden expired the legal strife. . . ." But the salvation that is in Jesus Christ is more than outward, legal, objective forgiveness. It is more than a right positioning of ourselves before God. Dealing with that matter is vitally important, and it is wonderful that Jesus' death can put us into a right legal standing with God, but there is more to it than that. There is a subjective freeing of the soul from the power of sin's grip. This is what Wesley is celebrating in this stanza. The salvation of Jesus Christ not only cancels out sin's debt but breaks its power over us. That is something worth having a thousand tongues to sing about.

The other stanza I truly love and wish that we would sing is this: "Murderers and all ye hellish crew, / ye sons of lust and pride, / believe the Savior died for you; / for me the Savior died." I love the bluntness of the language—"Murderers . . . ye hellish crew." The gospel invitation is for just such people. Sometimes it helps us to have language we cannot dress up or make dignified. It is the "hellish crew" for whom Christ died. Then note how Wesley places himself right in the middle of them all. Refusing to stand off from all the "sons of lust and pride," he boldly identifies with the sinfulness of all humanity as he adds "for me the Savior died."

I know I said I would comment on only two stanzas but I must not leave out the final one (in this version, the seventeenth). Wesley, already identified with humanity's sinfulness, now follows the lead of the Apostle Paul by declaring himself the chief of sinners and welcomes all to "feel your sins forgiven." Then he presents us with two of the finest lines in the entire hymn, "anticipate your heaven below, / and own that love is heaven." This is a tremendous understanding of the fact that Jesus' death and resurrection call us into life in the kingdom of God now, a life that is so filled with righteousness and peace and joy that it is a foretaste of the heaven to come. Even more, the supernatural love of God—agape—is so taking over our lives that we can own the fact that this love, multiplied and extended infinitely, is what heaven will be like.

RICHARD J. FOSTER

GOING DEEPER

John and Charles Wesley: Selected Writings and Hymns, edited by Frank Whaling (New York: Paulist, 1981). This book has excellent selections from the work of John Wesley and a number of the texts of Charles Wesley's hymns, as well as good historical and biographical background on both.

JOHN LAWSON, *The Wesley Hymns as a Guide to Scriptural Teaching* (Grand Rapids, MI: Francis Asbury Press [Zondervan], 1987). A splendid book illustrating the wedding of the Wesleys' mastery of Scripture and hymnology. Of special interest is Lawson's treatment of this hymn. On pp. 126–28 he reproduces the poem, fourteen stanzas of it; and there is scarcely a line of verse that doesn't have at least one scriptural resonance or reference. With the poem and the Scripture references, one has food for a month of prayer.

ARNOLD A. DALLIMORE, *A Heart Set Free: The Life of Charles Wesley* (Westchester, IL: Crossway, 1988). This is a fine treatment of Charles Wesley's life and work, showing his imperfections as well as his gifts.

Gerard Manley Hopkins

(1844–1889)

———

Gerard Manley Hopkins died relatively young, with most of his writing unpublished, and was not recognized as a major English writer until some forty years after his death. His style of writing broke new ground; he is considered one of the great innovators in English poetry, partly because of his use of simple, old-fashioned country words that have a strong resonance and power.

Born in Essex to a creative and literary family of High Anglican sympathies, he began writing poetry in his school days, much of it with a Christian purpose. At Balliol College, Oxford, he was converted to Roman Catholicism and soon afterward entered the Society of Jesus, known familiarly as the Jesuits, where he found a life of intense prayer and spiritual discipline.

Ordained a priest, he was sent to many different places in the United Kingdom, serving as a teacher, scholar, preacher, and administrator. Everywhere he found himself drawn to the outdoors, and he wrote poetry to celebrate the beauties of creation. Hopkins died of typhoid in June 1889 with his parents at his side; they had at last accepted his Roman Catholicism.

The two short poems that follow are songs of praise. In them Hopkins speaks of his personal vision of God the Creator and the beauty of God's creation. He also laments the inability of human beings to reverence God in his creation.

Hopkins asks why "generations have trod, have trod" over the earth but fail to grasp God's government and rule ("not reck his rod").

Notice how he, with his love of Celtic and Anglo-Saxon usage, will often choose a very simple, old word, like "pied" (multicolored) or "brindled" (multicolored) instead of our somewhat less interesting modern equivalents.

On Reading Hopkins's Poems

As with John Milton, Hopkins can best be understood in the hearing.

Before reading the poems aloud, you may want to mark the unfamiliar words Hopkins uses, like "reck" for "reckon" and "rod" for "reign or rule." Most of these are easy to decipher if you give them a little thought or consult a dictionary.

When you, or someone in your group, reads aloud, Hopkins's thought can sing out clearly.

As you read, identify with Hopkins. When you are dazzled, as he is, by the wonder of created things, isn't it natural to sing the praises of God?

GOD'S GRANDEUR

The world is charged with the grandeur of God.
   It will flame out, like shining from shook foil;
   It gathers to a greatness, like the ooze of oil
Crushed. Why do men then now not reck his rod?
Generations have trod, have trod, have trod;
   And all is seared with trade; bleared, smeared with toil;
   And wears man's smudge and shares man's smell: the soil
Is bare now, nor can foot feel, being shod.

And for all this, nature is never spent;
   There lives the dearest freshness deep down things;
And though the last lights off the black West went
   Oh, morning, at the brown brink eastward, springs—
Because the Holy Ghost over the bent
   World broods with warm breast and with ah! bright wings.

PIED BEAUTY

Glory be to God for dappled things—
   For skies of couple-colour as a brindled cow;
     For rose-moles all in stipple upon trout that swim;
Fresh firecoal chestnut-falls; finches' wings;
   Landscapes plotted and pieced-fold, fallow, and plough;
     And áll trádes, their gear and tackle and trim.

All things counter, original, spare, strange;
   Whatever is fickle, freckled (who knows how?)
     With swift, slow; sweet, sour; adazzle, dim;
He fathers-forth whose beauty is past change:
                    Praise him.

BIBLE SELECTION
Psalm 84

How lovely is your dwelling place,
    O LORD of hosts!
My soul longs, indeed it faints
    for the courts of the LORD;
my heart and my flesh sing for joy
    to the living God.

Even the sparrow finds a home,
    and the swallow a nest for herself,
    where she may lay her young,
at your altars, O LORD of hosts,
    my King and my God.
Happy are those who live in your house,
    ever singing your praise. *Selah*

Happy are those whose strength is in you,
    in whose heart are the highways to Zion.
As they go through the valley of Baca
    they make it a place of springs;
    the early rain also covers it with pools.
They go from strength to strength;
    the God of gods will be seen in Zion.

O LORD God of hosts, hear my prayer;
    give ear, O God of Jacob! *Selah*
Behold our shield, O God;
    look on the face of your anointed.

For a day in your courts is better
    than a thousand elsewhere.
I would rather be a doorkeeper in the house of my God
    than live in the tents of wickedness.
For the LORD God is a sun and shield;
    he bestows favor and honor.
No good thing does the LORD withhold
    from those who walk uprightly.

O Lord of hosts,
   happy is everyone who trusts in you.

DISCUSSION QUESTIONS

The following can be used for discussion within a small group, or used for journal reflections by individuals:

1. How can I make time to appreciate the beauty of God as expressed in his creation?
2. In what ways can I let my gratitude bubble up, in a style that comes naturally to me?
3. Have I been a faithful steward of God's gifts in creation? How can I remedy that?

SUGGESTED EXERCISES

The following exercises can be done by individuals, shared between spiritual friends, or used in the context of a small group. Choose one or more of the following:

1. Take a nature walk. Allow enough time for being in a place of natural beauty so that you will not be hurried or rushed. Relax and experience fully the splendor of God's creation wherever you discover it: in a sunrise, in light splintering across water, in an unfolding bud or a massive tree. Dwell in the experience and be grateful for it.
2. Buy a flower from a shop or take one from your garden, and enjoy it. Capture the experience in a way that is natural to you, in order to savor and continue it in a later time. Take a photograph; make a drawing or sketch; write about it in your journal. Share the experience with another person by describing the beauty that you saw.
3. Sing a hymn of praise that you may have stored in memory. From your treasure trove of remembered hymns, choose one that celebrates the beauty of creation. "There's a Wideness in God's Mercy Like the Wideness of the Sea" might be one such. Another, more recent, is "All the Ends of the Earth," based on Psalm 98.

REFLECTIONS

Hopkins has such a fully orbed doctrine of creation that it takes my breath away. No secularized, modern myth of "Mother Nature" for him. He sees the greatness and goodness of God the Creator around every bend, over every hill, under every rock. I love this in Hopkins because it is such a refreshing contrast to the detached, cold, meaningless, mechanistic view of the universe we post-Darwinian moderns have.

Right after reading these poems from Hopkins I took a hike in a lovely canyon area near our home. I was accompanied only by my carved redwood walking stick and a water bottle. In the springtime this canyon is filled with the sights and smells of columbine and larkspur, golden banner and Indian paintbrush. But spring is yet to come to this mountain canyon, and earth tones still dominate. Even the ponderosa pine are darker in winter, blending in with the browns of gambel oak and mountain mahogany.

The absence of leaf and flower makes the boulders of the canyon stand out in rugged relief. They are always here, of course, but in the winter they fill the landscape, like giant sentinels. I like the rock—hard and durable. I brush my hand over a conglomerate boulder studded with stones, all cemented together by ancient pressures.

Actually this is my favorite time of year in the canyon. In the spring and summer numerous hikers enjoy the beauties of flora and fauna: but few venture out in the winter. Often I can hike along miles of trail without sight of another Homo sapiens. So it is today. As a result I do not speak . . . but I do listen. Always I hear the rush of the stream winding through this little canyon. Its perpetual babble in a strange way both calms and energizes me. Other sounds abound: chipmunk and squirrel scratching for food in the underbrush, and in the trees high above I hear hawk and jay, American goldfinch and dark-eyed junco. The great variety of tracks in the snow remind me that I have many more neighbors than I ever see or hear.

The sun flees the canyon early, and I feel a chill beginning to set in. I pull my jacket tight around my ears, regretting my decision not to bring hat or gloves. Clutching the water bottle, my fingers feel icy. On the way back I meet a herd of deer grazing in a brown meadow. Several bound away, but others only watch in an uninterested sort of way, making sure this stranger does not come too close. They remind me that I am only a guest and visitor here; they are the permanent residents. The wind whistling through the trees and the thunder clouds rolling over the distant peaks are another reminder—a storm is blowing in from the north. Quickening my pace I finish the trail loop just as Venus begins to make her nightly appearance in the western sky.

Back home I think of the words of St. Augustine that the senses are "the messengers of God." Having seen and heard and smelled and touched I add my humble witness to that of Gerard Manley Hopkins, declaring, "The world is charged with the grandeur of God."

RICHARD J. FOSTER

GOING DEEPER

Gerard Manley Hopkins: A Selection of His Poems and Prose, edited by W. H. Gardner (Baltimore, MD: Penguin, 1961). A fine collection of the complete poems and letters, with extensive annotations.

BERNARD BERGONZI, *Gerard Manley Hopkins* (New York: Macmillan, 1977). This is a good biography, dealing with both literary and religious aspects of Hopkins's work.

PAUL MARIANI, *A Commentary on the Complete Poems of Gerard Manley Hopkins* (Ithaca, NY: Cornell University Press, 1970). Paul Mariani, a poet and biographer of poets, provides a close reading of the entire body of Hopkins's verse.

Andrew Murray

(1828–1917)

———

Born in Cape Town, South Africa, Andrew Murray became a renowned missionary leader (Dutch Reformed) and exerted wide influence with his devotional writings. His father was a Scottish Presbyterian minister serving the Dutch Reformed
Church. His mother's connections were Huguenot and Lutheran. No doubt their
influence encouraged him to be ecumenical in outlook.

Educated in Scotland and the Netherlands and ordained in 1848, Murray pastored several South African churches, then helped to found two institutions of
higher learning. Moderator of Cape Synod of the Dutch Reformed Church, he
was also president of the YMCA (1865) and the South Africa General Mission
(1888–1917).

Murray vigorously promoted the call to missions, especially Dutch Reformed
missions to blacks in the Transvaal and Malawi. He made large evangelistic tours
in South Africa; he also spoke at the Keswick and Northfield Conventions in
1895, greatly impressing British and American audiences. He received honorary
doctorates from the Universities of Aberdeen (1898) and Cape of Good Hope
(1907).

He is best remembered for his extensive devotional writings (240 volumes in
all), which continue to be widely read today.

Notice in these selections, which are taken from *The Best of Andrew Murray on
Prayer* and *With Christ in the School of Prayer*, how he calls us to a rich, personal
depth of devotion.

THE BEST OF ANDREW MURRAY ON PRAYER

The Glory of God

We have been speaking especially of the adoration of God the Father and the
need for sufficient time each day to worship Him in some of His glorious attributes. But we must remind ourselves that, in all our communion with the Father,
the presence and the power of the Son and the Spirit are absolutely necessary.

We must understand how our communion with the Father is conditioned by
the active and personal presence and working of the Lord Jesus. It takes time to

become fully conscious of the need we have of Him in every approach to God. But we can have confidence in the work that He is doing in us and assurance of His intimate love and presence as we make intercession.

So too the Holy Spirit, working in the depth of our heart, is the One who is able to reveal the Son within us. Through Him alone we have the power to know what and how to pray. Through Him we have the assurance that our prayer has been accepted.

Dear Christian, it is in tarrying in the secret of God's presence that you receive grace to abide in Christ and to be led by His Spirit. What food for thought—and worship!

New wonders of that glory

There is no more wonderful image in nature of the glory of God than we find in the starry heavens. Telescopes have long discovered the wonders of God's universe. By means of photography, new wonders of that glory have been revealed. A photographic plate fixed below the telescope will reveal millions of stars which otherwise could never have been seen by the eye. Man must step to one side and allow the glory of the heavens to reveal itself. The stars, at first wholly invisible, will leave their image on the plate.

What a lesson for the soul that longs to see the glory of God in His Word. Let your heart be as a photographic plate that waits for God's glory to be revealed. The plate must be prepared and clean; let your heart be prepared and purified by God's Spirit. "God blesses those whose hearts are pure, for they will see God" (Matt. 5:8). The plate must be immovable; let your heart be still before God in prayer. The plate must be exposed for several hours to receive the full impression of the farthest stars; let your heart take time in silent waiting upon God and He will reveal His glory.

If you keep silent before God and give Him time, He will leave within you impressions that will be as the rays of His glory shining in you.

WITH CHRIST IN THE SCHOOL OF PRAYER

The Chief End of Prayer

This was Jesus' goal when He was on earth: "I seek not mine own honor: I seek the honor of Him that sent me." In such words we have the keynote of His life. The first words of His High-Priestly prayer voice it: "Father glorify Thy Son, that Thy Son may glorify Thee. I have glorified Thee on earth: glorify me with Thyself"

(John 17:1,4). His reason for asking to be taken up into the glory He had with the Father . . .

Let us make His aim ours! Let the glory of the Father be the link between our asking and His doing!

Jesus' words come indeed as a sharp two-edged sword, dividing the soul and the spirit, and quickly discerning the thoughts and intents of the heart. In His prayers on earth, His intercession in heaven, and His promise of an answer to our prayers, Jesus makes His first object the glory of His Father. Is this our object, too? Or are self-interest and self-will the strongest motives urging us to pray? A distinct, conscious longing for the glory of the Father must animate our prayers . . .

Our object: God's glory

For the sake of God's glory, let us learn to pray well. . . . When we seek our own glory among men, we make faith impossible. Only the deep, intense self-sacrifice that gives up its own glory and seeks the glory of God wakens in the soul that spiritual susceptibility to Divine faith. The surrender to God and the expectation that He will show His glory in hearing us are essential. Only he who seeks God"s glory will see it in the answer to his prayer.

How do we accomplish this? Let us begin with a confession. The glory of God hasn't really been an all-absorbing passion in our lives and our prayers. How little we have lived in the likeness of the Son and in sympathy with Him for God and His glory alone. Take time to allow the Holy Spirit to reveal how deficient we have been in this. True knowledge and confession of sin are the sure path to deliverance.

Looking to Jesus

And then let us look to Jesus. In death He glorified God; through death He was glorified with Him. It is by dying—being dead to self and living for God—that we can glorify Him. This death to self, this life to the glory of God, is what Jesus gives and lives in each one who can trust Him for it. Let the spirit of our daily lives consist of the decision to live only for the glory of the Father as Christ did, the acceptance of Him with His life and strength working it in us, and the joyful assurance that we can live for the glory of God because Christ lives in us. Jesus helps us to live this way. The Holy Spirit is waiting to make it our experience, if we will only trust and let Him. Don't hold back through unbelief! Confidently do everything for the glory of God! Our obedience will please the Father. The Holy Spirit will seal us within the consciousness that we are living for God and his glory.

What quiet peace and power will be in our prayers when we know we are in perfect harmony with Christ, Who promises to do what we ask, "That the Father may be glorified in the Son." With our whole beings consciously yielded to the inspiration of the Word and Spirit, our desires will no longer be ours. They will be His, and their main purpose will be the glory of God. With increasing liberty we will be able in prayer to say, "Father! You know we ask it only for Your glory." Answers to prayer, instead of being mountains we cannot climb, will give us a greater confidence that we are heard. And the privilege of prayer will become doubly precious because it brings us into perfect unison with the Beloved Son in the wonderful partnership He proposes: "You *ask*, and *I do*, that the Father may be glorified in the Son."

Learning from Jesus
Lord, teach us to pray.

Blessed Lord Jesus! Once again I am coming to You. Every lesson You give me convinces me all the more deeply that I don't know how to pray properly. But every lesson also inspires me with hope that You are going to teach me what prayer should be. O my Lord! I look to you with courage. You are the Great Intercessor. You alone pray and hear prayer for the sole purpose of glorifying the Father. Teach me to pray as You do.

Let Your life and Your love of the Father take possession of me. A new longing is filling my soul that every day and every hour prayer to the glory of the Father will become everything to me. O my Lord! Please teach me this!

My God and my Father! Accept the desire of Your child who has seen that Your glory alone is worth living for. Show me Your glory. Let it overshadow me and fill my heart! May I dwell in it as Christ did. Tell me what pleases You, fulfill in me Your own good pleasure, so that I may find my glory in seeking the glory of my Father. Amen.

BIBLE SELECTION
Psalm 19:1–6, 14

The heavens are telling the glory of God;
   and the firmament proclaims his handiwork.
Day to day pours forth speech,
   and night to night declares knowledge.
There is no speech, nor are there words;
   their voice is not heard;
yet their voice goes out through all the earth,
   and their words to the ends of the world.

In the heavens he has set a tent for the sun,
which comes out like a bridegroom from his wedding canopy,
   and like a strong man runs its course with joy.
Its rising is from the end of the heavens,
   and its circuit to the end of them;
   and nothing is hid from its heat. . . .

Let the words of my mouth and the meditation of my heart
   be acceptable to you,
   O LORD, my rock and my redeemer.

DISCUSSION QUESTIONS

The following can be used for discussion within a small group, or used for journal reflections by individuals:

1. How can I expand my vision of what worship entails and where it takes place?
2. What kinds of activities can help with this?

SUGGESTED EXERCISES

The following exercises can be done by individuals, shared between spiritual friends, or used in the context of a small group. Choose one or more of the following:

1. Have your group meet (on a clear night) under the stars. Allow the splendor of the heavens to influence your praise of God. If starry nights are in short supply, consider sunset as an equally splendid option.
2. Keep a sky journal during the week. Notice the changing colors, the clouds, the thunderstorm patterns, sunlight, rain, snow, and hail. If you can make sketches or take photographs, do so. In a group, have the members compare notes about their skies; dialogue about how natural wonders can shape our ways of worshiping.
3. Spend some worship time in church or chapel outside a planned service. Consider how the place itself calls you more deeply to praise God.

REFLECTIONS

I first met Andrew Murray through his book With Christ in the School of Prayer. *It was a formative book for me, and while I may meander here and there in his other devotional writings it is to* With Christ *that I always return. It is the most sustained and carefully thought out discussion of prayer I have found. And it never fails to warm my heart.*

All of Murray's books deal with prayer in one form or another. This particular selection helps us to center on the glory of God through the prayer of adoration. Adoration is our most direct reply to God's perpetual outpouring of love into our soul. It is the spontaneous yearning of the heart to worship, honor, magnify, and bless God. Adoration is the air in which prayer breathes, the sea in which prayer swims. In adoration we enter the rarefied air of selfless devotion. We ask for nothing but to cherish God. We seek nothing but his exaltation. We focus on nothing but his goodness.

God's glory, you understand, is seen primarily in his goodness, and so for us to give glory to God means that we magnify his goodness. Now, to magnify something, you make it look larger, increasing it out of proportion. To talk about ourselves or our activities out of true proportion is dangerous indeed, but when we magnify God, we are on safe ground. We simply cannot say too much about God's goodness and love. The most exaggerated things we can think of will still be far below what is actually the case. So we can freely and joyfully join with the psalmist who calls us to worship saying, "O magnify the LORD *with me, and let us exalt his name together" (Ps. 34:3). In this we do no more than give the glory to God that is due his name.*

RICHARD J. FOSTER

GOING DEEPER

Of Andrew Murray's 240 works on the devotional life, some are especially well known, such as *Abide in Christ, Absolute Surrender, With Christ in the School of Prayer,* and *Waiting on God.* A great number of these works are still available in contemporary editions, many of which have modernized language. All Murray's writing stresses the importance of personal time given to study, worship, prayer, and devotion. His work is biblically centered, often commenting on or elaborating specific Scripture texts.

You may also want to try one of the Andrew Murray readers. A good one is Edward A. Elliott's *The Best of Andrew Murray on Prayer* (Urichsville, OH: Barbour Publishing, 1996).

Guidance

———

Martin Luther King Jr.

(1929–1968)

———

Martin Luther King Jr. was an eloquent African-American Baptist minister who led the civil rights movement in the United States from the mid-1950s until his death by assassination in 1968. Through his dynamic leadership, the movement was remarkably effective in removing racial barriers that had been firmly entrenched for many generations.

Rising to national prominence through the Southern Christian Leadership Conference, King advocated love and nonviolent action, insisting that such action was courageous and would work better than any violent protest. One signal triumph of this strategy was the massive March on Washington (1963), which he led personally.

A high point of this event was his "I Have a Dream" speech, given on the steps of the Lincoln Memorial. He was awarded the Nobel Prize for Peace in 1964. The United States Congress voted in 1986 to establish Martin Luther King Day, the third Monday in January, as a national holiday.

As a preacher, King was deeply formed by Southern black preaching and ministry: both his father and his maternal grandfather were Baptist preachers. But through his education (he held a Ph.D. from Boston University) he was also formed by contemporary Protestant theologians, among them Paul Tillich and Reinhold Niebuhr.

King's idea of God was active and personal; faith in God's guidance was essential. Vague notions such as "social progress" did not motivate him. Instead he was shaped by biblical stories, understanding God's prophetic work as an ongoing thing.

In standing firm against threats of violence against himself and his family, King chose Jesus as his fundamental model for action. "It was the Sermon on the Mount," he wrote, "rather than a doctrine of passive resistance, that initially inspired the Negroes of Montgomery to dignified social action. It was Jesus of Nazareth that stirred the Negroes to protest with the creative weapon of love."

In the reading that follows, taken from the essay "Walk with Freedom" published in 1956, King elaborates this vision of Christian courage and love.

WALK WITH FREEDOM

On Love and Non-Violence

This is a spiritual movement, and we intend to keep these things in the fore-front. We know that violence will defeat our purpose. We know that in our struggle in America and in our specific struggle here in Montgomery, violence will not only be impractical but immoral. We are outnumbered; we do not have access to the instruments of violence. Even more than that, not only is violence impractical, but it is *immoral*; for it is my firm conviction that to seek to retaliate with violence does nothing but intensify the existence of evil and hate in the universe.

Along the way of life, someone must have *sense* enough and morality enough to cut off the chain of hate and evil. The greatest way to do that is through love. I believe firmly that love is a transforming power that can lift a whole community to new horizons of fair play, good will and justice.

Love is our instrument

Love is our great instrument and our great weapon, and that alone. On January 30 my home was bombed. My wife and baby were there; I was attending a meeting. I first heard of the bombing at the meeting, when someone came to me and mentioned it, and I tried to accept it in a very calm manner. I first inquired about my wife and daughter; then after I found out that they were all right, I stopped in the midst of the meeting and spoke to the group, and urged them not to be panicky and not to do anything about it because that was not the way.

I immediately came home and, on entering the front of the house, I noticed there were some five hundred to a thousand persons. I came in the house and looked it over and went back to see my wife and to see if the baby was all right, but as I stood in the back of the house, hundreds and hundreds of people were still gathering, and I saw there that violence was a possibility.

It was at that time that I went to the porch and tried to say to the people that we could not allow ourselves to be panicky. We could not allow ourselves to retaliate with any type of violence, but that we were still to confront the problem with *love*.

One statement that I made—and I believe it very firmly—was: "He who lives by the sword will perish by the sword." I urged people to continue to manifest love, and to continue to carry on the struggle with the same dignity and with the same discipline that we had started out with. I think at that time the people did decide to go home, things did get quiet, and it ended up with a great deal of calmness and a great deal of discipline, which I think our community should be proud of and which I was very proud to see because our people were determined not to retaliate with violence.

Hold to non-violence

Some twenty-six of the ministers and almost one hundred of the citizens of the city were indicted in this boycott. But we realized in the beginning that we would confront experiences that make for great sacrifices, experiences that are not altogether pleasant. We decided among ourselves that we would stand up to the finish, and that is what we are determined to do. In the midst of the indictments, we still hold to this nonviolent attitude, and this primacy of love.

Even though convicted, we will not retaliate with hate, but will stand with love in our hearts, and stand resisting injustice, with the same determination with which we started out. We need a great deal of encouragement in this movement. Of course one thing that we are depending on, from not only other communities but from our own community, is prayer. We ask people everywhere to pray that God will guide us, pray that justice will be done and that righteousness will stand. And I think through these prayers we will be strengthened; it will make us feel the unity of the nation and the presence of Almighty God. For as we said all along, this is a spiritual movement.

BIBLE SELECTION
Matthew 26:47–56

While he was still speaking, Judas, one of the twelve, arrived; with him was a large crowd with swords and clubs, from the chief priests and the elders of the people. Now the betrayer had given them a sign, saying, "The one I will kiss is the man; arrest him." At once he came up to Jesus and said, "Greetings, Rabbi!" and kissed him. Jesus said to him, "Friend, do what you are here to do." Then they came and laid hands on Jesus and arrested him. Suddenly, one of those with Jesus put his hand on his sword, drew it, and struck the slave of the high priest, cutting off his ear. Then Jesus said to him, "Put your sword back into its place; for all who take the sword will perish by the sword. Do you think that I cannot appeal to my Father, and he will at once send me more than twelve legions of angels? But how then would the scriptures be fulfilled, which say it must happen in this way?" At that hour Jesus said to the crowds, "Have you come out with swords and clubs to arrest me as though I were a bandit? Day after day I sat in the temple teaching, and you did not arrest me. But all this has taken place, so that the scriptures of the prophets may be fulfilled." Then all the disciples deserted him and fled.

DISCUSSION QUESTIONS

The following can be used for discussion within a small group, or used for journal reflections by individuals:

1. In what ways do I look for God's guidance in my life?
2. What implications do I see in living as a peacemaker?
3. What actions in my past may have disappointed me—by showing me what I truly feel in contrast to what I may say I believe?

SUGGESTED EXERCISES

The following exercises can be done by individuals, shared between spiritual friends, or used in the context of a small group. Choose one or more of the following:

1. If you have been personally involved in any incident where it was possible to resist an injustice, recall this, relive it, and share it with a friend or with your group.
2. Tell stories from your own past—or true-life stories you know about—in which people were guided through times of danger or trial by being attentive to God's leading.
3. In the history of every nation there are stories of oppression and liberation. Reflect on the ones that directly affect your own attitudes and patterns of thought. Pray about these influences, asking for the influence of God's love in your understanding and your actions.

REFLECTIONS

Did you notice that this reading from Martin Luther King Jr. began and ended with the same words: "This is a spiritual movement"? Many people were never able to understand the methods of non-violent direct action of King and the movement that grew up around him. And they did not understand it because they simply were unable to grasp the simple fact that "this is a spiritual movement." Oh, they could understand non-violent direct action as a political tactic, and when it succeeded in its objectives they were all for it. But when it did not accomplish those objectives . . . well, that was a different matter.

Now, King did believe that violence was "impractical" and that non-violent direct action was the best way to achieve their objectives. But he believed more than this. He also believed that violence was "immoral." <u>And because violence was immoral he could not resort to it even when nonviolent direct action failed to accomplish his objectives. Where, I ask you, did he get this idea</u>? He got it straight from the Sermon on the Mount, for, as he said, "this is a spiritual movement."

What King understood (and what we are still trying to understand) is that someone, somewhere has to break the vicious cycle of violence in order to, as he put it, "cut off the chain of hate and evil." This vicious cycle has a name—the lex talionis, the law of retaliation. Negatively put it says, "You gore my ox, I gore your ox." Positively put it says, "You scratch my back, I scratch your back." And the lex talionis is written across the face of humanity. But <u>King saw that Jesus broke this vicious cycle of retaliation when he brought us the law of love.</u> This is why King could see that violence was immoral.

And what does this say to us today: about war, about abortion, about the death penalty, about the arms race, about poverty, about euthanasia? Can we in all these areas maintain a spirit of peace, reconciliation, and respect in protecting the unprotected? Certainly not by ourselves. <u>It would have to be a work of God; it would have to be a spiritual movement.</u>

RICHARD J. FOSTER

GOING DEEPER

A Testament of Hope: The Essential Writings of Martin Luther King, Jr., edited by James M. Washington (San Francisco: HarperSanFrancisco, 1991). This comprehensive work provides selections dealing with King's philosophy, sense of social concern, and political views. It includes his most famous sermons and public addresses. Historic essays and interviews are also included, together with excerpts from his books. There is a select bibliography and a good index.

MARTIN LUTHER KING, JR., A Knock at Midnight: Inspiration from the Great Sermons of Martin Luther King, Jr. (New York: Warner, 1998). Here eleven of Dr. King's most powerful sermons are collected, covering the full range of his preaching career. Also included are eleven introductions by such important ministers as Billy Graham and Archbishop Desmond Tutu.

John Ruusbroec

(1293–1381)

The fourteenth century, a time of social and religious unrest, brought a flourishing of spiritual writers. Outstanding among them is the Flemish contemplative John Ruusbroec (sometimes spelled *Ruysbroeck*, sometimes pronounced *Roycebroyk*). Many scholars, including Evelyn Underhill, have relied on him for clarity of description and explanation.

Born in Ruusbroec, a town near Brussels, which is now in Belgium, John was encouraged by his mother in holiness. At eleven he left home to live with his uncle, John Hinckaert, a priest and canon regular. He pursued priestly studies, was ordained in 1317, and served as an assistant parish priest in Brussels.

Then Ruusbroec, his uncle, and his uncle's friend Francis van Coudenberg, also a canon and man of great piety, went to live in a hermitage in the Forest of Soignes, in Groenendaal. By 1349 the community had grown; they became a religious institute of canons regular.

Ruusbroec devoted himself to writing about the life of devotion. His first and best-known work was *The Spiritual Espousals*. His treatise *The Kingdom of Lovers* was apparently over the heads of the Carthusians at Herne, who asked him for an explanation. Distressed that a copyist had sent it to the Carthusians without his knowledge, he responded with the stellar short work *The Little Book of Clarification*.

Ruusbroec wrote eleven treatises in all. Some of these were learned, meant for those much advanced in contemplation. Others were light, popular works, among these the delightful *Book of the Twelve Beguines*.

In the following selection, which is at the beginning of "The Interior Life," Book Two of *The Spiritual Espousals*, Ruusbroec wants us to be able to "see" in the way that Jesus invites us to do.

Notice that he mentions the powers of the memory, the understanding, and the will as sources of spiritual life. Memory, for Ruusbroec, is not just "remembering things"; it is a way of getting in touch with the divine.

THE SPIRITUAL ESPOUSALS

Christ Guides Us to Seeing

The wise virgin, that is, the pure soul which has abandoned earthly things and which lives for God through the virtues, has taken into the vessel of her heart the oil of charity and of virtuous works, together with the lamp of a spotless conscience. But whenever Christ the Bridegroom delays his coming with consolation and a new influx of gifts, the soul becomes drowsy, sleepy, and indolent. In the middle of the night, that is, when it is least expected, a spiritual cry resounds within the soul: "See, the bridegroom is coming. Go out to meet him." We now wish to speak of this seeing, and of an interior coming of Christ, and of a person's going out spiritually to meet him. We will clarify and explain these four points with respect to an interior exercise full of desire—the kind of life which many persons attain through the practice of moral virtues and interior zeal. . . .

The three things necessary for seeing
The first word which Christ says is "See." If a person wishes to see in a supernatural way in the interior life, three things are necessary. The first of these is the light of God's grace in a higher way than that which can be experienced in a life of exterior works without fervent interior zeal. The second is the stripping of all strange images and solicitude from the heart, so that a person may be free and imageless, delivered from attachments and empty of all creatures. The third thing which is necessary is a free turning of the will and a gathering together of all the bodily and spiritual powers in such a way that the will, unencumbered by any inordinate affection, might flow into the Unity of God and of the mind. This allows the rational creature to attain the sublime Unity of God and to possess it in a supernatural way. It is for this reason that God created heaven and earth and all that is in them, and it is likewise for this reason that he became a human being, taught us, lived for us, and himself became the way to this Unity. He died in the bond of love, ascended into heaven, and has opened up for us the same Unity through which we might possess eternal bliss.

The threefold unity which is in us naturally and supernaturally
Now note carefully: There is a threefold unity which is in everyone naturally and which is in good persons supernaturally as well. The first and highest unity is that which we have in God, for all creatures depend on this unity for their being, their life, and their preservation. If they were separated from God at this level, they would fall into nothingness and become nothing. This unity is in us essentially, by

nature, whether we are good or evil, and without our cooperation it neither sancti-fies nor saves us. We possess this unity within ourselves and yet above ourselves, for it both grounds and preserves our very being and life.

The second unity is also in us by nature. This is the unity of the higher powers, a unity from which they arise naturally as active powers; this is the unity of the spirit or of the mind. This is the same unity as the first, which is in God and depends on him, but here we are considering it as regards its activity and there as regards its essence; in each case the spirit is whole and entire according to the totality of its substance. We possess this unity within ourselves above the activity of the senses. From it arise the powers of the memory, the understanding, and the will—our entire power of performing spiritual activity. In this unity the soul is called spirit.

The third unity which is in us by nature is the ground of the bodily powers, that is, the unity of the heart, which is the beginning and source of our corporeal life. The soul possesses this unity in the body and in the life-giving center of the heart; from it flow all the works of the body and of the five senses. Here the soul is simply called soul, for it is the form of the body and animates the flesh by giving it life and keeping it alive.

These three unities exist naturally in a person and constitute a single life and kingdom. . . .

We now wish to go on and show how these three unities are more beautifully adorned and more nobly possessed when fervent interior exercises are added to those of the active life. When through charity and an upright intention a person offers himself in all his works and in his entire life to the glory and praise of God, and when he seeks rest in God above all things, then he should humbly and patiently, with self-surrender and firm confidence, await new riches and gifts—but always without anxiety as to whether God will bestow them or not. This is the way a person makes himself ready and capable of receiving an interior life full of desire. When the vessel is ready, the precious liquid is poured in. There is no more precious vessel than a loving soul and no more beneficial drink than the grace of God. It is in this way that a person will offer to God all his works and his entire life with a simple and upright intention and will also, above that intention, above himself, and above all things, rest in that sublime unity where God and the loving spirit are united without intermediary.

The enlightenment which occurs in the highest unity
. . .From out of [the] unity where the spirit rests above itself in God, Christ, the eternal truth, says, "See, the bridegroom is coming. Go out to meet him." It is Christ, the light of truth, who says "See," and it is through him that we are able to

see, for he is the light of the Father, without which there is no light in heaven or on earth. Christ's speaking within us is nothing other than an influx of his light and grace. This grace descends upon us in the unity of our higher powers and of our spirit. From this unity the higher powers actively flow forth in all the virtues by means of the power of grace, and to it they return in the bond of love. In this unity lie the power and the beginning and end of all creaturely activity, both natural and supernatural, insofar as it is performed in a creaturely way by means of grace, divine gifts, and the power proper to creatures.

God bestows his grace upon the unity of the higher powers so that a person may constantly practice the virtues by means of the power, richness, and impulse of grace, for God gives his grace for the sake of works, whereas he gives himself above all grace for the sake of enjoyment and rest. This unity of the spirit is where we are to dwell in the peace of God and in the richness of charity. Here all the multiplicity of the virtues comes to an end, and they live together in the simplicity of the spirit. . . .

The requisite conditions for obtaining this enlightenment
Christ now speaks in a spiritual way within a person who is devoted to him: "See." There are three things, as I said earlier, which make a person able to see in interior exercises. The first of these is the illumination of divine grace. This grace within a soul is like a candle in a lantern or other glass vessel, for it warms and brightens and shines through the vessel, that is, through a person who is good. It also reveals itself to a person who has it within himself, provided that he is careful in observing himself, and it reveals itself to others through him by means of his virtues and good example. This radiation of God's grace touches and moves a person promptly from within; this quick movement is the first thing which makes us able to see.

This same quick movement of God gives rise to the second prerequisite. This is from the person's side and consists in a gathering together of all his powers, from within and from without, in the unity of the spirit and the bond of love. The third thing which is necessary is freedom, so that without hindrance from sensible images a person can turn within as often as he wishes and as often as he thinks of his God. In other words, a person must be unattached to pleasure and pain, gain and loss, exaltation and humiliation, strange anxieties, and joy and fear, just as he must also not be bound to any creature.

These three things make a person able to see in interior exercises. If you possess them, then you have the foundation and the beginning of such exercises and of the interior life.

BIBLE SELECTION
Matthew 25:1–13

"Then the kingdom of heaven will be like this. Ten bridesmaids took their lamps and went to meet the bridegroom. Five of them were foolish, and five were wise. When the foolish took their lamps, they took no oil with them; but the wise took flasks of oil with their lamps. As the bridegroom was delayed, all of them became drowsy and slept. But at midnight there was a shout, 'Look! Here is the bridegroom! Come out to meet him.' Then all the bridesmaids got up and trimmed their lamps. The foolish said to the wise, 'Give us some of your oil, for our lamps are going out.' But the wise replied, 'No! there will not be enough for you and for us; you had better go to the dealers and buy some for yourselves.' And while they went to buy it, the bridegroom came, and those who were ready went with him into the wedding banquet; and the door was shut. Later the other bridesmaids came also, saying, 'Lord, lord, open to us.' But he replied, 'Truly I tell you, I do not know you.' Keep awake therefore, for you know neither the day nor the hour."

DISCUSSION QUESTIONS

The following can be used for discussion within a small group, or used for journal reflections by individuals:

1. In what ways am I conscious of such a gracious turning of the will in my own relationship to God? Explain.
2. In what ways can I relax into the love of God?

SUGGESTED EXERCISES

The following exercises can be done by individuals, shared between spiritual friends, or used in the context of a small group. Choose one or more of the following:

1. Ruusbroec discerned his call as one of solitude, spiritual discipline, and writing about spiritual experience in a time of social and religious unrest. Discuss whether you think we are living in a time of social and religious unrest and what we may feel guided to do because of the times we live in. Choose one of the suggestions as your exercise this week.

2. Discuss the ways that living a life of intimacy with the Father, Son, and Spirit allows us to consult God and be guided in our decisions, small and large. Though their roles cannot be sharply defined, try to determine where your guidance comes from in the next few days; write down your discoveries in a journal.

REFLECTIONS

Do not be disheartened if you found this Ruusbroec reading an uphill climb. He writes in an unfamiliar way and takes us places we are not used to going. A little unpacking of this selection may be helpful.

Ruusbroec begins with the three essential preparations for spiritual sight. In the background here is Jesus' observation that so many people are in such a spiritual condition that "seeing they do not see and hearing they do not hear," and he is helping us to overcome this spiritual blindness.

The three preparations he calls us to are these: first, the action of God's grace upon us as we seek him with an interior heart longing; second, a freeing of ourselves from outward attachments that would hinder an internal gaze of the soul upon God; and, third, the turning of our will toward God. These three—inward longing, detachment, and turning the will—are well recognized essentials in all the great devotional writers. We could only wish they were more common in the preaching and teaching of today.

Next Ruusbroec turns to a kind of ontology of the human person. He says that there are three essential realities about human beings: first, we live and breathe only because of the creating and sustaining power of God; second, the higher faculties of our ability to think (mind) and our ability to enter into relationship with God (spirit) are capacities given to us by the creative action of God; and, third, we are embodied spirits, that is, we are created in such a way that we express our spirituality through our bodies. Now, we today need much clearer thinking about an ontology of human beings, learning, for example, how the soul, body, mind, spirit, emotions, and will interact with each other. Ruusbroec is not a bad place to start.

Finally Ruusbroec helps us see that as we add "charity and an upright intention" to our lives we are enabled to "constantly practice the virtues by means of the power, richness, and impulse of grace." Let me restate what he is getting at here in as simple a way as I can: as we continually and lovingly press our will toward God the grace of God creates within us such an inward transformation of character that the moral virtues easily and naturally flow from us, in much the same way that beautiful music easily and naturally flows from an accomplished violinist. This is a goal worth our most earnest pursuit.

RICHARD J. FOSTER

GOING DEEPER

John Ruusbroec: The Spiritual Espousals and Other Works, edited by James A. Wiseman (New York: Paulist, 1985); a volume in *The Classics of Western Spirituality* series. This collection offers selections from *The Spiritual Espousals, The Sparkling Stone, A Mirror of Eternal Blessedness*, and *The Little Book of Clarification*. A prefatory essay by Louis Dupré, a philosopher of religion who is expert in mystical literature of the Low Countries, is also of value.

Ignatius Loyola

(1491–1556)

Ignatius Loyola is one of the most influential religious founders in Christian history. The religious order that he founded continues to have worldwide influence and is especially known for its work in education and spiritual formation.

Born at Casa de Torres in the province of Guipúzcoa, Spain, he became involved with affairs of court, first as a page and later as a courtier and soldier. Severely wounded in the defense of Pamplona (one leg was wounded and the other broken by cannon fire), Ignatius convalesced by reading the lives of saints and began to make bold resolves to live for Christ.

He went as a pilgrim to Montserrat and made an all-night vigil, vowing perpetual chastity and to live a spiritual life. During a long visit to the Dominicans at Manresa, he cared for the sick, did penance, and prayed for long times in a cave. There, beside the Cardoner River, he had a special experience of God.

Keeping a vow to visit the Holy Land, Ignatius got no farther than Jaffa because of the occupation of the Turks. He returned to studies (philosophy, theology, and Latin) in Barcelona, Salamanca, and Paris. Interrogated and imprisoned for his opinions and later released, he earned the M.A. in Paris in 1534.

By 1538 he had established a group of spiritual companions who took vows of poverty, chastity, obedience, and loyalty to Pope Paul III. By 1539 the pope gave spoken approval to his group (the Society of Jesus, informally known as Jesuits); solemn approval came the following year.

Other Jesuits were sent on long journeys while Ignatius remained at Rome, organizing, conducting vast correspondence, and doing apostolic work that included homes for orphans, catechumens, and penitent women. His *Spiritual Exercises* were approved by Paul III in 1538 and by his successor, Julius III, in 1550. In 1551 Ignatius opened the Roman College with an attendance of three hundred; the German College soon followed. His *Constitutions* had broad impact on religious life then and later. Obedience was fundamental, but medieval practices such as praying in choir (mandatory prayers chanted in common), wearing a fixed habit, and obligatory penances were done away with, leaving the Jesuits a freedom to enter into the contemporary scene. They could pray in private, say the Office rather than sing it, and wear the dress of the local clergy while traveling. Also, they could personalize their penetential practices, always under obedience to a confessor or superior.

Ignatius focused his energies on a spiritually renewed laity; his *Spiritual Exercises* were not to be read, but made, in intensive retreats pointed toward interior conversion. He himself was a contemplative, more taken up into mystical prayer as his life neared its end. Among his great contributions are the "Rules for the Discernment of Spirits," from which the following selection is taken.

THE SPIRITUAL EXERCISES

Rules for the Discernment of Spirits

Rules for distinguishing between different spiritual influences so that only good ones may be admitted, evil ones being rejected.

1. Those who go from mortal sin to mortal sin are usually influenced in this way: the enemy proposes certain illusory delights, causing them to imagine sensual pleasures and enjoyments, the more effectively to keep them under the sway of their vicious and sinful course. The good spirit deals with these same people in the opposite way, working on their consciences by reason to induce compunction and remorse.

2. The contrary prevails with those who are making earnest progress in self-purification, rising from good to better in the service of God our Lord. In these cases it is typical of the evil spirit to cause regret and sadness, using fallacious arguments to disturb them and impede their progress. On the other hand, the role of the good spirit is to provide courage and strength, to console and inspire, to move to tears, all in a spirit of peace. Everything is made easy, all obstacles are removed, to enable the soul to continue in virtue.

3. Spiritual comfort: this is the name I give to any interior movement experienced by the soul, causing it to glow with love for its Creator and Lord, the effect of which is that it can no longer love any earthly creature in itself, but only in the Creator of them all. The name also applies to the shedding of tears leading to love of God, either out of sorrow for sin or for the sufferings of Christ our Lord, or for other reasons directly concerned with His service and praise. Lastly, comfort is the name given to any growth in faith, hope or charity, or to any inward joy which summons or draws a man to the things of the next world, to the saving of his own soul, bringing the soul to peace and tranquillity in its Creator and Lord.

4. Spiritual distress: this is the name I give to whatever is opposite to the foregoing—darkness of soul, disquiet of mind, an attraction to what is coarse and earthly, all restlessness proceeding from different temptations and disturbances, such as the temptation tending to destroy faith, hope and charity; the condition in

which the soul finds itself listless, apathetic, melancholy, like one cut off from its Creator and Lord. Inasmuch as comfort and distress are opposed, the thoughts that spring from the former are contrary to those springing from the latter.

5. In a period of distress we are not to alter anything, but should remain firm and unyielding in our resolutions and the purpose of mind in which we found ourselves on the day preceding such distress, or in the purpose in which we found ourselves in the preceding comfort. For in times of comfort it is the good spirit that guides us by his counsel, whereas in distress it is the evil spirit; but the latter's counsel will never bring us to a right decision.

6. Though in principle we should not alter our previous resolutions in periods of distress, it is of great value to strive in a sense opposed to the distress; for instance by more insistence on prayer, meditation, close examination, and by making an effort to practice some appropriate penance.

7. When in distress, a man should reflect that God is testing him by leaving him to his own resources in his struggle against the different assaults and temptations of the enemy; he can succeed with the help of God, which is always there, even though he is not clearly aware of it. God has indeed withdrawn any great warmth of feeling, intensity of love and extraordinary grace, but He has left grace enough for the man's eternal salvation.

8. In this state he should also strive to abide in patience, which is the antidote to the trials that beset him. He should also reflect that he will soon be comforted, and should put forth all his efforts against this distress, as described in the sixth rule.

9. There are three chief reasons why we experience distress:

(a) Because we are listless, apathetic and careless in our spiritual exercises; it is on account of our own faults that our spiritual comfort is withdrawn.

(b) To test our worth, and to show how far we are able to advance in His service and praise without that great reward of comforts and extraordinary favours.

(c) To give us clear understanding and insight, to enable us to have a deep inner conviction that of ourselves we are powerless to produce or sustain a flood of devout feelings, intense love, tears or any other spiritual comfort, but that this is all a gratuitous gift of God our Lord. We are not, that is, to build on another's foundations, getting above ourselves in pride and empty boasting, claiming as our own the devout feelings or other features of spiritual comfort.

10. In a period of comfort a man should think about his conduct in the distress that will ensue, building up his strength afresh for that experience.

11.   When experiencing comfort he should be careful to keep himself humble and modest, recalling how worthless he is in time of distress, when he is without the favour of this comfort. Contrariwise, a man who is in a state of distress should reflect that he can do a great deal with the grace that is sufficient to withstand all his enemies, finding strength in his Creator and Lord.

12.   The enemy is like a woman, weak in face of opposition, but correspondingly strong when not opposed. In a quarrel with a man, it is natural for a woman to lose heart and run away when he faces up to her; on the other hand, if the man begins to be afraid and to give ground, her rage, vindictiveness and fury overflow and know no limit. In the same way, it is typical of the enemy to collapse and lose heart, his assaults turning tail, when a man who is training himself in spirituality faces up to the enemy's assaults, doing the precise opposite to what is suggested. On the other hand, if the retreatant begins to feel panic and to lose heart at these assaults, there is no animal on earth so savage as is the enemy of our human nature in the ever-growing malice with which he carries out his evil plan.

13.   He is also like a seducer in his desire to remain disguised and undetected. If that sort of schemer pays dishonourable court to the daughter of a good father or the wife of a good husband, he wants his words and suggestions not to be disclosed; he is greatly upset if the daughter or the wife tells the father or the husband about his deceitful words and his dishonourable purpose, since he easily recognizes that he will not then realize the plan he has embarked on.

So is it with the enemy of our human nature. When he introduces into a faithful soul his lying suggestions, he is very anxious that these should be accepted and kept secret. But he is far from pleased when their victim discloses them to a good confessor or someone else versed in spiritual matters, who is acquainted with the ill-disposed designs of the tempter, who then realizes that his wicked attempt must fail, once his obvious tricks are revealed.

14.   Or again he acts like a military commander in his attempts to overcome and seize the object he has set his heart on. An officer in command of an army takes up a position, makes a reconnaissance to discover the strength and disposition of troops in a fortified post and launches his attack at the weakest point. Similarly, the enemy of our human nature makes a tour of inspection of our virtues — theological, cardinal and moral. Where he finds us weakest and most defective in which pertains to our eternal salvation, he attacks at that point, seeking to overthrow us.

Greater discernment of spirits

Rules for the same purpose, with a more precise way of distinguishing between different spiritual influences . . .

1.   The characteristic effect produced by God and His angels in their spiritual operations is a genuine lightness of heart and spiritual joy, eliminating all the disturbing sadness engendered by the enemy, whilst his characteristic activity is to resist such lightness of heart and spiritual comfort, alleging specious reasons, subtle suggestions and sophistries without end.

2.   Spiritual comfort with no previous occasion giving rise to it comes from our Lord God alone. It is the Creator's prerogative to come into and leave the soul, to move it with inspirations of love for His Divine Majesty. "With no previous occasion" means without any preceding awareness or knowledge of anything which might induce such comfort in the soul, by means of its own acts of intellect and will.

3.   Granted some occasion, a sense of comfort may be produced in the soul either by the good angel or the bad one, though with opposing ends in view. The good angel has in view the soul's progress, that it may grow by advancing from what is good to what is better. The evil spirit, contrariwise, tries to draw it to his own perverted designs and wickedness of will.

4.   It is typical of the evil spirit to transform himself into an angel of light, to go in by the devout soul's way but to come out his own way; I mean he introduces sound and pious thoughts, suited to the piety of that soul; but then, little by little, he tries to achieve his own purposes, by dragging the soul down to his secret designs and corrupt purposes.

5.   We should pay great attention to the entire train of thought. If beginning, middle and end are wholly sound, tending to what is completely innocent, this is a sign of the good angel; but the train of thought suggested sometimes leads to something that is bad or at least distracting, or less good than what the soul had originally proposed to do; sometimes it undermines our strength of mind or disturbs us by destroying our peace and tranquillity of mind and the unperturbed condition already obtaining: these are clear signs that the thoughts come from the evil spirit, the enemy of our progress and everlasting salvation.

6.   When the enemy of mankind is perceived and known by his serpent's tail, the evil conclusion to which he leads men, the person so tempted will find it useful afterwards to retrace the course of his thoughts, beginning with the good ideas originally suggested and the way in which he was gradually brought down from the heights of spiritual satisfaction and joy to accept the other's corrupt purpose. The understanding and noting of this experience will help him to be on his guard in future against the enemy's usual tricks.

7.   When souls are advancing from good to better, the touch of the good angel is soft, light and gentle, like a drop of water making its way into a sponge. The touch of the evil angel is rough, accompanied by noise and disturbance, like a drop of water falling on stone. But their action is the opposite with those who are going from bad to worse. The reason is that the state of soul is either contrary or similar to these angels. When it is contrary they make their way in with perceptible noise and sensation; when it is similar they come in quietly, like a man coming into his own house when the door is open.

8.   When the comfort has no preceding occasion, whilst it is true that this cannot be illusory, since it can come only from God our Lord, as we have said, yet the spiritual recipient must scrutinize the process with great care. He must distinguish exactly the specific time of the actual comforting from the subsequent stage when the soul is still glowing with the favour conferred on it, a sort of afterglow from the comforting which is now over. In this second stage the soul often makes different resolutions and plans which are not the direct result of the action of God our Lord. They may be due to the soul's own activity, based on established habits of mind or the implications of ideas or judgements previously formed; they may be the result of the action of the good and evil spirit. So they have to be very carefully scrutinized before we can give them complete credit and put them into effect.

BIBLE SELECTION
Psalm 91

You who live in the shelter of the Most High,
    who abide in the shadow of the Almighty,
will say to the LORD, "My refuge and my fortress;
    my God, in whom I trust."
For he will deliver you from the snare of the fowler
    and from the deadly pestilence;
he will cover you with his pinions,
    and under his wings you will find refuge;
    his faithfulness is a shield and buckler.
You will not fear the terror of the night,
    or the arrow that flies by day,
or the pestilence that stalks in darkness,
    or the destruction that wastes at noonday.

A thousand may fall at your side,
   ten thousand at your right hand,
   but it will not come near you.
You will only look with your eyes
   and see the punishment of the wicked.

Because you have made the LORD your refuge,
   the Most High your dwelling place,
no evil shall befall you,
   no scourge come near your tent.

For he will command his angels concerning you
   to guard you in all your ways.
On their hands they will bear you up,
   so that You will not dash your foot against a stone.
You will tread on the lion and the adder,
   the young lion and the serpent you will trample under foot.

Those who love me, I will deliver;
   I will protect those who know my name.
When they call to me, I will answer them;
   I will be with them in trouble,
   I will rescue them and honor them.
With long life I will satisfy them,
   and show them my salvation.

DISCUSSION QUESTIONS

The following can be used for discussion within a small group, or used for journal reflections by individuals:

1. What times of distress or desolation have I had? How have I reacted?
2. What responses should I have to times of comfort or consolation? What would help me with this?

SUGGESTED EXERCISES

The following exercises can be done by individuals, shared between spiritual friends, or used in the context of a small group. Choose one or more of the following:

1. If someone in the group is facing a major decision or is faced with a large difficulty and feels comfortable bringing it before the group, let the discussion apply Ignatius's rules of discernment to the question at hand.
2. Discuss, or write in your journal about, a big life decision that seemed hard to make. What struggles accompanied that decision? Were you able to wait for the influence of the "good angel" that Ignatius mentions?

REFLECTIONS

Of all the literature on the discernment of spirits I think Ignatius of Loyola is the very best. He is so wise, so clear, so direct. It makes me wonder about the experiences necessary for such clarity—the extended prayer times in that cave near the Cardoner River perhaps? Whatever and whenever Ignatius's experiences we can be deeply grateful for the help these "rules for the discernment of spirits" can give us as we seek to distinguish the movement of God upon the soul from that of Satan and his minions.

Most of these counsels of Ignatius are so straightforward and clear that you need no explanation or commentary from me. As you read you will know almost immediately how to apply them to given situations. Hence these three general observations will suffice.

First, notice the contrasts he draws between the spiritual comforts that come from God and the spiritual distresses that come from the enemy (other translations call them "consolations" and "desolations"). The comforts are characterized by things like peace and clarity, quietness and inward joy. The distresses, on the other hand, are characterized by things like confusion and restlessness, hopelessness and apathy. You might put it this way: God draws and encourages, Satan pushes and condemns. The difference is palpable.

Second, watch for how many of Ignatius's counsels are simply good common sense. For example: when we are in the midst of spiritual distress we should never change a decision or resolution. Or consider this one: when we are in the light (spiritual comfort) we should plan out how we will handle ourselves when we are in the dark (spiritual distress). All good, practical, soul counsel.

Third, let his metaphors and analogies delight and instruct you. For example: Satan is like a false lover who always tries to hide his motives, or like a military leader who is always looking for the point of greatest weakness in his adversary. Or, this gem of a contrast: "the touch of the good angel is soft, light, and gentle, like a drop of water making its way into a sponge. The touch of the evil angel is rough, accompanied by noise and disturbance, like a drop of water falling on a stone."

RICHARD J. FOSTER

GOING DEEPER

The Spiritual Exercises of St. Ignatius, edited and translated by Anthony Mottola, foreword by Robert W. Gleason (New York: Doubleday, 1989). These spiritual exercises are designed to be administered in a retreat setting over a four-week period. However, an attentive reading of them can be of great benefit in understanding the approach of Ignatius and his followers.

JOSEPH A. TETLOW, *Ignatius Loyola, Spiritual Exercises* (New York: Crossroad, 1992); a volume in the *Spiritual Legacy* series. Still another treatment (and translation) of Ignatius's renowned exercises. Tetlow's introduction has a rousing account of Ignatius's life.

WILLIAM A. BARRY, *Finding God in All Things: A Companion to the Spiritual Exercises of St. Ignatius* (Notre Dame, IN: Ave Maria, 1991). This book of reflections on the spiritual teachings of Ignatius Loyola is an excellent treatment by a noted Jesuit spiritual director and retreat leader.

PHILIP CARAMAN, *Ignatius Loyola: A Biography of the Founder of the Jesuits* (San Francisco: Harper & Row, 1990). Caraman is a fine writer, and this account of the life of Ignatius has both depth and breadth.

G. K. Chesterton

(1874–1936)

———

Gilbert Keith Chesterton was a writer, journalist, illustrator, and Christian apologist. Born in London to an artistic and literary middle-class family, he attended London's Slade School of Art and later studied English literature at University College, London.

Chesterton's work changed noticeably as his thought matured. At first he was a romantic, intuitive writer. Work from this early period he later repudiated and destroyed.

Chesterton married Frances Blogg in 1901. During this period he gained notoriety as a journalist-illustrator, contributing extensively to the *Daily News*, the *Illustrated London News*, and *G. K.'s Weekly*. Soon he was famous, a large man easily recognized by eccentric dress: a cape, a sombrero, and a sword stick.

As thousands of provocative essays poured from his pen, Chesterton moved into Christian apologetics, defending orthodox Christian belief with book-length arguments. His beliefs were utterly traditional; his methods of argument fresh and original.

By 1914, exhausted by his own productivity, Chesterton was almost routed by a breakdown; he was hit hard in 1918 by the death of his brother Cecil. In 1922, Chesterton became a Roman Catholic.

Though his work is neither formal nor scholarly, he is considered a profound thinker. Besides his prolific writing, Chesterton also gave weekly radio broadcasts in his later years. In 1936 the Roman Catholic Church named him "Defender of the Faith."

In the following selection, "Enjoying the Floods and Other Disasters," which appeared in the July 21, 1906, issue of the *Illustrated London News*, Chesterton characteristically uses humor to invite us into a more childlike and trusting faith.

THE ILLUSTRATED LONDON NEWS

Enjoying the Floods and Other Disasters

I feel an almost bitter envy on hearing that London has been flooded in my absence, while I am in the mere country. [An exceptional rainfall in London on June 30, over two inches in twenty-four hours, caused serious floods there and in nearby counties.] My own Battersea has been, I understand, particularly favoured as a meeting of the waters. Battersea was already, as I need hardly say, the most beautiful of human localities. Now that it has the additional splendour of great sheets of water there must be something quite incomparable in the landscape (or waterscape) of my own romantic town. Battersea must be a vision of Venice. The boat that brought the meat from the butcher's must have shot along those lanes of rippling silver with the strange smoothness of the gondola. The greengrocer who brought cabbages to the corner of the Latchmere Road must have leant upon the oar with the unearthly grace of the gondolier. There is nothing so perfectly poetical as an island; and when a district is flooded it becomes an archipelago.

The joy of inconveniences

Some consider such romantic views of flood or fire slightly lacking in reality. But really this romantic view of such inconveniences is quite as practical as the other. The true optimist who sees in such things an opportunity for enjoyment is quite as logical and much more sensible than the ordinary "Indignant Ratepayer" who sees in them an opportunity for grumbling. Real pain, as in the case of being burnt at Smithfield [where the Protestant martyrs were burned during the reign of Queen Mary] or having a toothache, is a positive thing; it can be supported, but scarcely enjoyed. But, after all, our toothaches are the exception, and as for being burnt at Smithfield, it only happens to us at the very longest intervals. And most of the inconveniences that make men swear or women cry are really sentimental or imaginative inconveniences—things altogether of the mind.

Waiting for a train

For instance, we often hear grown-up people complaining of having to hang about a railway station and wait for a train. Did you ever hear a small boy complain of having to hang about a railway station and wait for a train? No; for to him to be inside a railway station is to be inside a cavern of wonder and a palace of poetical pleasures. Because to him the red light and the green light on the signal are like a new sun and a new moon. Because to him when the wooden arm of the signal falls down suddenly, it is as if a great king had thrown down his staff as a signal and started a shrieking tournament of trains. I myself am of little boys' habit in this matter. They also serve who only stand and wait for the two fifteen. Their meditations may be full of rich and fruitful things; and many of the most purple hours of my life have been passed at Clapham Junction, which is now, I suppose, under water. I have been there in many moods so fixed and mystical that the water might well have come up to my waist before I noticed it particularly. But in the case of all such annoyances, as I have said, everything depends upon the emotional point of view. You can safely apply the test to almost every one of the things that are currently talked of as the typical nuisance of daily life.

We are comic creatures

For instance, there is a current impression that it is unpleasant to have to run after one's hat. Why should it be unpleasant to the well-ordered and pious mind? Not merely because it is running, and running exhausts one. The same people run much faster in games and sports. The same people run much more eagerly after an uninteresting little leather ball than they will after a nice silk hat. There is an idea that it is humiliating to run after one's hat; and when people say it is humiliating they mean that it is comic. It certainly is comic; but man is a very comic creature, and most of the things he does are comic—eating for instance. And the most comic things of all are exactly the things that are most worth doing—such as making love. A man running after a hat is not half as ridiculous as a man running after a wife.

Hat-hunting on a windy day

Now a man could, if he felt rightly in the matter, run after his hat with the manliest ardour and the most sacred joy. He might regard himself as a jolly huntsman pursuing a wild animal, for certainly no animal could be wilder. In fact, I am inclined to believe that hat-hunting on windy days will be the sport of the upper classes in the future. There will be a meet of ladies and gentlemen on some high ground on a gusty morning, who will be told that the professional attendants have started a hat in such-and-such a thicket, or whatever be the technical term. Notice that this employment will in the fullest degree combine sport with humanitarianism; it will soothe the consciences of many who will find themselves conscientiously unable to join in what they considered more cruel sports. The runaway hat has all the tantalizing and even demoniac qualities of a living enemy. The hat can double like a hare. The hat can leap like a stag. The hat can turn to bay like a lion. But while its pursuers will thus have all the fierce cunning and violent variety of the chase, they would not have the feeling that they were actually inflicting pain; for modern philosophers are all agreed that hats have no feelings; though modern philosophers know nothing whatever about the matter, any more than about most others. Still, the hunters would feel that they were not inflicting pain. Nay, they would feel that they were inflicting pleasure, rich, almost riotous pleasure, upon the people who were looking on. When last I saw an old gentleman running after his hat in Hyde Park, I told him that a heart so benevolent as his ought to be filled with peace and thanks at the thought of how much unaffected pleasure his every gesture and bodily attitude were at that moment giving to the crowd.

A *jammed drawer*

The same principle can be applied to every other typical domestic worry. A gentleman trying to get a fly out of the milk or a piece of cork out of his glass of wine often imagines himself to be irritated. Let him think for a moment of the patience of anglers sitting by dark pools, and let his soul be immediately irradiated with gratification and repose. Again, I have known some people of very modern views driven by their distress to the use of theological terms to which they attached no doctrinal significance, merely because a drawer was jammed tight and they could not pull it out. A friend of mine was particularly afflicted in this way. Every day his drawer was jammed, and every day in consequence it was something else that rhymes to it. But I pointed out to him that this sense of wrong was really subjective and relative; it rested entirely upon the assumption that the drawer could, should, and would come out easily. "But if," I said, "you picture to yourself that you are pulling against some powerful and oppressive enemy, the struggle will become merely exciting and not exasperating. Imagine that you are tugging up a life-boat out of the sea. Imagine that you are roping up a fellow-creature out of an Alpine crevass. Imagine even that you are a boy again and engaged in a tug-of-war between French and English." Shortly after saying this I left him; but I have no doubt at all that my words bore the best possible fruit. I have no doubt that every day of his life he hangs on to the handle of that drawer with a flushed face and eyes bright with battle, uttering encouraging shouts to himself, and seeming to hear all round him the roar of an applauding ring.

Inconvenience rightly considered

So I do not think that it is altogether fanciful or incredible to suppose that even the floods in London may be accepted and enjoyed poetically. Nothing beyond inconvenience seems really to have been caused by them; and inconvenience, as I have said, is only one aspect, and that the most unimaginative and accidental aspect of a really romantic situation. An adventure is only an inconvenience rightly considered. An inconvenience is only an adventure wrongly considered. The water that girdled the houses and shops of London must, if anything, have only increased their previous witchery and wonder. For as the Roman Catholic priest in the story said: "Wine is good with everything except water," and on a similar principle, water is good with everything except wine. Last week may be said to have exhibited teetotalism on a gigantesque scale. To have water, water everywhere, and not a drop to drink seems to me to put that element exactly to its proper use. The whole human race has exhibited as one consistent principle the principle that those who saw most of the water drank least of it. Fishermen, sailing men, divers, and all others have always acted upon the idea that there might be any amount of water outside them, but none inside them.

A *poetical event*

The actual impression of the tempest must have been something almost recalling the Flood. It would have been very impressive if an enormous ark could have been built on the top of Piccadilly (let us say) and all the beasts fit for sacrifice could have gone up two by two and entered into the ark. London cabhorses, one would instinctively think, are beasts fit for sacrifice. London cabmen, in the opinion of many persons, are beasts fit for sacrifice or, at any rate, beasts fit for something. And as for cab-owners, the Marquesses and other wealthy persons who own cabs, it would seem on the first impression that they simply cry out for the sacrificial knife. But to suppose this is to misunderstand the original principle of sacrifice. The beast fitted for sacrifice must be spotless, healthy, and perfect; this seldom applies to the cab-horse, not often to the cabman, and never (for all practical purposes) to the man in the cab. . . .

I will not, however, carry too far the comparison with the original Deluge. I will not suggest that the people in the ark should send out a postman (let us say) who should not return, and then send out a policeman who should return with a branch of olive in his mouth. I will not suggest that in future ages children will have little arks of wood made to commemorate the event, with little wooden figures of spotted cab-horses and brightly coloured County Councillors. It is enough for me that this was in all probability the most poetical event that has happened for a long time in the London that I love; since it is out of the area of great earthquakes. And it is enough for me, it is far too much for me (it has broken my heart), that I was not there to see it.

BIBLE SELECTION
Matthew 8:23–27

And when he got into the boat, his disciples followed him. A windstorm arose on the sea, so great that the boat was being swamped by the waves; but he was asleep. And they went and woke him up, saying, "Lord, save us! We are perishing!" And he said to them, "Why are you afraid, you of little faith?" Then he got up and rebuked the winds and the sea; and there was a dead calm.

They were amazed, saying, "What sort of man is this, that even the winds and the sea obey him?"

DISCUSSION QUESTIONS

The following can be used for discussion within a small group, or used for journal reflections by individuals:

1. How can I best be guided by unusual or exceptional events? What does it take to see such situations as benevolent?
2. Must religious experience be always a solemn affair? What funny episodes have been connected to my relationship with God?

SUGGESTED EXERCISES

The following exercises can be done by individuals, shared between spiritual friends, or used in the context of a small group. Choose one or more of the following:

1. Make a list of the funniest people you can think of: comedians, film personalities, personal friends, cartoonists, or cartoon characters. What might these people have to say to us about spiritual life in accordance with God's grace?
2. Tell stories about storms, floods, power failures, and such. Were any of these incidents actually pleasant affairs?

REFLECTIONS

By now you may be wondering what in the world this Chesterton reading has to do with the spiritual discipline of guidance. For that matter you may be wondering what it has to do with the spiritual life at all! It feels like he is giving us aimless ramblings on the "inconveniences" of a London flood, of waiting in a railway station, chasing silk hats, jammed drawers, a fly in your milk, a piece of cork in your wine. You may ask, "What is the point of it all?" Oh, I assure you there is a point to it, a very definite point.

If I could borrow a phrase from St. Paul to encapsulate Chesterton's point, "I want you to be free from anxieties" (1 Cor. 7:23). But, of course, the point is not exactly the point. I mean, just to say "do not be anxious" is not nearly as much fun as Chesterton saying, "I have known some people of very modern views driven by their distress to the use of theological terms to which they attached no doctrinal significance, merely because a drawer was jammed tight and they could not pull it out. A friend of mine was particularly afflicted in this way. Every day his drawer was jammed, and every day in consequence it was something else that rhymes to it."

Part of the delight in this selection is the journey Chesterton takes us on in arriving at the point. It is a journey that pokes fun at our foibles, that laughs in the face of our grim earnestness, that teases us out of our seriousness. You see, it is an occupational hazard of religious people to take life (and themselves) far too seriously. This is because life is serious business: heaven and hell are serious matters; sin and repentance and obedience are serious concerns. But, "Be not anxious" is the way we are to deal with all of life's seriousness. Frankly, most of the "momentous issues" we face in our daily living are not in the least momentous. Most of the time whether a decision goes this way or that makes little difference; our lives will go on. To be sure, there are decisive moments and genuinely tragic events, but they are much fewer than we imagine. So Chesterton, in his inimitable way, is inviting us to relax, enjoy the little "inconveniences" of our days, and rest easy in the God who has the whole world in his hands.

RICHARD J. FOSTER

GOING DEEPER

G. K. Chesterton's principal works of Christian apologetic are *Orthodoxy* (1908), *The Everlasting Man* (1925), and *The Catholic Church and Conversion* (1926). The first two of these make every argument for Christian orthodoxy, and no direct argument for Roman Catholic belief. It is possible that Chesterton was influenced toward Roman Catholicism because of the widespread prejudice against it, as in his own famous saying, "It is impossible to be just to the Catholic Church . . . The moment [people] try to be fair to it they begin to be fond of it" (*Collected Works*, Vol. 3, *The Catholic Church and Conversion* [San Francisco: Ignatius, 1990], p. 92). His religious biographies are also quite worthwhile: *St. Francis of Assisi* (1923) and *St. Thomas Aquinas* (1933). His fiction includes fairy tales, fantastic novels (among these *The Man Who Was Thursday* [1908]), and a detective fiction series, *The Father Brown Stories* (collected 1929).

Celebration

———

Christina Rossetti

(1830–1894)

Christina Rossetti, an English poet, was the daughter of a distinguished Italian political exile who became Professor of English at King's College, London. Her brother, Dante Gabriel Rossetti, more famous than she, was also a poet and a painter. They lived in a time of high creativity in which the religious imagination often furnished material for artistic and literary works. A devout High Anglican who engaged in many charitable works, Rossetti wrote a large number of poems, although she was a semi-invalid for much of her life.

The Nativity is the theme of the poem that follows. Notice how vividly Rossetti sets the scene, a wintry setting worthy of an English Christmas. She is intense and visionary, looking beyond the first Christmas to the Lord's second coming, "when he comes to reign." Her contrasts are steep and wide, as they are in Mary's Magnificat (Luke 1:46–55). Heaven and earth are always in tension; riches and poverty, and God's triumphant power revealed in a small and humble space—these high contrasts of the Infancy Narratives become this poet's material as well.

Rossetti's intense spirituality comes most forcefully in the last verse, which by itself stands as a wonderful prayer of Christmas celebration and joy.

A CHRISTMAS CAROL

In the bleak mid-winter
  Frosty wind made moan,
Earth stood hard as iron,
  Water like a stone;
Snow had fallen, snow on snow,
  Snow on snow,
In the bleak mid-winter
  Long ago.

Our God, Heaven cannot hold him,
  Nor earth sustain;
Heaven and earth shall flee away
  When he comes to reign:

In the bleak mid-winter
  A stable-place sufficed
The Lord God Almighty
  Jesus Christ.

Enough for him whom cherubim
  Worship night and day,
A breastful of milk
  And a mangerful of hay;
Enough for him whom angels
  Fall down before,
The ox and ass and camel
  Which adore.

Angels and archangels
  May have gathered there,
Cherubim and seraphim
  Thronged the air,
But only his mother
  In her maiden bliss
Worshipped the Beloved
  With a kiss.

What can I give him,
  Poor as I am?
If I were a shepherd
  I would bring a lamb,
If I were a wise man
  I would do my part—
Yet what I can I give him,
  Give my heart.

BIBLE SELECTION
Luke 2:1–20

In those days a decree went out from Emperor Augustus that all the world should be registered. This was the first registration and was taken while Quirinius was governor of Syria. All went to their own towns to be registered.

Joseph also went from the town of Nazareth in Galilee to Judea, to the city of David called Bethlehem, because he was descended from the house and family of David. He went to be registered with Mary, to whom he was engaged and who was expecting a child. While they were there, the time came for her to deliver her child. And she gave birth to her firstborn son and wrapped him in bands of cloth, and laid him in a manger, because there was no place for them in the inn.

In that region there were shepherds living in the fields, keeping watch over their flock by night. Then an angel of the Lord stood before them, and the glory of the Lord shone around them, and they were terrified. But the angel said to them, "Do not be afraid; for see—I am bringing you good news of great joy for all the people: to you is born this day in the city of David a Savior, who is the Messiah, the Lord. You will find a child wrapped in bands of cloth and lying in a manger." And suddenly there was with the angel a multitude of the heavenly host, praising God and saying,

> "Glory to God in the highest heaven,
>   and on earth peace among those whom he favors!"

When the angels had left them and gone into heaven, the shepherds said to one another, "Let us go now to Bethlehem and see this thing that has taken place, which the Lord has made known to us." So they went with haste and found Mary and Joseph, and the child lying in the manger. When they saw this, they made known what had been told them about this child; and all who heard it were amazed at what the shepherds told them. But Mary treasured all these words and pondered them in her heart. The shepherds returned, glorifying and praising God for all they had heard and seen, as it had been told them.

DISCUSSION QUESTIONS

The following can be used for discussion within a small group, or used for journal reflections by individuals:

1. In what ways can I apply the story of the birth of Jesus to my experience every day?
2. How do I celebrate the transformed order of salvation that God has brought about in Jesus Christ?

3. Notice how the poet expresses inadequacy when she says (at first) that she has little to give the Christ child. Are there times when I share her sense of inadequacy? Is this a good or a bad thing?

SUGGESTED EXERCISES

The following exercises can be done by individuals, shared between spiritual friends, or used in the context of a small group. Choose one or more of the following:

1. Have each member of the group assemble some materials that depict the Nativity. Perhaps, for this session, someone can provide a Christmas crèche or stable scene. Reflect on the power of this much-celebrated scene. What does it say to us about the meaning of God's grace?
2. Tell stories about your personal encounters with the poor. Why should the poor circumstances in which Jesus comes to us become a cause of joy and rejoicing? What does his poverty say to us?
3. Sing familiar Christmas carols. Don't plan which ones you will sing ahead of time, just sing the ones everybody knows. Rejoice in the feeling of fellowship that springs up in the group.
4. Play a Christmas tape or CD, and use the time for prayer and meditation.

REFLECTIONS

The Christian Christmas story is filled with a wonder and an enchantment that makes our modern embellishments pale by comparison. All our plastic Santa Clauses and reindeer icons, all our flashing tinsel decorations, all our champagne-laden office parties—they all crumple in a heap whenever we try to wrap our mind around the miracle of God come in the flesh.

Christina Rossetti's poem gives us the Christmas story in all its stark magnificence: "A stable-place sufficed" . . . "A breastful of milk" . . . "a mangerful of hay" . . . "The ox and ass and camel." Next, she adds not plastic paraphernalia but the celestial realities we glimpse so faintly: angels and archangels, cherubim and seraphim, all in heavenly celebration. Then Rossetti does something startling, something I like a lot. Immediately after lifting us up into the panoramic heights of heaven's worship she moves in close and frames our vision with a single scene; a mother's worshipful kiss upon a newborn Child.

With such dazzling realities all around Rossetti recognizes her own poverty, and we see it in us too. What can she give him? Only her heart. Us too.

But, now, we must ask ourselves: How do we in our circumstances give Jesus our heart? What intentions and plans might it involve? What decisions might we make? What actions might we take? Good queries not just on Christmas day but on every day.

RICHARD J. FOSTER

GOING DEEPER

CHRISTINA GEORGINA ROSSETTI, *Poems,* selected and arranged by Kathleen Jarris (New York: Philosophical Library, 1956). Rossetti has tremendous skill as a poet with a strong lyrical quality and spiritual force even when her subject is not precisely religious. This collection shows us Christina's range: ballads, love lyrics, sonnets, and religious verse.

Frederick Buechner

(1926–)

———

Frederick Buechner, an ordained Presbyterian minister, is the author of more than twenty celebrated works of fiction and nonfiction. His later work, especially, reflects the importance to him of Christian faith. His novels, including *Godric* and *Brendan*, often celebrate Christian themes in historical settings. He also writes fiction about modern life and its dilemmas, such as *The Book of Bebb*. Many people have been helped by Buechner's memoirs, in which he reveals his own faith struggles. Among these are *Sacred Journey, Telling Secrets*, and *A Room Called Remember*.

In *Peculiar Treasures: A Biblical Who's Who*, Buechner provides a number of cameo treatments of biblical figures, often with a very amusing and lighthearted tone. They are treated in alphabetical order, everyone from Aaron to Zacchaeus.

"What struck me more than anything else as I re-acquainted myself with this remarkable rag-bag of people," Buechner writes, "was both their extraordinary aliveness and their power to make me feel more alive myself for having known them. Even across all the centuries, they still have the power to bring tears to the eyes and send shivers up the spine. And more besides." He also expresses a hope that the book will be as much fun to read as it was for him to write it.

In the following selection, which is taken from *Peculiar Treasures*, Buechner allows us to appreciate some of the humor of the biblical story—humor that is inherent in the story itself, but that the author emphasizes in his retelling. Besides being "a fun read," this selection allows us to delight in God's way with human beings. It helps us to practice the discipline of celebration.

PECULIAR TREASURES

Sarah's Laughter

Quantitatively speaking, you don't find all that much laughter in the Bible, but, qualitatively, there's nothing quite like it to be found anywhere else. There are a couple of chapters in the Book of Genesis that positively shake with it. Sarah was never going to see ninety again, and Abraham had already hit one hundred, and when the angel told them that the stork was on his way at last, they both of them almost collapsed. Abraham laughed "till he fell on his face" (Gen. 17:17), and Sarah stood cackling behind the tent door so the angel wouldn't think she was being rude as the tears streamed down her cheeks. When the baby finally came, they even called him Laughter—which is what Isaac means in Hebrew—because obviously no other name would do.

Laughter mixed up in the Bible
Laughter gets mixed up with all sorts of things in the Bible and in the world too, things like sneering, irony, making fun of, and beating the competition hollow. It also gets mixed up with things like comedians and slipping on banana peels and having the soles of your feet tickled. There are times when you laugh to keep from crying like when the old wino staggers home in a party hat, or even in the midst of crying like when Charlie Chaplin boils his shoe for supper because he's starving to death. But one hundred percent, bonded, aged-in-the-wood laughter is something else again.

Making merry till the cows come home
It's the crazy parrot-squawks that issue out of David as he spins like a top in front of the Ark (2 Sam. 6:16–21).

It's what the psalms are talking about where they say, "When the Lord had rescued Zion, then our mouth was filled with laughter" (Ps. 126:1–2), or where they get so excited they yell out, "Let the floods clap their hands, let the hills sing for joy together!" because the Lord has come through at last (Ps. 98:8).

It's what the Lord himself is talking about when he says that on the day he laid the cornerstone of the earth "the morning stars sang together, and all the sons of God shouted for joy" (Job 38:7), and it's what the rafters ring with when the Prodigal comes home and his old crock of a father is so glad to see him he almost has a stroke and "they began to make merry" and kept on making merry till the cows came home (Luke 15:24).

Blessed laughter
It's what Jesus means when he stands in that crowd of cripples and loners and odd-balls and factory rejects and says, "Blessed are you that weep now, for you shall laugh" (Luke 6:21).

Nobody claims there's a chuckle on every page, but laughter's what the whole Bible is really about. Nobody who knows his hat from home-plate claims that getting mixed up with God is all sweetness and light, but ultimately it's what that's all about too.

Ecstatic laughter

Sarah and her husband had plenty of hard knocks in their time, and there were plenty more of them still to come, but at that moment when the angel told them they'd better start dipping into their old age pensions for cash to build a nursery, the reason they laughed was that it suddenly dawned on them that the wildest dreams they'd ever had hadn't been half wild enough (Gen. 17, 18, 21).

BIBLE SELECTION
Genesis 17:1–9, 15–22; 18:1–15; 21:1–7

When Abram was ninety-nine years old, the LORD appeared to Abram, and said to him, "I am God Almighty; walk before me, and be blameless. And, I will make my covenant between me and you, and will make you exceedingly numerous." Then Abram fell on his face; and God said to him, "As for me, this is my covenant with you: You shall be the ancestor of a multitude of nations. No longer shall your name be Abram, but your name shall be Abraham; for I have made you the ancestor of a multitude of nations. I will make you exceedingly fruitful; and I will make nations of you, and kings shall come from you. I will establish my covenant between me and you, and your offspring after you throughout their generations, for an everlasting covenant, to be God to you and to your offspring after you. And I will give to you, and to your offspring after you, the land where you are now an alien, all the land of Canaan, for a perpetual holding; and I will be their God."

God said to Abraham, "As for you, you shall keep my covenant, you and your offspring after you throughout their generations. . . ."

God said to Abraham, "As for Sarah your wife, you shall not call her Sarai, but Sarah shall be her name. I will bless her, and moreover I will give you a son by her. I will bless her, and she shall give rise to nations; kings of peoples shall come from her." Then Abraham fell on his face and laughed, and said to himself, "Can a child be born to a man who is a hundred years old? Can Sarah, who is ninety years old, bear a child?" And Abraham said to God, "O that Ishmael might live in your sight!" God said, "No, but your wife Sarah shall bear you a son, and you shall name him Isaac. I will establish my covenant with him as an everlasting covenant for his offspring after him. As for Ishmael, I have heard you; I will bless him and make him fruitful and exceedingly numerous; he shall be the father of twelve princes, and I will make him a great nation. But my covenant I will establish with Isaac, whom Sarah shall bear to you at this season next year." And when he had finished talking with him, God went up from Abraham.

The LORD appeared to Abraham by the oaks of Mamre, as he sat at the entrance of his tent in the heat of the day. He looked up and saw three men standing near him. When he saw them, he ran from the tent entrance to meet them, and bowed down to the ground. He said, "My lord, if I find favor with you, do not pass by your servant. Let a little water be brought, and wash your feet, and rest yourselves under the tree. Let me bring a little bread, that you may refresh yourselves, and after that you may pass on—since you have come to your servant." So they said, "Do as you have said." And Abraham hastened into the tent to Sarah, and said, "Make ready quickly three measures of choice flour, knead it, and make cakes." Abraham ran to the herd, and took a calf, tender and good, and gave it to the servant, who hastened to prepare it. Then he took curds and milk and the calf that he had prepared, and set it before them, and he stood by them under the tree while they ate.

They said to him, "Where is your wife Sarah?" And he said, "There, in the tent." Then one said, "I will surely return to you in due season, and your wife Sarah shall have a son." And Sarah was listening at the tent entrance behind him. Now Abraham and Sarah were old, advanced in age, it had ceased to be with Sarah after the manner of women. So Sarah laughed to herself, saying "After I have grown old, and my husband is old, shall I have pleasure?" The LORD said to Abraham, "Why did Sarah laugh, and say, 'Shall I indeed bear a child, now that I am old?' Is anything too wonderful for the Lord? At the set time I will return to you, in due season, and Sarah shall have a son." But Sarah denied, saying, "I did not laugh"; for she was afraid. He said, "Oh yes, you did laugh."

The LORD dealt with Sarah as he had said, and the LORD did for Sarah as he had promised. Sarah conceived and bore Abraham a son in his old age, at the time of which God had spoken to him. Abraham gave the name Isaac to his son whom Sarah bore him. And Abraham circumcised his son Isaac when he was eight days old, as God had commanded him. Abraham was a hundred years old when his son Isaac was born to him. Now Sarah said, "God has brought laughter for me; everyone who hears will laugh with me." And she said, "Who would ever have said to Abraham that Sarah would nurse children? Yet I have borne him a son in his old age."

DISCUSSION QUESTIONS

The following can be used for discussion within a small group, or used for journal reflections by individuals:

1. What aspects of my life do I grieve about? Which ones do I celebrate?
2. How can my predicaments and confusing moments become a source of delight and celebration?

SUGGESTED EXERCISES

The following exercises can be done by individuals, shared between spiritual friends, or used in the context of a small group. Choose one or more of the following:

1. Have members of the group tell their "funniest Bible stories." Were there some Bible stories that we misunderstood as children? Have our children made us laugh about biblical things in ways we didn't think possible?
2. Identify Bible stories or passages (not necessarily funny ones) that deal especially with gladness and rejoicing, such as Acts 8:26–39; 3:1–9; Luke 10:1–12,17–20; Philippians 4:4. Read one or two of these stories during the coming days.

REFLECTIONS

Do any of us really wonder why Abraham and Sarah laughed at the heavenly announcement of a child-to-be? We would laugh too; laugh in disbelief, laugh at the absurdity of it all. The Scripture tells us, "It had ceased to be with Sarah after the manner of women." That was a polite way of saying she was no longer ovulating. Now, they may not have had all the vast medical information we have at our fingertips on conception and birth, but they knew enough to say with confidence that Sarah could not have a child. No way.

But then we hear the query that is as much for us as it is for Abraham and Sarah: "Is anything too wonderful for the Lord?" Well, there we have it. I mean, when it is put that way we have no option but to agree; yes, indeed, nothing is too wonderful for the Lord! But even so . . .

You see, we also laugh in disbelief because, like Abraham and Sarah, we are so often living in and counting on the "flesh." The flesh says very simply, "I will rely *upon what I can do in my own natural abilities and strengths without any reference to God." And, may I just say, many things can be done in the power of the flesh. I have seen whole churches built in the power of the flesh. But <u>we cannot do the work of the Spirit in the power of the flesh, and Isaac was a work of the Spirit.</u>*

But, now comes the great reversal for Abraham and Sarah. They had laughed in disbelief, but now, with baby Isaac in their presence, they are ushered into the laughter of celebration. Sarah, we are told, exclaims, "God has brought laughter for me; everyone who hears will laugh with me" (Gen. 21:6). <u>The laughter of doubt was transformed into the laughter of praise. The latter laughter is the better laughter.</u>

RICHARD J. FOSTER

GOING DEEPER

FREDERICK BUECHNER, *Peculiar Treasures: A Biblical Who's Who* (San Francisco: HarperSanFrancisco, 1993).

FREDERICK BUECHNER, *Son of Laughter* (San Francisco: HarperSanFrancisco, 1994). In this short work of fiction Buechner retells the story of Jacob with a light touch and in a humorous way.

W. DALE BROWN, *Of Fiction and Faith: Twelve American Writers Talk About Their Vision and Their Work* (Grand Rapids: Eerdmans, 1997). See Chapter 2, "Frederick Buechner: Doubt and Faith," an interview in which Buechner describes how faith animates him as a writer, why he avoids the term "Christian writer," and how Scripture has formed him in his writing.

Pierre Teilhard de Chardin

(1881–1955)

———

Pierre Teilhard de Chardin was born in Sarcenat, France (the province of Auvergne); child of a devout Catholic family, he entered the Jesuits in 1899, studied in the United Kingdom (Jersey and Hastings), and was ordained in 1911.

He had met two major figures in paleontology and fixed on this for his life's work, earning a doctorate from the Sorbonne in Paris. Teilhard also served as a stretcher bearer in Morocco during World War I.

His work as a paleontologist led to worldwide travels: Central Asia, India, Burma. After 1946 he worked principally in New York and Paris.

Teilhard was known for two kinds of writing.

First was his scientific writing, in which he proposed a large-scale theory of cosmic life ascending through humanity toward an ultimate Omega Point, or ending, in Jesus Christ. Needless to say, his joining of the physical and spiritual realms was controversial. He was prevented by his religious superiors from accepting a professorship at the College of France in 1948; his work did not receive an imprimatur, or approval by the Roman Catholic Church for publication. Teilhard gracefully accepted these setbacks; much of his writing remained to be published after his death. His scientific views have been questioned, but his fidelity to Christ, never.

His second sort of writing was spiritual treatises. Among these *The Divine Milieu* and the *Hymn of the Universe* are especially well known.

In the selection that follows, taken from a collection of essays entitled *On Love and Happiness*, Teilhard is giving a sermon at the marriage of a couple who have been raised in different parts of the world: Asia and France.

Notice how he celebrates that by alluding often to world traveling: journeys, discoveries, navigation. Always, his thoughts are focused on Jesus Christ.

ON LOVE AND HAPPINESS

At the Wedding of Odette Bacot and Jean Teilhard d'Eyry
(14 June 1928)

Mademoiselle, my dear Jean,

When I look at you both here, united for all time, my old professional habits reassert themselves, and I cannot help glancing back at the two roads—your two roads—which for so long seemed to be independent of one another, have just suddenly converged, and here and now, in a moment, are about to run as one. And you will not be surprised that, presented with a meeting so unexpected and yet prepared for so long, I am filled with wonder and joy, as though I were witnessing another of life's triumphs.

Your road, Jean, began far from here, under the heavy clouds of the tropics, in the flat paddy-fields enclosed by the blue silhouette of Cape Saint-Jacques. It called for nothing less than this vigorous mixture of cold Auvergne and the Far East worthily to continue in you a fearless, far-ranging mother, and that legendary "Uncle Georges," too. When I was only a child, I used occasionally to gaze with admiration at his face, beside the already whitehaired grandmother, in that rather dark, and half-Chinese, drawing room in the Rue Savaron.

By tradition, and by birth, you are of Asia; and that is why, from time to time, you have gone back to Asia to breathe in its quality.

Journeys of heart and mind

But what are these journeyings of the heart and mind? Only you could draw up that itinerary, the stages and detours through which your being had to travel before the emergence in the end of the man you are today. At home, as a young cadet, everywhere, what influences were at work, what meetings came about, what attractions were felt, what choices made! . . . How slender the fibers in the web from which our lives are suspended!

Finally, having found your way through the shifting labyrinth of external and internal forces, you have succeeded in finding your soul. In this inner domain (for it is within you much more than outside you) to which life has brought you, are you not going to find yourself alone and lost? Men are crowded together and have to force their way along our roads, metaled or earthen; even in the skies they are already beginning to find themselves cramped. But in the thousand times vaster and more complex domain of the mind, each one of us, the more he is human (and therefore unique), the more he is condemned by his very success to wander, endlessly lost. You might well have feared, Jean, that where such a succession of chances had driven your ship no other vessel, except by some even greater chance, would be found.

When two minds meet

And it was then, Mademoiselle, in that very habitation of souls in which it seemed impossible that two beings should find one another, that you, like the princess in a fairy story, quite naturally appeared. That, among some thousands of human beings, the eyes of two individuals should meet is in itself a remarkable and precious coincidence: what, then, can we say when it is two minds that meet?

While you, Jean, were engaged in the long circumnavigation during which the real core of every living creature—its power to love—was maturing within you, you, Mademoiselle, were following a different curve, the rhythm of whose approach was nevertheless wonderfully harmonized; and so the two of you were passing through those successive cycles whose culmination we are witnessing here today.

Through your family origins you, too, blossomed on a stem whose roots lie deep in one of France's ancient provinces—Touraine instead of Auvergne—which has about it something warmer and gentler; and, to crown this, you had that finishing touch which only the atmosphere of Paris can give. From your childhood you, too, learned to revere that same historic academy and the exact science of honorable warfare. In a circle of three children—which included yet another Jacqueline—with an exceptional mother, you, too, received that generously liberal upbringing, firmly based on Christian principles, which has given so wonderfully harmonious a balance to your development. And so it was—with how astonishing a symmetry in your destinies—that, without realizing it, you were gradually moving towards your meeting with the man who, in equal ignorance, was moving towards you.

What brought them together

I referred, a moment ago, to fairy tales. Who was the fairy who, without ever breaking her thread, worked alone to weave today into one perfect whole the double web of your two lives?

Was it only chance that blindly worked this miracle? Must we really resign ourselves to believing that the value of the loveliest things around us depends simply on what is unpredictable, unusual, and in consequence impermanent, in the confluence of the elements from which they seem to us to have emerged?

True enough, there are days when the world appears to be one vast chaos. Great, indeed, is the confusion; so great that if we look at ourselves we may very well reel with dizziness at the prospect of our very existence. With such heavy odds against us, is it not most improbable that we should find ourselves whole and entire, and living—as single individuals, let alone as two? We wonder, then, whether true wisdom may not consist in holding on to every chance that comes our way, and immediately drawing all we can from it. It would be madness, surely, to take any further risk with the future and to strive after a life that is even more improbable because even more elevated.

For years now, Jean, my work has been such that every day of my life has necessarily been lived under the shadow of the improbability of life's successes. And once again it is this improbability which I meet today when I look at the happiness of both of you together.

So: since you have asked me to speak today, allow me to tell you what, after a long confrontation with the splendid reality of the world, is my dearest and most profound conviction. I began, like everyone else, by being impressed by the superior importance, among events, that must be accorded to what comes lower down the scale, and to the past. Then, unless I was to cease to understand anything that goes on within me or around me, I was obliged to shift my point of view and accord absolute supremacy to the future and the greater.

The energies of the soul

No, I believe what gives the universe around us its consistence is not the apparent solidity of the ephemeral materials from which bodies are made. Rather is it the flame of organic development which has been running through the world since the beginning of time, constantly building itself up. With all its weight behind it, the world is being impelled upon a center which lies ahead of it. Far from being impermanent and accidental, it is souls, and alliances of souls, it is the energies of souls, that alone progress infallibly, and it is they alone that will endure.

What is imponderable in the world is greater than what we can handle.

What radiates from living beings is more valuable than their caresses.

What has not yet come is more precious than what is already born.

That is why what I want to say to you now, Jean—what I want to say to both of you—is this:

"If you want, if both of you want, to answer the summons (or respond to the grace, for that is the better word) which comes to you today from God-animated life, then take your stand confidently and unhesitatingly on tangible matter; take that as an indispensable bulwark—but, through and above that matter, put your faith in the bulwark of the intangible."

Put your faith in the spirit that lies behind you; by that I mean the long series of unions similar to your own which throughout the ages have accumulated, to pass on to you, a great store of healthy vigor, of wisdom and of freedom. Today this treasure is entrusted to your keeping. Remember that you are responsible for it to God and the universe.

Life prolonging itself

Put your faith, then, in the spirit that lies ahead of you. Creation never comes to a halt. It is through you two that life seeks to prolong itself. Your union, therefore, must not be a self-enclosed embrace; let it express itself in that deliberate act, infinitely more unifying than any inactivity, which consists in an effort directed towards one and the same, ever-greater, passionately loved, goal.

And finally, in a phrase that sums up all the rest, put your faith in the spirit which dwells between the two of you. You have each offered yourself to the other as a boundless field of understanding, of enrichment, of mutually increased sensibility. You will meet above all by entering into and constantly sharing one another's thoughts, affections, dreams, and prayer. There alone, as you know, in spirit which is arrived at through the flesh, you will find no surfeit, no disappointments, no limits. There alone the skies are ever open for your love; there alone lies the great road ahead.

At this very moment can you not feel this spirit, to which I am urging you, concentrating upon you; can you not feel its mantle spread over you?

The united love of so many kinsfolk and friends gathered together, the warmth and purity of wishes transmitted, through some subtle medium, from Auvergne, from Touraine or Poitou, and from the Côte d'Argent, too; the blessings sent by those whom we no longer see; and above all the infinite tenderness of Him who sees in you two, forming one, the welding of one more precious link in his great work of creative union.

In very truth, grander than the external, material ceremonial which surrounds and honors you, it is the accumulated forces of an invisible loving-kindness which fill this church.

I pray that this spiritual ardor may come down upon your nascent love, and preserve it for eternal life. Amen.

BIBLE SELECTION
Isaiah 61:10–11

I will greatly rejoice in the LORD,
  my whole being shall exult in my God;
for he has clothed me with the garments of salvation,
  he has covered me with the robe of righteousness,

as a bridegroom decks himself with a garland,
    and as a bride adorns herself with her jewels.
For as the earth brings forth its shoots,
    and as a garden causes what is sown in it to spring up,
so the Lord GOD will cause righteousness and praise
    to spring up before all the nations.

DISCUSSION QUESTIONS

The following can be used for discussion within a small group, or used for journal reflections by individuals:

1. Are there important meetings that have especially changed our lives for the better or have led us into good paths? How do we celebrate those?
2. What has been the role in our faith lives of family and national origins? How can we observe and celebrate that influence?

SUGGESTED EXERCISES

The following exercises can be done by individuals, shared between spiritual friends, or used in the context of a small group. Choose one or more of the following:

1. Remember and tell stories about wedding celebrations. Are these sometimes surprising events? Reflect on grace as a way of confronting the unexpected.
2. Describe an experience of foreign travel, or friendship with a person from a foreign country, and how it has affected your attitude.
3. Organize a gathering of friends or family. Celebrate your commonalities and differences.

REFLECTIONS

I first met Pierre Teilhard de Chardin through The Phenomenon of Man, *that breathtaking journey through the history and insights of paleontology that ultimately emerges into "Omega Point"—the intensely unified "hyper-personal" community of persons brought about by means of "Christogenesis." I was especially intrigued by the introduction by Sir Julian Huxley, like Teilhard a man of science but far removed from Teilhard's religious convictions. Then came* The Future of Man *and* The Divine Milieu. *I will leave it to your imagination to consider the extent (small, I assure you) that I understood of those sweeping intellectual adventures.*

I say all of this to underscore what a delight and pleasure it is to have this wedding sermon, which places such an intimate face upon such a towering intellect. What a carefully crafted, individualized wedding sermon! It is a refreshing contrast to the Xerox weddings of today. And I am not just referring to those fly-by-night weddings made famous by the Las Vegas advertisers. In our churches, even our best churches, when was the last time you heard such a preciously personalized sermon?

It is so very appropriate, this sermon by Teilhard. Marriage is the commitment of a lifetime, demanding careful preparation, loving nurture, and dogged determination. Such radical and permanent commitment deserves a wedding sermon that shares these same qualities. It makes me wish I could have slipped into a back pew during that wedding so long ago, just to feel "the accumulated forces of an invisible loving-kindness which fill this church." But, then, in a way I have.

RICHARD J. FOSTER

GOING DEEPER

Pierre Teilhard de Chardin's short works of spiritual reflection are rich with insight and invite the reader into prayer. Among the best are *The Divine Milieu* and *Hymn of the Universe*. Another very accessible work by Teilhard is *Letters from a Traveller*, which includes many letters to his cousin, Marguerite Teillard-Chambon [*sic*], who was his great spiritual friend.

DORAN MCCARTY, *Teilhard de Chardin* (Waco, TX: Word Books, 1976). A Baptist scholar and theologian summarizes the life's work of Pierre Teilhard de Chardin, critiques his thought, and describes his spirituality.

John Henry Newman

(1801–1890)

———

John Henry Newman's *Parochial and Plain Sermons* originally ran to eight volumes, though they are now available in one. They were preached when Newman was an Anglican, from the pulpit of the Church of St. Mary the Virgin, in Oxford, on Sundays and feast days. Most of the Christian themes that Newman would explore over his lifetime are treated in these sermons, which show his intellectual power, his poetic streak, and his moral and spiritual backbone.

It is worth noting that in his later years Newman avoided the kind of religious partisanship that he thought might give offense to the Church of England. When other Roman Catholics wanted him to take the lead in founding a Catholic college at Oxford, Newman was not eager to do so. Oxford University was the bastion of Anglicanism; Newman did not want to appear to be baiting the Anglicans. By now Catholic students were readily entering the various Oxford colleges, and certain religious biases against Roman Catholics were beginning to fade. Newman did not want to prolong that misery.

Although a great part of his contribution to thought and ideas came out of religious controversy, it seems likely that the role of controversialist was thrust upon him. Newman's great preoccupation was with the truths of Christianity as he saw them.

He worried more about skepticism and what we would now call secularism than about the differences between Protestants and Catholics.

In the following selections, which are taken from *Parochial and Plain Sermons*, Newman helps us to practice the discipline of celebration. The first, "Religious Joy," is a Christmas sermon (Book 8, Sermon 17); the second, "Christ, a Quickening Spirit," is an Easter sermon (Book 2, Sermon 13). Notice how Newman urges us to be cheerful and good-tempered and continually reminds us that the knowledge of our salvation should help us in this. God's love, he suggests, should "sweep away the vexations of life by its own richness and strength."

Sometimes, he suggests, our rejoicing should be sober and subdued. Even then, our peace and joy will be even fuller because of that seriousness.

For more about Newman's personal life story, see the "Introduction to the Author," which appears on page 62.

PAROCHIAL AND PLAIN SERMONS

Religious Joy

> "And the angel said unto them, Fear not: for, behold, I bring you good tidings of great joy, which shall be to all people. For unto you is born this day in the city of David a Saviour, which is Christ the Lord." (Luke 2:10–11)

There are two principal lessons which we are taught on the great Festival which we this day celebrate, lowliness and joy. This surely is a day, of all others, in which is set before us the heavenly excellence and the acceptableness in God's sight of that state which most men have, or may have, allotted to them, humble or private life, and cheerfulness in it. If we consult the writings of historians, philosophers, and poets of this world, we shall be led to think great men happy; we shall be led to fix our minds and hearts upon high or conspicuous stations, strange adventures, powerful talents to cope with them, memorable struggles, and great destinies. We shall consider that the highest course of life is the mere pursuit, not the enjoyment of good.

But when we think of this day's Festival, and what we commemorate upon it, a new and very different scene opens upon us. First, we are reminded that though this life must ever be a life of toil and effort, yet that, properly speaking, we have not to seek our highest good. It is found, it is brought near us, in the descent of the Son of God from His Father's bosom to this world. It is stored up among us on earth. No longer need men of ardent minds weary themselves in the pursuit of what they fancy may be chief goods; no longer have they to wander about and encounter peril in quest of that unknown blessedness to which their hearts naturally aspire, as they did in heathen times. The text speaks to them and to all, "Unto you," it says, "is born this day in the city of David a Saviour, which is Christ the Lord."

Nor, again, need we go in quest of any of those things which this vain world calls great and noble. Christ altogether dishonoured what the world esteems, when He took on Himself a rank and station which the world despises. No lot could be more humble and more ordinary than that which the Son of God chose for Himself.

So that we have on the Feast of the Nativity these two lessons—instead of anxiety within and despondence without, instead of a weary search after great things,—to be cheerful and joyful; and, again, to be so in the midst of those obscure and ordinary circumstances of life which the world passes over and thinks scorn of. . . .

Great joy

"Fear not," said the Angel, "for behold I bring you good tidings of great joy, which shall be to all people. For unto you is born this day in the city of David a Saviour, which is Christ the Lord." And then, when he had finished his announcement, "suddenly there was with the Angel a multitude of the heavenly host, praising God and saying, Glory to God in the highest, and on earth peace, good will towards men." Such were the words which the blessed Spirits who minister to Christ and His Saints, spoke on that gracious night to the shepherds, to rouse them out of their cold and famished mood into great joy; to teach them that they were objects of God's love as much as the greatest of men on earth; nay more so, for to them first He had imparted the news of what that night was happening. His Son was then born into the world. Such events are told to friends and intimates, to those whom we love, to those who will sympathize with us, not to strangers. How could Almighty God be more gracious, and show His favour more impressively to the lowly and the friendless, than by hastening (if I may use the term) to confide the great, the joyful secret to the shepherds keeping watch over their sheep by night?

The Angel then gave the first lesson of mingled humility and joyfulness; but an infinitely greater one was behind in the event itself, to which he directed the shepherds, in that birth itself of the Holy Child Jesus. This he intimated in these words: "Ye shall find the babe wrapped in swaddling clothes, lying in a manger." Doubtless, when they heard the Lord's Christ was born into the world, they would look for Him in kings' palaces. They would not be able to fancy that He had become one of themselves, or that they might approach Him; therefore the Angel thus warned them where to find Him, not only as a sign, but as a lesson also.

Great mystery

"The shepherds said one to another, Let us now go even unto Bethlehem, and see this thing which is come to pass, which the Lord hath made known to us." Let us too go with them, to contemplate that second and greater miracle to which the Angel directed them, the Nativity of Christ. St. Luke says of the Blessed Virgin, "She brought forth her first-born Son, and wrapped Him in swaddling clothes, and laid Him in a manger." What a wonderful sign is this to all the world, and therefore the Angel repeated it to the shepherds: "Ye shall find the babe wrapped in swaddling clothes, lying in a manger." The God of heaven and earth, the Divine Word, who had been in glory with the Eternal Father from the beginning, He was at this time born into this world of sin as a little infant. He, as at this time, lay in His mother's arms, to all appearance helpless and powerless, and was wrapped by Mary in an infant's bands, and laid to sleep in a manger. The Son of God Most High, who created the worlds, became flesh, though remaining what

He was before. He became flesh as truly as if He had ceased to be what He was, and had actually been changed into flesh. He submitted to be the offspring of Mary, to be taken up in the hands of a mortal, to have a mother's eye fixed upon Him, and to be cherished at a mother's bosom. A daughter of man became the Mother of God—to her, indeed, an unspeakable gift of grace; but in Him what condescension! What an emptying of His glory to become man! and not only a helpless infant, though that were humiliation enough, but to inherit all the infirmities and imperfections of our nature which were possible to a sinless soul. What were His thoughts, if we may venture to use such language or admit such a reflection concerning the Infinite, when human feelings, human sorrows, human wants, first became His? What a mystery is there from first to last in the Son of God becoming man! Yet in proportion to the mystery is the grace and mercy of it; and as is the grace, so is the greatness of the fruit of it. . . .

Rejoice in the Lord

Take these thoughts with you, my brethren, to your homes on this festive day; let them be with you in your family and social meetings. It is a day of joy: it is good to be joyful—it is wrong to be otherwise. For one day we may put off the burden of our polluted consciences, and rejoice in the perfections of our Saviour Christ, without thinking of ourselves, without thinking of our own miserable uncleanness; but contemplating His glory, His righteousness, His purity, His majesty, His overflowing love. We may rejoice in the Lord, and in all His creatures see Him. We may enjoy His temporal bounty, and partake the pleasant things of earth with Him in our thoughts; we may rejoice in our friends for His sake, loving them most especially because He has loved them.

"God has not appointed us unto wrath, but to obtain salvation through our Lord Jesus Christ, who died for us, that whether we wake or sleep, we should live together with Him" (1 Thess. 5:9–10). Let us seek the grace of a cheerful heart, an even temper, sweetness, gentleness, and brightness of mind, as walking in His light, and by His grace. Let us pray Him to give us the spirit of ever-abundant, ever-springing love, which overpowers and sweeps away the vexations of life by its own richness and strength, and which above all things unites us to Him who is the fountain and the centre of all mercy, loving kindness, and joy.

Christ, a Quickening Spirit

O blessed day of the Resurrection, which of old time was called the Queen of Festivals, and raised among Christians an anxious, nay contentious diligence duly to honour it! Blessed day, once only passed in sorrow, when the Lord actually rose, and the disciples believed not; but ever since a day of joy to the faith and love of the Church!

In ancient times, Christians all over the world began it with a morning salutation. Each man said to his neighbour, "Christ is risen"; and his neighbour answered him, "Christ is risen indeed, and hath appeared unto Simon."

Even to Simon, the coward disciple who denied Him thrice, Christ is risen; even to us, who long ago vowed to obey Him, and have yet so often denied Him before men, so often taken part with sin, and followed the world, when Christ called us another way. "Christ is risen indeed, and hath appeared to Simon!" to Simon Peter the favoured Apostle, on whom the Church is built, Christ has appeared.

Christ dispenses blessings

He has appeared to His Holy Church first of all, and in the Church He dispenses blessings, such as the world knows not of.

Blessed are they if they knew their blessedness, who are allowed, as we are, week after week, and Festival after Festival, to seek and find in that Holy Church the Saviour of their souls! . . .

But we, who trust that so far we are doing God's will, inasmuch as we are keeping to those ordinances and rules which His Son has left us, we may humbly rejoice in this day, with a joy the world cannot take away, any more than it can understand.

Truly, in this time of rebuke and blasphemy, we cannot but be sober and subdued in our rejoicing; yet our peace and joy may be deeper and fuller even for that very seriousness. For nothing can harm those who bear Christ within them. Trial or temptation, time of tribulation, time of wealth, pain, bereavement, anxiety, sorrow, the insults of the enemy, the loss of worldly goods, nothing can "separate us from the love of God, which is in Christ Jesus our Lord" (Rom. 8:30).

Christ within us

This the Apostle told us long since; but we, in this age of the world, over and above his word, have the experience of many centuries for our comfort. We have his own history to show us how Christ within us is stronger than the world around us, and will prevail. We have the history of his fellow-sufferers, of all the Confessors and Martyrs of early times and since, to show us that Christ's arm "is not shortened, that it cannot save"; that faith and love have a real abiding-place on earth; that, come what will, His grace is sufficient for His Church, and His strength made perfect in weakness; that, "even to old age, and to hoar hairs, He will carry and deliver" her; that, in whatever time the powers of evil give challenge, Martyrs and Saints will start forth again, and rise from the dead, as plentiful as though they had never been before, even "the souls of them that were beheaded for the witness of Jesus, and for the Word of God, and which had not worshipped the beast, neither his image, neither had received his mark upon their foreheads, or in their hands" (Rev. 20:4).

Meantime, while Satan only threatens, let us possess our hearts in patience; try to keep quiet; aim at obeying God, in all things, little as well as great; do the duties of our calling which lie before us, day by day; and "take no thought for the morrow, for sufficient unto the day is the evil thereof" (Matt. 6:34).

BIBLE SELECTION
1 Peter 1:3–9

Blessed be the God and Father of our Lord Jesus Christ! By his great mercy he has given us a new birth into a living hope through the resurrection of Jesus Christ from the dead, and into an inheritance that is imperishable, undefiled, and unfading, kept in heaven for you, who are being protected by the power of God for a salvation ready to be revealed in the last time. In this you rejoice, even if now for a little while you have had to suffer various trials, so that the genuineness of your faith—being more precious than gold that, though perishable, is tested by fire—may be found to result in praise and glory and honor when Jesus Christ is revealed. Although you have not seen him, you love him; and even though you do not see him now, you believe in him and rejoice with an indescribable and glorious joy, for you are receiving the outcome of your faith, the salvation of your souls.

DISCUSSION QUESTIONS

The following can be used for discussion within a small group, or used for journal reflections by individuals:

1. Are there some specific ways that we as Christians can keep our spirits up and remain cheerful, even in difficult times?
2. How can I cultivate a "festival spirit" on ordinary days?

SUGGESTED EXERCISES

The following exercises can be done by individuals, shared between spiritual friends, or used in the context of a small group. Choose one or more of the following:

1. Describe the best things about Christmas. What are the events we associate with this time?
2. Name the customs associated with Easter that seem to capture the discipline of celebration.
3. Have a Christmas or an Easter celebration on any day or evening of the year. Play music associated with this time; offer refreshments. Are there any other customs, like almsgiving, that might be appropriate? Include them.

REFLECTIONS

It is instructive, isn't it, this juxtaposition of a Christmas sermon and an Easter sermon? Birth and resurrection—an interesting comparison and contrast.

Swaddling clothes and a manger are the symbols of Christ's birth. Powerful symbols. Remember the manger was a feeding trough for animals, and swaddling clothes were the poor's means of dressing and diapering their young. In these symbols God sanctified the ordinary, intertwined the sacred with the secular, wedded the spiritual to the material.

The symbol of the resurrection is an empty tomb. Interesting, isn't it, that even in the most explosive spiritual reality in human history God gives us a material sign, an empty tomb? Just like at Christmas.

But the contrasts are even more striking than the comparisons. Christmas is a condensation, Easter is a conquest. Christmas is a humbling, Easter is a triumph. These are not in opposition to each other, you understand, only the double rhythm of divine kenosis and dunamis.

Of the two festivals Easter is the greater. As Newman reminds us it used to be called "the Queen of Festivals." That is not to speak disparagingly of Christmas; it is only to remind us to keep our focus on the center of our faith. Christmas does not speak the final word of Christian witness. That word is reserved for Easter: "Christ is risen." He is risen indeed!

RICHARD J. FOSTER

GOING DEEPER

JOHN HENRY NEWMAN, *Parochial and Plain Sermons* (San Francisco: Ignatius, 1987). Many different times of feasting and celebration are touched on in this collection of Newman's Anglican sermons.

BRIAN MARTIN, *John Henry Newman: His Life and Work* (Mahwah, NJ: Paulist, 1990). This sympathetic study of Newman combines elements from his life story with a critical study of his accomplishments. The author, a lecturer at Oxford University, recreates the ambience that affected Newman. A number of black-and-white illustrations are included, along with a bibliography and index.

Readings for the Fifth Week

———

John Wesley

Hannah More

Frederick William Faber

Amy Carmichael

John Wesley

(1703–1791)

———

John Wesley is a key figure in the history of Christianity, a powerful force in evangelical Protestantism. With his brother Charles he began to pursue enthusiastic religious devotion during his teens and especially at Oxford University.

Ordained an Anglican minister, Wesley broke with Church of England custom by engaging in itinerant, outdoor preaching to large assemblies of poor, working-class people throughout the British Isles. His preaching tours took him (chiefly on horseback) more than a quarter of a million miles; he delivered forty thousand sermons, sparking an intense religious revival. His zeal came from a genuine depth of devotion, well described in his account of a personal experience on May 24, 1738.

In the evening I went very unwillingly to a [meeting] in Aldersgate Street, where one was reading Luther's preface to the *Epistle of the Romans*. About a quarter before nine, while he was describing the change which God works in the heart through faith in Christ, I felt my heart strangely warmed. I felt I did trust in Christ, Christ alone, for my salvation; and an assurance was given me that he had taken away *my* sins, even *mine*, and saved *me* from the law of sin and death.

This assurance Wesley found himself able to convey persuasively to many thousands of grateful souls, by urging them to <u>a complete reliance on the blood of Christ</u>.

In the following selection, which is taken from Chapter 3 of *The New Birth*, "The Firstfruits [*sic*] of the Spirit," notice that Wesley means to encourage us in dealing with our sinfulness. Note also how close he stays to Scripture texts in order to extend this assurance.

THE NEW BIRTH

The Firstfruits of the Spirit

Sins of infirmity

There is no condemnation for "sins of infirmity," as they are sometimes called, resulting from involuntary defects of our human finitude. Perhaps it is better instead to call them simply *"infirmities,"* or "human frailties," in order that we may not seem to lend legitimacy to sin, or to excuse it in any way by coupling it too directly with human finitude. Although "sin of infirmity" remains an ambiguous and somewhat dangerous expression, by it I mean primarily involuntary failings. One example would be saying something we believe to be true, though in fact it later proves to be false. Another example: hurting our neighbor without knowing or intending it, or even when we intended to do good. Although these are deviations from the holy, acceptable, and perfect will of God, yet they should not properly be called sins because they lack the element of being willed. Thus they do not add any guilt to the conscience of "those who are in Christ Jesus." They cause no alienation or breach between God and the faithful. They do not cloud the light of God's shining. They are in no way inconsistent with the general character of one who "walks not after the lower nature, but after the Spirit."

Unpreventable sins

There is no condemnation to believers for anything conceivable that is beyond their power to prevent. This refers both to inward attitudes and outward actions, both to doing something and to leaving something undone. For example, suppose the Lord's Supper is celebrated but you do not partake of it because of sickness—an omission indeed, but one you cannot help. There is here no condemnation and no guilt, because there is no choice. Paul writes: "Provided there is an eager desire to give, God accepts what a man has; he does not ask for what he has not" (2 Cor. 8:12). . . .

Sins of surprise

Then there are so-called sins of surprise; for example, when one who is usually patient speaks or acts in a way that violates the command to love the neighbor due to some sudden or violent temptation. These cases are far more difficult to analyze. It is not easy to fix a general rule concerning misdeeds of this sort. We cannot flatly say either that persons are or are not condemned for these types of highly uncharacteristic behavior. Whenever a believer is overtaken in a fault by surprise, however, there must be some degree of guilt proportional to the degree of concurrence of the will. In proportion as a sinful desire, word, or action is more or less voluntary, so we may suppose that God is more or less displeased; and there is more or less of a burden of guilt to bear.

If so, then there may be some "sins of surprise" that rightly elicit a sense of guilt and condemnation. Admittedly, in some instances our being surprised is due to some wilful and culpable neglect. Perhaps we could have been attentive to something that could have been prevented or shaken off before the temptation came. We might have been adequately forewarned that trials and dangers were at hand and yet have said in our hearts: "A little more slumber, a little more folding of the hands in rest." Suppose one later falls unaware into a trap that might easily have been avoided. Inattentiveness is hardly an excuse, for one might have foreseen and averted the danger. Falling, even by surprise, in such an instance as this is, in effect, a wilful sin and, as such, must expose the sinner to condemnation, both from God and from one's own conscience.

Sins of disobedience

On the other hand, there may be sudden assaults, either from the world or the god of this world, and frequently from our own distorted imaginings, which we did not, and hardly could have, foreseen. Believers who are weak in faith may be overcome by these assaults; they may become inordinately angry or think badly of others with only a very slight concurrence of the will. In such a case, God—who jealously cares for their souls—would undoubtedly show them that they have acted foolishly, in order to convince them that they had swerved away from the perfect law, from the mind which was in Christ. Consequently, they would feel grieved with a godly sorrow and lovingly ashamed before God. But they do not need to feel condemned. God does not charge them with folly, but has compassion, even "as a father has compassion on his children" (Ps. 103:12). This is why their hearts do not condemn them. For even in the midst of that sorrow and shame they can still say:

> God is indeed my deliverer.
> I am confident and unafraid;
> for the LORD is my refuge and defence
> and has shown himself my deliverer.
> And so you shall draw water with joy
> from the springs of deliverance (Isa. 12:2).

You of little faith

It is fitting that we try to draw some practical inferences from all this.

Why are you afraid of your past? For there is now no condemnation of past sins "for those who are united with Christ Jesus" (Rom. 8:1), when the "law of the Spirit has set you free" (Rom. 8:1). O you of little faith! Even though your sins were once more in number than the sand, so what? You are now in Christ Jesus! "Who will be the accuser of God's chosen ones? It is God who pronounces acquittal; then who can condemn?" (Rom. 8:33).

All the sins you have committed from your childhood right up to the moment when you were "accepted as his sons through Jesus Christ" (Eph. 1:5) are driven away as chaff. They are gone. They are lost. They are swallowed up. They are remembered no more. You are now "born" from spirit (John 3:6). Why are you afraid? Why be troubled even about what happened before you were born? Throw away your fears! "For the spirit that God gave us is no craven spirit, but one to inspire strength, love, and self-discipline" (2 Tim. 1:7). Know your calling! Rejoice in God your Savior and give thanks to God your Father through Him.

How Christ frees us

Some will say, "But I have once again done serious wrongs, even after receiving this redemption. I seem like a lost cause. I still feel deep remorse." It is fitting that you feel a proportional remorse after doing wrong. For it is God who has awakened this very feeling in you. But you are now invited to transcend it in trust. Hasn't the Spirit also enabled you to say, "But in my heart I know that my vindicator lives, and that he will rise last to speak in court" (Job 19:25); and "the life I now live is not my life, but the life which Christ lives in me; and my present bodily life is lived by faith in the Son of God" (Gal. 2:20). It is that faith that cancels all that is past, and in it there is no condemnation. At whatever time you truly believe in the name of the Son of God, all your sins prior to that time vanish like the morning dew. "Christ set us free, to be free men. Stand firm, then, and refuse to be tied to the yoke of slavery again" (Gal. 5:1). Christ has once again made you free from the power of sin, as well as from its guilt and punishment. So do not become entangled again in the yoke of bondage—its twisted desires, distorted emotions, its vile words and works, the most desperate bondage this side of hell. Refuse to be caught again in bondage to slavish, tormenting fear or self-condemning guilt. . . .

Look inward, honestly

There is no condemnation for any inward sin still remaining in those who "walk by the Spirit." Even though sin may seem to cling tenaciously to everything we do, we are not guilty as long as we do not give way to it. So do not be disturbed because some ungodly imaginations remain in your heart. Do not feel dejection because you still come short of the glorious image of God; or because pride, self-will, or unbelief cling to all your words and works. Do not be afraid to face candidly all these distortions of your heart. Know yourself as you are known. Desire fervently of God that you may not think more highly of yourself than you ought to think. Let your continuous prayer be:

> Show me, as my soul can bear,
>> The depth of inbred sin;
> All the unbelief declare,
>> The pride that lurks within.

As God hears your prayer, he will let you see your heart. Then he will show you in entirety the spirit to which you belong. Then take care that your faith does not fail you, or that your protection is not torn from you. Now you are free to see yourself quite openly even at your lowest, to be humbled in the dust, to see yourself as nothing, less than nothing, and empty. At that very moment you may still "set your troubled hearts at rest, and banish your fears" (John 14:27). Remember that you, even you, have an Advocate "with the Father, Jesus Christ, and he is just" (1 John 2:1). Hold fast to the recollection that "as the heaven stands high above the earth" (Ps. 103:11), so is God's love higher even than my sins.

God is merciful

God is merciful to you, a sinner! Precisely the sinner you are! God is love, and Christ has died! That means: the Father himself loves you! You are his child! God will not withhold from you anything that is for your good. Is it not good that the whole body of sin, which is now crucified in you, should be destroyed? It shall be done! You shall be cleansed "from all that can defile flesh or spirit" (2 Cor. 7:1). Is it not good that nothing should remain in your heart but the pure love of God alone? Take joy in all of this. "Love the Lord your God with all your heart, with all your soul, with all your mind, and with all your strength"; and "love your neighbor as yourself" (Mark 12:30, 31). Stand firm in the "conviction of his power to do what he had promised" (Rom. 4:21). It is your part patiently to continue in the work of faith and the labor of love, in cheerful peace, humble confidence, and with calm and accepting, but fervent, expectation, to wait until the zeal of the Lord of hosts shall perform this work in you.

Leap and walk

If those who are "in Christ" and "walk in the Spirit" are not condemned for sins of infirmity or for involuntary failings or for anything they are unable to prevent, then take care, all you who have newly born faith in God's mercy, that you do not just at this point give the devil a huge advantage. You are still unformed and weak, lacking in clear insight and deep knowledge. You are more vulnerable than words can express, more prone to error than you can imagine. For you do not yet understand faith as fully as you intend. So do not let this weakness and untested judgment, or any of its fruits which you are not yet able to avoid, shake your basic faith, your filial trust in God, or disturb your peace or joy in the Lord. The very idea that sin must be willed can itself be dangerously misapplied, so it is wiser and safer if it is applied only to the case of weakness and infirmities.

If you have stumbled, O seeker of God, do not just lie there fretting and bemoaning your weakness! Patiently pray: "Lord, I acknowledge that every moment I would be stumbling if you were not upholding me." And then get up! Leap! Walk! Go on your way! "Run with resolution the race" in which you are entered (Heb. 12:1).

Just love God

My last point: Even if you find yourself for a moment to your amazement doing exactly what your soul otherwise detests, this is still not reason to feel overburdening guilt. Let us hope that your being surprised is not due to your own carelessness or wilful neglect. If, while you believe, you are suddenly overtaken in a fault, then let the Lord immediately hear your cry of grief. It will then be felt by you as a healing ointment. Pour out your heart before God. Declare your trouble. Pray with all your might to God who is fully able "to sympathize with our weaknesses" (Heb. 4:15). God wants to establish, strengthen, and settle your soul and not allow you to fall again; but, meanwhile, God is not harshly disapproving of you. So why should you be afraid? You have no reason to fall into the grip of the fear that "brings with it the pains of judgment" (1 John 4:18).

Just love God who loves you. That is sufficient. The more deeply you love, the stronger you will feel. And as soon as you have learned to love God with all your heart, "if you give fortitude full play you will go on to complete a balanced character that will fall short in nothing" (James 1:4). Wait in peace for that hour when "God himself, the God of peace," will "make you holy in every part, and keep you sound in spirit, soul, and body, without fault when Our Lord Jesus Christ comes" (1 Thess. 5:23)!

BIBLE SELECTION
1 John 2:12–14

I am writing to you, little children,
  because your sins are forgiven on account of his name.
I am writing to you, fathers,
  because you know him who is from the beginning.
I am writing to you, young people,
  because you have conquered the evil one.
I write to you, children,
  because you know the Father.
I write to you, fathers,
  because you know him who is from the beginning.
I write to you, young people,
  because you are strong
  and the word of God abides in you,
    and you have overcome the evil one.

DISCUSSION QUESTIONS

The following can be used for discussion within a small group, or used for journal reflections by individuals:

1. What dangers might there be in becoming overconfident about our salvation?
2. How can I be confident of God's forgiveness and still maintain an appropriate sense of sin?

SUGGESTED EXERCISES

The following exercises can be done by individuals, shared between spiritual friends, or used in the context of a small group. Choose one or more of the following:

1. Arrange a definite time to review your recent actions. If you find some wrongdoing, seek forgiveness and make amends.
2. Make a list of your past sins. Decide whether one or more of them continues to worry you. If God has forgiven you, do you need to forgive yourself?

Consider doing the following in private, at a whiteboard or blackboard. Write a brief description of the worrisome sin or sins, and then erase the board vigorously. Thank God for sins forgiven, and make a fresh start.

REFLECTIONS

It is so refreshing to read someone who takes sin seriously as a subject about which we can actually have knowledge. Most today, even among religious leaders, avoid the subject like the plague. And those who do talk about it usually do so only to rail against it. Here we have someone who deals with sin as a body of knowledge and who further believes that guidance can be given on how to deal with both the sin nature and the habits of sin.

The distinction Wesley is making between "sins of infirmity," "sins of surprise," "sins of disobedience," and so forth has to do with gradations of intention, human will, and voluntary choice. This is an ancient distinction but one that is little understood today. It is not understood for two reasons: first, we today lack a proper ontology of the human person, hence we do not know how the will fits into the overall makeup of personality, and, second, we deny volition on all sides. The last thing we want today is to be responsible for our intents and actions, and so we merely deny the function of the will and our ability to take up a freely chosen course of action for our lives. I think Wesley's option holds out more promise for successful living.

Did you notice the great pastoral care Wesley gives throughout this selection? He helps people understand the failures and shortcomings that should not be considered sin proper and relieves people of excessive guilt over those matters. And even in areas where sin is recognized for what it is and dealt with, he is so very pastoral: "God wants to establish, strengthen, and settle your soul and not allow you to fall again; but, meanwhile, God is not harshly disapproving of you. So why should you be afraid? You have no reason to fall into the grip of the fear that 'brings with it the pains of judgment' (1 John 4:18)."

RICHARD J. FOSTER

GOING DEEPER

John and Charles Wesley: Selected Writings and Hymns, edited by Frank Whaling (New York: Paulist, 1981); a volume in *The Classics of Western Spirituality* series. This book has excellent selections from the work of John Wesley and a number of the texts of Charles Wesley's hymns, as well as good historical and biographical background on both.

The New Birth, edited by Thomas C. Oden (San Francisco: Harper & Row, 1984). This book includes five widely read meditations by John Wesley. Among these are "The New Birth," "The Firstfruits of the Spirit," "The Spirit of Bondage and of Adoption," "The Marks of the New Birth," and "On Working Out Our Own Salvation." Oden's preface provides historical background and clarification.

The John Wesley Reader, edited by Al Bryant (Waco, TX: Word, 1983). Readable selections from John Wesley's journals and sermons. They are grouped around themes, such as "Seasonings from the Sermon on the Mount" and "The Path of Patience," along with Bible citations for each selection.

Other John Wesley volumes of interest include *John Wesley's Fifty-Three Sermons,* edited by Edward A. Sugden (Nashville, TN: Abingdon, 1983), and *The Journal of John Wesley* (Tring, UK: Lion Publishing, 1986).

Hannah More

(1745–1833)

———

Hannah More was a poet, playwright, and spiritual writer. One of five daughters born to a schoolmaster and his wife in the neighborhood of Bristol, England, Hannah showed literary talent, enough to bring her into contact with exalted literary circles in London that included Dr. Samuel Johnson, Sir Joshua Reynolds and his sister, political leader Edmund Burke, and the distinguished actor David Garrick and his wife, Eva.

More achieved some fame as a writer of poems and plays, yet was uncomfortable with the literary scene. Evangelically minded, she began reading works by John Newton, a former slave trader who after his conversion had become the rector of a London Church. He is happily remembered for the words of the hymn "Amazing Grace." He was also a strong advocate for abolition and became Hannah More's spiritual adviser. Another acquaintance was William Wilberforce who spearheaded the abolitionists" cause.

Under such influences, More left her London circle to live at Cowslip Green, a country house near Bristol. Her retirement was facilitated by an annuity settled on her by a man who had jilted her. But her retirement did not afford much solitude.

Many distinguished visitors came to call; concerned for the poor in her Somerset neighborhood, she and her sisters set up Sunday schools and weekday schools; through her writings she helped to agitate against slavery, aligning herself with John Newton, Wilberforce, and the Clapham Sect. Their efforts helped abolish slavery in 1833.

Despite chronic asthma and bronchitis Hannah More was able to write widely popular Christian reflections. The earnings from these were substantial; she used them to establish poor schools in the Mendip Hills near Bristol, and greatly advanced the cause of literacy in her generation.

The following selection is taken from *Religion of the Heart*, originally published in 1811 under the title *Practical Piety*. Chapter 11, "On the Comparatively Small Faults and Virtues," has been condensed; the English has been edited and modernized.

Notice the vigor of More's writing and the force of her opinions. Conscience, she suggests, is "a sudden flash from heaven." Procrastination should not be excused, but noticed. She seems to be having a conversation with us across the centuries.

RELIGION OF THE HEART

Comparatively Small Faults and Virtues

The "Fishers of Men," as if exclusively bent on catching the greater sinners, often make the openings of the moral net so wide that it cannot retain sinners of more ordinary size which everywhere abound. Their catch might be more abundant, if the net were woven tighter so the smaller, slipperier sinner could not slide through. Such souls, having happily escaped entanglement, plunge back again into their native element, enjoy their escape, and hope for time to grow bigger before they are in danger of being caught.

It is important to practice the smaller virtues, to avoid scrupulously the lesser sins, and to bear patiently with minor trials. . . .

Reject what is wrong—seize what is right

God has furnished the body with senses, and the soul with conscience, an instinct to avoid the approach of danger and a spontaneous reaction to any attack whose suddenness and surprise allows no time for thoughtful consideration. . . .

By cherishing this quick sense of rectitude—this sudden flash from heaven, which is in fact the motion of the Spirit—we intuitively reject what is wrong before we have time to examine why it is wrong, and seize on what is right before we have time to examine why it is right. Should we not then be careful how we extinguish this sacred spark? . . .

The acquisition of even the smallest virtue is actually a conquest over the opposite vice and doubles our moral strength. The spiritual enemy has one subject less, and the conqueror one virtue more.

By being negligent in small things, we are not aware how much we injure Christianity in the eyes of the world. How can we expect people to believe that we are in earnest in great points when they see that we cannot withstand a trivial temptation? At a distance they hear with respect of our general characters. Then they get to know us and discover the same failings, littleness, and bad tempers as they have been accustomed to encounter in the most ordinary persons. . . .

Cultivate the inferior duties

Our neglect of inferior duties is particularly injurious to the minds of our families. If they see us "weak and infirm of purpose," peevish, irresolute, capricious, passionate or inconsistent in our daily conduct, they will not give us credit for those higher qualities which we may possess and those superior duties which we may be more careful to fulfil. . . . Seeing us so defective in the daily course of our behavior at home, though our children may obey us because they are obliged to it, they will neither love nor esteem us enough to be influenced by our instruction or advice. . . .

But there is a still more serious point of view to consider. Do small faults, continually repeated, always retain their original weakness? Is a bad temper which is never repressed not worse after years of indulgence than when we first gave the reins to it? Does that which we first allowed ourselves under the name of harmless levity on serious subjects, never proceed to profaneness? Does what was once admired as proper spirit, never grow into pride, never swell into insolence? Does the habit of loose talking or allowed exaggeration never lead to falsehood, never move into deceit? Before we positively determine that small faults are innocent, we must try to prove that they shall never outgrow their primitive dimensions. We must make certain that the infant shall never become a giant.

For example, *procrastination* is reckoned among the most excusable of our faults, and weighs so lightly on our minds that we scarcely apologize for it. But, what if, from mere sloth and indolence, we had put off giving assistance to one friend under distress, or advice to another under temptation. Can we be sure that had we not delayed we might have preserved the well-being of the one, or saved the soul of the other? . . .

Indecision, though it is not so often caused by reflection as by the lack of it, may be just as mischievous, for if we spend too much time in balancing probabilities, the period for action is lost. While we are busily considering difficulties which may never occur, reconciling differences which perhaps do not exist, and trying to balance things of nearly the same weight, the opportunity is lost for producing that good which a firm and bold decision would have effected.

Idleness, though itself the most inactive of all the vices, is however the path by which they all enter, the stage on which they all act. Though supremely passive itself, it lends a willing hand to all evil. It aids and encourages every sin. If it does nothing itself, it connives all the mischief that is done by others.

Vanity is exceedingly misplaced when ranked with small faults. It is under the guise of harmlessness that it does all its mischief. Vanity is often found in the company of great virtues, and by mixing itself in it, mars the whole collection. The use our spiritual enemy makes of it is a master stroke. When he cannot prevent us from doing right actions he can accomplish his purpose almost as well by making us vain about them. When he cannot deprive others of our good works he can defeat the effect in us by poisoning our motive. When he cannot rob others of the good effect of the deed, he can gain his point by robbing the doer of his reward.

Irritability is another of the minor miseries. Life itself, though sufficiently unhappy, cannot devise misfortunes as often as the irritable person can supply impatience. Violence and belligerence are the common resource of those whose knowledge is small, and whose arguments are weak. Anger is the common refuge of insignificance. People who feel their character to be slight, hope to give it weight by inflation. But the blown balloon at its fullest distension is still empty.

Trifling is ranked among the venial faults. But, consider that time is one grand gift given to us in order that we may secure eternal life. If we trifle away that time so as to lose that eternal life, then it will serve to fulfil the very aim of sin. A life devoted to trifles not only takes away the inclination, but the capacity for higher pursuits. . . .

Vanity the source

Vanity is at the bottom of almost all, may we not say, of all our sins. We think more of distinguishing than of saving ourselves. We overlook the hourly occasions which occur for serving, aiding and comforting those around us, while we perform an act of well-known generosity. The habit in the former case, however, better shows the disposition and bent of the mind, than the solitary act of splendor. The apostle does not say whatsoever _great_ things ye do, but "whatsoever things ye do, do _all_ to the glory of God" (1 Cor. 10:31) . . .

What we refer to here are habitual and unresisted faults: habitual, because they go unresisted, and allowed because they are considered to be too insignificant to call for resistance. . . .

We must, however, be careful not to entangle our consciences with groundless apprehensions. We have a merciful Father, not a hard master to deal with. We must not harass our minds with a suspicious dread, as if the Almighty were laying snares to entrap us. Nor should we be terrified with imaginary fears, as if He were on the watch to punish every casual error. Being immutable and impeccable is not part of human nature. He who made us best knows of what we are made. Our compassionate High Priest will bear with much infirmity and will pardon much involuntary weakness. . . .

Enjoin small duties

But small services, scarcely perceptible to any eye but his for whom they are made, bear the true character of love to God, as they are the infallible marks of charity to our fellow creatures.

By enjoining small duties, the spirit of which is everywhere implied in the Gospel, God's intention seems to be to make the great ones easier for us. He makes the light yoke of Christ still lighter, not by lessening duty, but by increasing its ease through its familiarity. These little habits at once indicate the sentiment of the soul and improve it.

It is an awesome consideration, and one which every Christian should bring home to our own bosoms, whether or not small faults willfully persisted in, may in time not only dim the light of conscience, but extinguish the spirit of grace. Will indulgence in small faults ultimately dissolve all power of resistance against great evils? We should earnestly seek to remember that perhaps among the first objects which may meet our eyes when we open them on the eternal world, may be a tremendous book. In that book, together with our great and actual sins, may be recorded in no less prominent characters, an ample page of omissions and of neglected opportunities. There we may read a list of those good intentions, which indolence, indecision, thoughtlessness, vanity, trifling, and procrastination served to frustrate and to prevent.

BIBLE SELECTION
Romans 12:1–2

I appeal to you therefore, brothers and sisters, by the mercy of God, to present your bodies as a living sacrifice, holy and acceptable to God, which is your spiritual worship. Do not be conformed to this world, but be transformed by the renewing of your minds, so that you may discern what is the will of God— what is good and acceptable and perfect.

DISCUSSION QUESTIONS

The following can be used for discussion within a small group, or used for journal reflections by individuals:

1. How have I experienced increases in virtue? Do any specific incidents come to mind?
2. Have I noticed small faults in other people? In myself? How would I describe or characterize them?

SUGGESTED EXERCISES

The following exercises can be done by individuals, shared between spiritual friends, or used in the context of a small group. Choose one or more of the following:

1. Ask a close friend whom you trust to mention a few of your small faults and small virtues. Try not to flinch or be defensive. After you have talked, pray privately about these faults. Work on them as the Spirit directs.

2. Do a workshop-style discussion on some of the faults that Hannah More mentions: procrastination, indecision, idleness, vanity, irritability, and trifling (a modern equivalent would be time-wasting). Beside each one of the small faults, write down the corresponding virtue. Can we add other small faults (and corresponding virtues) to her list? Discuss some ways we can work on these defects and whether we need to "live with" and "tolerate" certain discouraging habits.

REFLECTIONS

We need to take this essay on the small virtues and faults with utmost seriousness. Frankly, the battle is won or lost precisely in the trifling areas of life. We will be wise to take to heart the counsel of the prophet Zechariah not to despise "the day of small things" (4:10).

Why are these small matters of such importance? Hannah More gives two reasons. One, the practice of virtue overcomes vice: "The acquisition of even the smallest virtue is actually a conquest over the opposite vice and doubles our moral strength." Two, small vices inevitably lead to greater vices: "We must make certain that the infant shall never become a giant."

I would like to add a reason of my own to these two important matters that Hannah More has discussed. My reason is simply this: it is the small fidelities that are most helpful in training the heart toward God. These thousands upon thousands of little actions of righteousness and peace and joy in the Holy Spirit slowly but surely change our heart. More than any other thing the small corners of life reveal who we truly are. The large virtues most often occur in a public forum and usually we are able to put on a good front when we know others are watching. It is in the unguarded moment, however, when no one is watching that what is really in our heart comes to the surface. And may the revelation of our heart be a cause for rejoicing in the goodness of God.

RICHARD J. FOSTER

GOING DEEPER

Religion of the Heart: Hannah More, edited and "mildly modernized" by Hal M. Helms (Orleans, MA: Paraclete, 1993). A group of selected readings from Hannah More, along with a biography and introduction by the editor.

JEREMY AND MARGARET COLLINGWOOD, *Hannah More* (Tring, UK: Lion Publishing, 1990). Jeremy Collingwood, Vicar of Hotwells, and his wife, Margaret, a writer, collaborated on this biography of Hannah More. Hotwells was the neighborhood where Hannah More lived shortly before her death.

Frederick William Faber

(1814–1863)

Born in Calverley, Yorkshire, England, of Huguenot descent, Faber attended Harrow School and Balliol College and later University College, Oxford, of which he became a fellow.

In his university days Faber became gradually persuaded by John Henry Newman's arguments and joined the Tractarian Movement; he received Anglican ordination in 1839 and became rector of Elton, Northamptonshire.

During two extended tours of the Continent (1839–43) Faber became enamored of Roman Catholic rites and devotions; returning in 1844, he began to advocate Roman Catholic doctrine and practices. He also wrote a life of St. Wilfrid.

In 1845 both Faber and Newman were received into the Roman Catholic Church. The following year Faber founded a religious community, the Wilfridians, or Brothers of the Will of God. In 1847 he was ordained priest; he influenced his entire parish to become Roman Catholics. In 1848, when Newman founded the Oratory of St. Philip Neri, at Old Oscott, Birmingham, Faber brought himself and many of his community into the Oratory as novices.

In 1849 Newman sent Faber to found the Oratory in London and named him its superior. Here Faber flowered in fervent devotional services and good works, founding poor schools, helping the afflicted, organizing processions, writing hymns, and giving sermons. He was a popular spiritual leader and confessor, and his spiritual writing was much loved.

Besides his series of forty-nine *Lives of the Saints*, he also wrote a number of works on the spiritual life, among these *All for Jesus, Growth in Holiness*, and *The Creator and Creature*. In 1854 the Oratory moved to South Kensington, where Faber spent the last years of his life devoted to prayer and the care of souls.

In the selection that follows, which is taken from *The Creator and the Creature*, notice the joyful, almost childlike picture that Faber paints of what it is to be a creature under God's rule. His aim is like the Almighty's, to flood our spiritual lives with sunshine.

THE CREATOR AND THE CREATURE

What It Means to Be a Creature

Let us sit down upon the top of this fair hill. The clear sunshine and the bright air flow into us in streams of life and gladness, while our thoughts are lifted up to God, and our hearts quietly expand to love. . . . There at our feet is the gigantic city, gleaming with an ivory whiteness beneath its uplifted but perpetual canopy of smoke. . . . There, in every variety of joy and misery, of elevation and depression, three million souls are working out their complicated destinies. . . . What a mingled scene it is of God and man! . . .

What is our uppermost thought? It is that we live, and that our life is gladness. . . . How did we come to live? Why do we live? How do we live? What is our life? Where did it come from? Whither is it going? What was it meant for? All that the sun shines upon is real; and we are real too. Are we to be the beauty of a moment, part of earth's gilding, to warm ourselves in the sun for a while, and glitter, and add to the hum of life on the planet, and then go away, and go nowhere? . . .

We are creatures

We are creatures. What is it to be a creature? Before the sun sets in the red west, let us try to have an answer to our question. We find ourselves in existence today . . . We have been alive and on the earth so many years, so many months, so many weeks, so many days. . . . We know nothing of what has gone before us . . .

So it is with the creature man. He finds himself in existence. . . . He has no notion why it was that his particular soul rather than any other soul, was called into being, and put into his place. Not only can he conceive a soul far more noble and devout than his, but he sees, as he thinks, peculiar deficiencies in himself, in some measure disqualifying him for the actual position in which God has placed him. And how can he account for this? Yet God must be right. . . . He clearly has a work to do, and came here simply to do it . . . Every step which a creature takes, when he has once been created, increases his dependence on the Creator. . . . This is, in fact, his true blessedness—to be ever more and more enclosed in the hand of God who made him. The Creator's hand is the creature's home. . . .

Three conclusions about the creature

Now let us go back to the man we left sitting on the hilltop in the brightness of the summer sun. We have to draw some conclusions about him from what has been already said: and the first is this. As *"creature"* is his name, his history, and his condition . . . He must behave as what he is. . . . He must be made up of fear, of obedience, of submission, of humility, of prayer, of repentance, and above all, of love. As fire warms and frost chills, as the moon shines by night and the sun by day, as birds have wings and trees have leaves, so must man, as a creature, conduct himself as such, and do those virtuous actions, which are chiefly virtues because they are becoming to him and adapted to his condition. . . .

Our second conclusion about this [creature] is that, whatever may be his attainments or his inclinations, the only knowledge worth much of his time and trouble, the only science which will last with him and stand him in good stead, consists in his study of the character of God. He received everything from God. He belongs to Him. He is surrounded by Him. His fate is in God's hands. His eternity is to be with God, in a companionship of unspeakable delights. Or if it is to be in exile from Him, it is the absence of God which will be the intolerableness of his misery. His own being implies God's being; and he exists, not for himself, but for God. . . .

Our third conclusion is that, if God is to be the subject of man's intellectual occupations, God must be equally the object of his moral conduct. God must have his whole heart as well as his whole mind. . . .

These three conclusions are inevitable results of . . . being a creature. . . . A creature means "All for God." Holiness is an unselfing ourselves. . . .

The creature's end is God

If we take all the peculiarities of the creature and throw them into one, if we sum them all up and express them in the ordinary language of Christian doctrine, we should say that they came to this—that as man was not his own beginning, so also he is not his own end. His end is God; and man belies his own position as a creature when he swerves from this his sole true end. . . .

To make God always our end is always to remember that we are creatures; and to be a saint is always to make God our end. Hence to be a saint is always to remember and to act on the remembrance, that we are creatures. . . .

If we examine the falls of both angels and men, we shall see that what lay at the root of them was a forgetfulness that they were creatures, or a perverse determination to be something more. Whether the angels contemplated their own beauty and rested with an unhallowed complacency in themselves as their end, or whether they would not bow to the divine counsel of the Incarnation and the exaltation of Christ's human nature above their own, in both cases they forgot themselves as creatures, and demanded what it was not becoming in a creature to demand. You shall be as gods, was the very motive which the tempter urged in order to push man to his ruin. . . . The knowledge of God was the object of Adam's envy . . . In both cases . . . the angels and man . . . would not acquiesce in their created position. Can anything show us more plainly the importance of keeping always before us the fact that we are creatures?

God became a creature

Yes! we may go still higher. We say of our Blessed Lord that He is our example as well as our mediator. Yet he was God as well as man. What is this then but saying that of such consequence was it to the happiness of man that he should know how to behave himself as a creature, that it was necessary the Creator should take a created nature, and come Himself to show how to wear it? Thus one of the many known reasons of the sublime mystery of the Incarnation was that the Creator Himself might show the creature how he should behave as a creature. . . . The mysteries of Jesus are man's studies of the beauty of holiness. . . .

If we turn from our Lord's example to His work for us as our mediator, the same truth meets us in another shape. . . . Speaking of His intercession the apostle says that "in the days of His flesh He was heard because He feared," and again he speaks of the Crucifixion in the same way, "He was obedient unto death, even the death of the Cross." It was as if Jesus redeemed the world especially by acknowledging in an infinitely meritorious manner through His created nature the sovereignty and dominion of the Creator.

The creature loves and serves God

To sum up briefly . . . it appears, that to be a creature is a very peculiar and cognizable thing, that it gives birth to a whole set of duties, obligations, virtues and proprieties, that it implies a certain history past and future . . . and that it involves, without reference to any additional mercies, the precise obligation of loving our Creator supremely as our sole end, and of serving Him from the motive of love.

BIBLE SELECTION
Psalm 24:1–6

The earth is the LORD's and all that is in it,
　　the world, and those who live in it;
for he has founded it on the seas,
　　and established it on the rivers.

Who shall ascend the hill of the LORD?
　　And who shall stand in his holy place?
Those who have clean hands and pure hearts

who do not lift up their souls to what is false,
    and do not swear deceitfully.
They will receive blessing from the LORD,
    and vindication from the God of their salvation.
Such is the company of those who seek him,
    who seek the face of the God of Jacob.

DISCUSSION QUESTIONS

The following can be used for discussion within a small group, or used for journal reflections by individuals:

1. How can the thought of being a creature help me to experience the order of grace?
2. What kinds of rebelliousness keep me from thinking of myself as a creature?

SUGGESTED EXERCISES

The following exercises can be done by individuals, shared between spiritual friends, or used in the context of a small group. Choose one or more of the following:

1. Take some time this week to put yourself in a place where you can reflect on God as Creator: a place of natural beauty, perhaps, or a place where beautiful works of art can be seen, or possibly a visit to a formal garden. What thoughts come to mind about the relationship between Creator and creature?
2. Write your own brief meditation on what it is to be a creature.

REFLECTIONS

I loved Frederick Faber even before I really met him. As a very young Christian I came across A. W. Tozer's The Knowledge of the Holy *and devoured it. Inside that book Tozer quoted eleven of Faber's poems, and while I knew nothing of Faber himself, his poems (hymn lyrics, really) became a way for me to meditate upon God.*

As a college student, studying the attributes of God was a delightful and absorbing spiritual exercise. During those years I memorized a stanza from Faber that touched me profoundly and has, in fact, stayed with me to this day:

Only to sit and think of God,
    Oh what a joy it is!
To think the thought, to breathe the Name
    Earth has no higher bliss.

While I may have puzzled over the various arguments for the doctrine of the Trinity, I could always settle into Faber's simple doxology:

O Blessed Trinity!
    O simplest Majesty!
        O Three in One!
Thou art for ever God alone.
    Holy Trinity!
    Blessed equal Three.
    One God, we praise Thee.

While I might scratch my head over the philosophical debates between the eternalness of matter and the self-existence of God, I found both head and heart instructed by these lines of Faber's:

Timeless, spaceless, single, lonely,
    Yet sublimely Three,
Thou art grandly, always, only
    God in Unity!
Lone in grandeur, lone in glory,
Who shall tell Thy wondrous story?
    Awful Trinity!

Or I might marvel at the distinctions between the Creator and the creature, which is incidentally the theme of this reading. <u>*God is forever wholly Other*</u>*: incomprehensible, self-existent, self-sufficient, infinite, immutable, omniscient, omnipotent, omnipresent, transcendent, imminent, holy, sovereign, just, good, merciful, and ever loving.*

The contrast to the creature is too obvious to need enumeration. And yet in spite of the distance between the Creator and the creature God freely and lovingly reaches out to you and to me and invites our responding love and worship. Faber one last time:

How dread are Thine eternal years,
*   O everlasting Lord!*
By prostrate spirits day and night
*   Incessantly adored!*

How beautiful, how beautiful
*   The sight of Thee must be,*
Thine endless wisdom, boundless power,
*   And awful purity!*

Oh how I fear Thee, living God!
*   With deepest, tenderest fears,*
And worship Thee with trembling hope,
*   And penitential tears.*

RICHARD J. FOSTER

GOING DEEPER

FREDERICK WILLIAM FABER, *The Creator and Creature* (Rockford, IL: Tan Books & Publishers, 1961). Throughout this book Faber develops with high Victorian creativity his notion of God the Creator and human creatures and how we should respond to God's forgiveness and love.

FREDERICK WILLIAM FABER, *Hymns* (Baltimore and New York: John Murphy Company, 1880). Out of print for perhaps a century, this 500-page book contains all of Faber's hymns and is worth hunting the libraries and second-hand shops for a copy. As with Charles Wesley, there wasn't a religious thought that Faber didn't put into a hymn.

Poet and Priest: Selected Letters by Frederick William Faber from 1833–1863, edited by Raleigh Addington (London: D. Brown and Sons, 1974). In this volume the precise historical development of Faber's ideas and religious convictions becomes clear.

Amy Carmichael

(1867–1951)

———

Amy Carmichael was born in County Down, Northern Ireland, but spent most of her life as a missionary in Asia. She came to Jesus Christ early and developed a sense of social concern.

At the age of seventeen she was leading a Sunday school class for the poor mill girls of Belfast in a Presbyterian church hall. The class swelled to 500. By the age of twenty-four, Amy felt a call to the mission field. First she sailed to Japan to win souls for Jesus Christ but became ill after fifteen months and had to return to England.

In 1895, having recovered, she again volunteered, this time for service in India under the sponsorship of a Church of England mission society. By now, Amy Carmichael's gifts were already well known. She gave a moving farewell message at the Keswick convention.

Amy arrived in the Tinnevelly region of India when she was twenty-nine. Four years later the missionary band moved to Dohnavur, where she helped the Dohnavur Fellowship found a major healing and training center, staffed with workers from around the world.

In 1931 a fall left Carmichael an invalid for the rest of her life. Even so, she wrote extensively. Her books also pioneered in the use of illustrative photography.

From 1901 onward Amy Carmichael worked against a practice that shocked her, temple traffic in children, in which children were dedicated to temple gods by marriage ceremonies. As a corollary, the British missionaries were opposing the entrenched caste system, as the following reading from her autobiographical writings will show. Eventually this practice was abolished not by the British, but by the people of India themselves.

In this selection, taken from the anthology *Spiritual Witness*, notice how firm and confident is Amy Carmichael's opposition; she is relying on God's help. Also, she honors the higher traditions of India and is sensitive to differences of culture even while opposing what she believes is wrong.

SPIRITUAL WITNESS

The Traffic of the Temple

When, on March 7, 1901, we first heard from the lips of a little child the story of her life in a temple house, we were startled and distressed. Our hearts were penetrated with the conviction that such a story ought to be impossible in a land ruled by a Christian power.

The subject was new to us. We knew nothing of the magnitude of what may be called "the secret traffic of India"—a traffic in little children, mere infants oftentimes, for wrong purposes; and we did not appreciate, as we do now, the delicacy and difficulty of the position from a Government point of view, facing the quiet might of the forces on the other side. And though with added knowledge comes an added sense of responsibility, and a fear of all careless appeal to those whose burden is already so heavy, yet with every fresh discovery the conviction deepens that something should be done—and done, if possible, soon—to save at least this generation of children, or some of them, from destruction.

By temple children we mean children dedicated to gods or in danger of being so dedicated. Dedication to gods implies a form of marriage which makes ordinary marriage impossible. The child is regarded as belonging to the gods. In southern India, where religious feeling runs strong and the great temples are the centers of Hindu influence, the traffic is worked upon religious lines. . . . Something of the same kind exists in other parts of India, and the traffic under another name is common in provinces where temple service as we have it in the south is unknown.

Again, in some areas, owing to the action of the native Government, temple service as such is not recognized. Children in danger of wrong cannot, strictly speaking, be called temple children. Yet there is need for legislation which shall touch all houses where little children are being brought up for the same purpose. The subject is immense and involved, and the thought of it suggests a net thrown over millions of square miles of territory, so finely woven as to be almost invisible, but so strong in its mesh that in no place yet has it ever given way. And the net is alive; it can feel and it can hold.

We ourselves became only gradually aware of what was happening about us. As fact after fact came to light, we were forced to certain conclusions which we could not doubt were correct. . . .

An *alien spirit*

The thing we fight is not India or Indian, in essence or development. It is something alien to the old life of the people. . . . It is like a parasite which has settled upon the bough of some noble forest tree—on it, but not of it. The parasite has gripped the bough with strong and interlacing roots, but it is not the bough.

We think of the real India as we see it in the thinker—the seeker after the unknown God, with his wistful eyes. "The Lord beholding him loved him," and we cannot help loving as we look. And there is the Indian woman hidden away from the noise of crowds, patient in her motherhood, loyal to the light she has. We see the spirit of the old land there; and it wins us and holds us, and makes it a joy to be here to live for India.

The true India is sensitive and very gentle. There is a wisdom in its ways, none the less wise because it is not the wisdom of the West. This spirit which trafficks in children is callous and fierce as a ravening beast; and its wisdom descendeth not from above, but is earthly, sensual, devilish. And this spirit, alien to the land, has settled upon it and made itself at home in it, and so become a part of it that nothing but the touch of God will ever get it out. We want that touch of God: "Touch the mountains, and they shall smoke." That is why we write.

Pray for the children

For we write for those who believe in prayer—not in the emasculated modern sense, but in the old Hebrew sense, deep as the other is shallow. We believe there is some connection between knowing and caring and praying, and what happens afterward. Otherwise we should leave the darkness to cover the things that belong to the dark. . . .

"Only pray?" does someone ask? Prayer of the sort we mean never stops with praying. "Whatsoever he saith unto you, do it" is the prayer's solemn afterword; but the prayer we ask is no trifle. "Arise, cry out in the night; in the beginning of the night watches pour out thine heart like water before the Lord; lift up thine hands toward Him for the life of thy young children."

The story of the children is the story of answered prayer. If any of us were tempted to doubt whether, after all, prayer is a genuine transaction and answers to prayer no figment of the imagination—but something as real as the tangible things about us—we have only to look at some of our children. . . .

A *dear little babe*

In October, 1908, we were told of two children whose mother had recently died. They were with their father in a town some distance from Dohnavur. . . . We prayed a rather tentative prayer. "If the children exist, save them."

For three months we heard nothing; then a rumor drifted across to us that the elder of the two had died in a temple house. The younger, six months old, was still with her father. On Christmas eve our informant arrived in the compound with his usual unexpectedness. The father was near, but would not come nearer because the following day being Friday (a day of ill-omen), he did not wish to discuss matters concerning the child; he would come on Saturday.

On Saturday he came, carrying a dear little babe with brilliant eyes. She almost sprang from him into our arms, and we saw she was mad with thirst. She was fed and put to sleep, and hardly daring yet to rejoice (for the matter was not settled with the father), we took him aside and discussed the case with him.

Serious difficulties

There were difficulties. A temple woman had offered a large sum for the child and had also promised to bequeath her property to her. He had heard, however, that we had little children who had all but been given to temples and had come to reconnoiter rather than to decide.

The position was explained to him, but the temple meant to him everything that was worshipful. How could anything that was wrong be sanctioned by the gods? The child's mother had been a devout Hindu; and so we went deeper and deeper into things with him. It was evident he became more and more reluctant to leave the little one with us. "Her mother would have felt it shame and eternal dishonor."

We were in the little prayer room, a flowery summerhouse in the garden, when this talk took place. On either side are the nurseries, and playing on the wide verandahs were happy, healthy babes. Their merry shouts filled the spaces in the conversation. Sometimes a little toddling thing would find her way across to the prayer room and break in upon the talk with affectionate caresses. To our eyes everything looked so happy, so incomparably better than anything the temple house could offer.

The issue of caste

It was difficult to adjust one's mental vision so as to understand that of the Hindu beside us, to whose thought all the happiness was as nothing because these babes would be brought up without caste. In the temple house caste is kept most carefully. If a temple woman breaks the rules of her community, she is outcasted, excommunicated. "You do not keep caste! You do not keep caste!" the father repeated over and over in utter dismay. It was nothing to him that the babes were well and strong and as happy as the day was long, nothing to him that cleanliness reigned, as far as constant supervision could ensure it, through every corner of the compound.

We did not profess to keep caste; we welcomed every little child in danger of being given to temples, irrespective altogether of her caste. All castes were welcome to us, for all were dear to our Lord. This was beyond him, and he declared he would never have brought his child to us had he understood it before. "Let her die rather. There is no disgrace in death." As he talked and expounded his views, he argued himself further and further away from us in spirit, until he became disgusted with himself for ever having considered giving the baby to us.

Waiting upon God

All this time the baby lay asleep, and as we looked at the little face and noted the "mother-want," the appealing expression of pitiful weariness even in sleep, it was all we could do to turn away and face the almost inevitable result of the conversation. Once the father, a splendid-looking man, tall and dignified, rose and stood erect in sudden indignation. "Where is the babe? I will take her away and do as I will with her. She is my child!"

We persuaded him to wait awhile as she was asleep, and we went away to pray. Together we [of the fellowship] waited upon God, whose touch turns hard rocks into standing water and flint stone into a springing well, beseeching him to deal with that father's heart and make it melt and yield. And as we waited, it seemed as if an answer of peace was distinctly given to us, and we rose from our knees at rest. But just at that moment the father went to where his baby slept in her cradle, and he took her up and walked away in a white heat of wrath.

The little one was in an exhausted condition, for she had not had suitable food for at least three days. It was the time of our land-winds, which are raw and cold to south India people. It seemed that the answer of peace must mean peace after death of cold and starvation. It would soon be over, we knew—twenty-four hours, more or less, and those great wistful eyes would close, and the last cry would be cried. But even twenty-four hours seemed long to think of a child in distress, and her being so little did not make it easier to think of her dying like that.

The baby brought back

So on Sunday morning I shut myself up in my room, asking for quick relief for her, or—but this seemed almost asking too much—that she might be given back to us. And as I prayed, a knock came at the door, and a voice called joyously, "Oh, Amma, Amma, come! The father stands outside the church; he has brought the baby back!"

But the child was almost in collapse. Without a word he dropped the cold, limp little body into our arms and prostrated himself till his forehead touched the dust. We had no time to think of him; we hardly noted his extraordinary submission, for all our thought was for the babe. There was no pulse to be felt; only those far-too-brilliant eyes looked alive. We worked with restoratives for hours, and at last the little limbs warmed and the pulse came back. But it was a bounding, unnatural pulse, and the restlessness which supervened confirmed the tale of the brilliant eyes—the little babe had been drugged.

An unremitting fight with death

From that day on till our prayer day, January 6, it was one long, unremitting fight with death. We wrote to our medical comrade in Neyoor and described the symptoms, which were all bad. He could give us little hope. Gradually the brilliance passed from the eyes, and they became what the Tamils call "dead." The film formed after which none of us had ever seen recovery. Then we gathered round the little cot in the room we call Tranquillity, and we gave the babe her Christian name, Vinala, the Spotless One; for we thought that very soon she would be without spot and blameless, another little innocent in that happy band of innocents who see His face.

On the evening of January 5, friends of our own mission who were with us seemed to lay hold for the life of the child with such fresh earnestness and faith that we ourselves were strengthened. Next morning we believed we saw a change in the little, deathlike face, and that evening we were sure the child's life was coming back to her.

God had worked

It was not till then we thought of the father, who after signing a paper made out for him by our pastor, had returned to his own town. When we heard all that had occurred, we saw how our God had worked for us. It was not fear of his baby's death that had moved the man to return her to us. "What is the death of a babe? Let her die across my shoulders!" After all persuasions had failed, we had tried threats: the thing he proposed to do was illegal. The Collector (chief magistrate) would do justice. The father was not afraid of the law. "What care I for your Collector? How can he find me if I choose to lose myself? How can you prove anything against me?"

In that he spoke the truth. There are ways by which the intention of the law concerning children can be easily and successfully circumvented. Our pleadings had not touched him. "Is she not my child? Was her mother not my wife? Who has the right to come between this child of mine and me, her father?" And so saying, he had departed without the slightest intention of coming back again.

But a Power with which he did not reckon had him in sight; and a Hand was laid upon him, and it bent him like a reed. We hope some ray of a purer light than he had ever experienced found its way into his darkened soul and revealed to him the sin of his intention. But we only know that he left his child and went back to his own town. God had heard: God had answered.

BIBLE SELECTION
Mark 9:33–37

Then they came to Capernaum; and when he was in the house he asked them, "What were you arguing about on the way?" But they were silent, for on the way they had argued with one another who was the greatest. He sat down, called the twelve, and said to them, "Whoever wants to be first must be last of all and servant of all." Then he took a little child and put it among them; and taking it in his arms, he said to them, "Whoever welcomes such a child in my name welcomes me, and whoever welcomes me welcomes not me but the one who sent me."

DISCUSSION QUESTIONS

The following can be used for discussion within a small group, or used for journal reflections by individuals:

1. What are the arguments for opposing a practice you see and disapprove of? What arguments can I think of for leaving things as they are?
2. What can we learn from missionaries, both in our own countries and on foreign shores? How can we best follow their example?

SUGGESTED EXERCISES

The following exercises can be done by individuals, shared between spiritual friends, or used in the context of a small group. Choose one or more of the following:

1. Write a personal reflection on the way you react to pictures of sick or ailing children in foreign countries, far away.
2. Discuss the idea of personal vocation, using Amy Carmichael's younger life as a model. She began teaching Sunday school at seventeen; she felt a call to the mission field at twenty-four and was firmly advanced in mission work by the age of twenty-nine. How has your own sense of vocation come about?

What about "second vocations," taking on second careers in later life? Make these matters part of a group discussion or private reflection.

REFLECTIONS

There is a naive notion today that all religious beliefs are to be given equal deference, that none are to be thought superior to any other, and that we are all to live as one big happy family. <u>Such a position comes from a false notion of tolerance</u>. Now, all religious views do deserve to be understood, and understood within their own cultural and worldview setting. But not all religious views are to be tolerated. Some beliefs are downright evil. I know, I know, many today will rise up in self-righteous protest asking, "So, how do we know what is evil?" in much the same way that jesting Pilate asked of Jesus, "What is truth?" But, of course, such armchair quibblers would have no problem denouncing any view that, in effect, stated, "My religious belief is that you and your kind are to be wiped off the face of the earth." All of a sudden evil beliefs become much easier to identify.

Amy Carmichael in this selection faced just such an evil belief system, and she was not afraid to call it so: "This spirit which trafficks in children is callous and fierce as a ravening beast; and its wisdom descendeth not from above, but is earthly, sensual, devilish." The temple slave system was evil in much the same way that the American slave system was evil. Both were evil and both needed opposing even though both were condoned, even encouraged, by particular teachings (distorted teachings, I would insist), in the one case from Hinduism and in the other from Christianity.

Notice how sensitively Amy Carmichael worked her way through the tangled issues of tradition and culture, nation and government, without once flinching on the vital point of this matter as an enormous evil. <u>Always she affirms the very best in the cultural tradition of her adopted land</u>: "We see the spirit of the old land there; and it wins us and holds us, and makes it a joy to be here to live for India." It is a cultural sensitivity that she possessed at the beginning of the twentieth century that we who live at the beginning of the next century would do well to emulate.

Finally, I find her approach to prayer so very refreshing. I mean first and foremost that she actually believed in prayer. And then she acted upon her belief. (People always act upon their beliefs, of course, which is exactly why we so seldom do the kind of prayer work she did—we simply do not believe in prayer as she did.) Those working in social justice ministries—indeed all of us whatever our calling—would do well to study with care her story of the father with the six-month-old child. She teaches us volumes.

RICHARD J. FOSTER

GOING DEEPER

Spiritual Witness: Classic Christian Writings of the Twentieth Century, edited by Sherwood Eliot Wirt (Wheaton, IL: Crossway, 1991). This selection from works of Christian writers includes a longer text of the account by Amy Carmichael.

Christian Literature Crusade of Fort Washington, PA, has brought back into print some of Amy Carmichael's books: *Gold by Midnight* (1992), *If* (1992), *Mountain Breezes* (1999), and *Rose from Brier* (1980).

ELIZABETH R. SKOGLUND, *Amma: The Life and Words of Amy Carmichael* (Grand Rapids, MI: Baker Book House, 1994). This book incorporates a biography of Carmichael and selections from some of her important works.

Acknowledgments

─

Grateful acknowledgment is made to the following for permission to reprint material copyrighted or controlled by them.

Baker Book House for excerpt from "A Fast on Criticalness," *A Closer Walk* by Catherine Marshall, edited by Leonard E. LeSourd, 1986, pp. 102–4. Copyright © 1986 by Calen, Inc. Used by permission of Paulist Press, Inc.

Ballantine Books for excerpts from: (1) "Experiments in Prayer," *The Healing Light* by Agnes Sanford, pp. 6–16. Copyright © 1947, 1972 by Macalester Park Publishing Company. (2) *Instrument of Thy Peace: Meditations on the Prayer of St. Francis of Assisi*. Copyright © 1968, 1982 by The Seabury Press, Inc.

Barbour Publishing, Inc., for excerpt from *The Best of Andrew Murray on Prayer: A Daily Devotional*, compiled by Edward A. Elliott. Copyright © MCMXCVII by Barbour Publishing, Inc.

Bear & Company, Santa Fe, New Mexico, for "Letter Thirty-six," from *Hildegard of Bingen's Book of Divine Works with Letters and Songs*, edited and introduced by Matthew Fox. Copyright © 1987 by Bear & Company, Inc. Used with permission.

Bible Reading Fellowship for extracts from *Learning the Language of Prayer* by Joyce Huggett, 1997. Copyright © 1994 by Joyce Huggett. Used with permission.

Burns & Oates for excerpt from *The Spiritual Exercises of Saint Ignatius*, translated by Thomas Corbishley, S.J. Copyright © 1963 by Thomas Corbishley, S.J. Used with permission.

Cambridge University Press for excerpt from *The Journal of George Fox*, edited by John L. Nickalls, 1952. Reprinted with the permission of Cambridge University Press.

Caux Edition, Caux, Switzerland. Original French edition: *Vivre à l'écoute* by Paul Tournier, 1984. Used with permission.

Christian Literature Crusade for excerpts from *Gold Cord* and *Lotus Buds* by Amy Carmichael. Used with permission.

Christian Publications for excerpt from *The Pursuit of God* by A. W. Tozer. Copyright © 1982. Used with permission.

Concordia Publishing House for excerpt from *Luther's Works*, Volume 21. Copyright © 1956, 1984 by Concordia Publishing House. As it appears in "Do

Not Be Anxious," *The Place of Trust* by Martin Luther, edited by Martin E. Marty (San Francisco: HarperSanFrancisco, 1983), pp. 1–11. Used with permission of Concordia Publishing House.

Cowley Publications for excerpt from *Teach Us to Pray* by André Louf, translated by Hubert Hoskins. Copyright © 1974 Darton, Longman and Todd Ltd.

Darton, Longman and Todd Ltd. for excerpt from *Moment of Christ* by John Main, published and copyright © 1984 by Darton, Longman and Todd Ltd., and used by permission of the publishers.

David Higham Associates for excerpt from *Creed or Chaos?* by Dorothy L. Sayers (London: Hodder & Stoughton, 1949). Copyright © 1949 The Trustees of Anthony Fleming, deceased. Copyright renewed in the USA: Copyright © 1974 The Trustees of Anthony Fleming, deceased.

Division of Christian Education of the National Council of Churches of Christ in the USA for excerpts from *The Holy Bible: New Revised Standard Version*. Used by permission. All rights reserved.

Doubleday for excerpt from *Breakthrough: Meister Eckhart's Creation Spirituality in New Translation*, with introduction and commentaries by Matthew Fox. Copyright © 1980 by Matthew Fox. Used by permission of Doubleday, a division of Random House, Inc.

Georges Borchardt, Inc., for "At the Wedding of Odette Bacot and Jean Teilhard d'Eyry," *On Love and Happiness* by Pierre Teilhard de Chardin (New York: Harper & Row Publishers, Inc., 1984). Originally published in French as *Sur Le Bonheur and Sur L'Amour* by Editions du Seuil. Copyright © 1966 by Editions du Seuil. Reprinted by permission of Georges Borchardt, Inc.

Gill and Macmillan, Dublin, for: (1) "The Letter on Prayer," *The Cell of Self-Knowledge: Early English Mystical Treatises* by Margery Kempe and others, adapted and translated by Charles Crawford. Translation copyright © 1981 by Charles Crawford. Used with permission. (2) Excerpt from "The Fourth Stage," *A Mirror of Simple Souls* by an Anonymous Thirteenth-Century French Mystic, edited, translated, and adapted by Charles Crawford. Translation and introduction copyright © 1981 by Charles Crawford. Used with permission.

HarperCollins Publishers (UK) for excerpts from *The Lion and the Honeycomb: The Religious Writings of Tolstoy*, edited by A. N. Wilson, 1987. English translation of Russian text copyright © 1987 by William Collins & Co. Ltd. Used with permission.

HarperCollins Publishers (USA) for: (1) "The Firstfruits of the Spirit," *The New Birth* by John Wesley, a modern English edition by Thomas C. Oden. Copyright © 1984 by Thomas C. Oden. Reprinted by permission of HarperCollins Publishers, Inc. (2) Excerpt from *The Long Loneliness: The*

Autobiography of Dorothy Day. Copyright © 1952 by HarperCollins Publishers. Reprinted by permission of HarperCollins Publishers, Inc. (3) Excerpt from "Sarah," *Peculiar Treasures: A Biblical Who's Who* by Frederick Buechner. Copyright © 1979 by Frederick Buechner. Reprinted by permission of HarperCollins Publishers, Inc. (4) Excerpt from *A Testament of Devotion* by Thomas R. Kelly. Copyright © 1941 by Harper & Row Publishers, Inc. Renewed 1969 by Lois Kelly Stabler. Reprinted by permission of HarperCollins Publishers, Inc.

Rolland Hein for excerpt from "The Cause of Spiritual Stupidity," *Creation in Christ* by George MacDonald, edited by Rolland Hein, 1976, pp. 261–5. Used with permission of Rolland Hein.

Henry William Griffin for excerpt from *The Imitation of Christ* translated by William Griffin. Copyright © 1999 by Henry William Griffin. All rights reserved. Used with permission.

Hodder and Stoughton Publishers for excerpt from *Ring of Truth* by J. B. Phillips. Copyright © 1967 by J. B. Phillips. Used with permission.

Moyer Bell, Kymbolde Way, Wakefield, Rhode Island 02879 for excerpts from *The Simone Weil Reader* edited by George A. Panichas. Copyright © 1977 by George A. Panichas.

Newman Press, Westminster, Maryland, for "What It Is to Be a Creature," *The Creator and the Creature, Or, The Wonders of Divine Love* by Frederick William Faber, 1961 (1858).

Nile Mission Press for "The Secret of Leadership," *The Way of the Sevenfold Secret* by I. Lilias Trotter, pp. 39–46.

Paraclete Press for excerpt from *Religion of the Heart* by Hannah More, edited by Hal Helms. Copyright © 1993 by the Community of Jesus Inc. Used by permission of Paraclete Press.

Paulist Press for: (1) excerpt from *Francis and Clare: The Complete* Works, translated and with an introduction by Regis J. Armstrong, OFM Cap. and Ignatius C. Brady, O.F.M. Preface by John Vaughn, O.F.M., pp. 192–3. Copyright © 1982 by The Missionary Society of St. Paul the Apostle in the State of New York. Used by permission of Paulist Press, Inc. (2) Excerpt from *Hadewijch: The Complete Works*, translated and introduced by Mother Columba Hart, O.S.B., with a preface by Paul Mommaers, S.J., pp. 2–5, 15–16. Copyright © 1980 by The Missionary Society of St. Paul the Apostle in the State of New York. Used by permission of Paulist Press, Inc. (3) Excerpt from *Espousals*, Book Two from *John Ruusbroec: The Spiritual Espousals and Other Works*, translated and with an introduction by James A. Wiseman, O.S.B., preface by Louis Dupré, pp. 71–6. Copyright © 1985 by James A. Wiseman, O.S.B. Used by permission of Paulist Press, Inc. (4) Excerpt from "The Way of Holiness": "Is There a Shorter Way?" from *Phoebe Palmer: Selected Writings*, edited by Thomas C. Oden, 1988, pp. 166–71. Copyright © 1988 by Thomas C. Oden. Used by permission of Paulist Press, Inc. (5) Excerpt from *The Lord's Sermon on the Mount* by St. Augustine, translated by John J. Jepson, S.S., with an introduction and notes by the editors (Newman Press, 1948). Volume 5 of the Ancient Christian Writers series. Copyright © 1948 by Rev. Joseph Plumpe and Rev. Johannes Quasten. Used by permission of Paulist Press, Inc. (6) Excerpt from *The Cloud of Unknowing*, edited with an introduction by James Walsh, S.J. and a preface by Simon Tugwell, O.P., 1981. Copyright © 1981 by The Missionary Society of St. Paul the Apostle in the State of New York. Used by permission of Paulist Press, Inc. (7) Excerpt from William Law, *A Serious Call to a Devout and Holy Life, Etc.*, edited from the first edition by Paul G. Stanwood, with an introduction by Austin Warren and Paul G. Stanwood and a preface by John Booty, 1978. Copyright © 1978 by The Missionary Society of St. Paul the Apostle in the State of New York. Used with permission of Paulist Press, Inc. (8) Excerpt of *Richard of St. Victor: The Twelve Patriarchs, The Mystical Ark, Book Three of the Trinity*, translated and with an introduction by Grover A. Zinn, and with a preface by Jean Chatillon, 1979. Copyright © 1979 by The Missionary Society of St. Paul the Apostle in the State of New York. Used by permission of Paulist Press, Inc.

Random House, Inc., for excerpt from *Gift from the Sea* by Anne Morrow Lindbergh. Copyright © 1955, 1975, renewed 1983 by Anne Morrow Lindbergh. Reprinted by permission of Pantheon Books, a division of Random House, Inc.

Resurrection Press for "Reconcile Your Past" from *Loving Yourself for God's Sake* by Adolfo Quezada. Copyright © 1997 by Adolfo Quezada. Used by permission of Resurrection Press, Mineola, NY 11501.

Sands & Co. Publishers for "God of My Daily Routine" from *Encounters with Silence* by Karl Rahner, translated by James M. Demske, 1960, pp. 45–52.

Templegate Publishers, PO Box 5152, Springfield, IL 62705-5152, for excerpts from *What Is Contemplation?* by Thomas Merton. Copyright © 1978 The Trustees of the Merton Legacy Trust.

A. P. Watt Ltd., on behalf of the Royal Literary Fund for "Enjoying the Floods and Other Disasters" by G. K. Chesterton, *The Illustrated London News*, 1905–1907, as it appears in *G. K. Chesterton: Collected Works* vol. XXVII (San Francisco: Ignatius Press, 1986) pp. 238–48. Used with permission.

Writers' House Inc. for excerpt from "Walk with Freedom," *Fellowship* 22 (May 1956), pp. 5–7; as it appears in *A Testament of Hope: The Essential Writings of Martin Luther King, Jr.*, edited by James Melvin Washington (New York:

HarperCollins Publishers, 1986), pp. 83–4. Copyright © 1963 by Martin Luther King, Jr., copyright renewed 1991 by Coretta Scott King. Reprinted by arrangement with The Heirs to the Estate of Martin Luther King, Jr., Writers House Inc., as agent for the proprietor.

Indexes

ALPHABETICAL INDEX OF WRITERS

CHRONOLOGICAL INDEX OF WRITERS

SCRIPTURE INDEX

WHAT IS RENOVARÉ?

RENOVARÉ (from the Latin meaning "to renew") is an infrachurch movement committed to the renewal of the Church of Jesus Christ in all its multifaceted expressions. Founded by bestselling author Richard J. Foster, RENOVARÉ is Christian in commitment, international in scope, and ecumenical in breadth.

In *The Renovaré Spiritual Formation Bible*, we observe how God spiritually formed his people through historical events and the practice of Spiritual Disciplines that is The With-God Life. RENOVARÉ continues this emphasis on spiritual formation by placing it within the context of the two-thousand-year history of the Church and six great Christian traditions we find in its life—Contemplative: The Prayer-Filled Life; Holiness: The Virtuous Life; Charismatic: The Spirit-Empowered Life; Social Justice: The Compassionate Life; Evangelical: The Word-Centered Life; and Incarnational: The Sacramental Life. This balanced vision of Christian faith and witness was modeled for us by Jesus Christ and was evident in the lives of countless saints: Antony, Francis of Assisi, Susanna Wesley, Phoebe Palmer, and others. The With-God Life of the People of God continues on today as Christians participate in the life and practices of local churches and look forward to spending eternity in that "all-inclusive community of loving persons with God himself at the very center of this community as its prime Sustainer and most glorious Inhabitant."

In addition to offering a balanced vision of the spiritual life, RENOVARÉ promotes a practical strategy for people seeking renewal by helping facilitate small spiritual formation groups; national, regional, and local conferences; one-day seminars; personal and group retreats; and readings from devotional classics that can sustain a long-term commitment to renewal. RENOVARÉ Resources for Spiritual Renewal, Spiritual Formation Guides, and *The Renovaré Spiritual Formation Bible*—books published by HarperOne—seek to integrate historical, scholarly, and inspirational materials into practical, readable formats. These resources can be used in a variety of settings, including small groups, private and organizational retreats, individual devotions, and church school classes. Written and edited by people committed to the renewal of the Church, all of the materials present a balanced vision of Christian life and faith coupled with a practical strategy for spiritual growth and enrichment.

For more information about RENOVARÉ and its mission, please log on to its Web site (www.renovare.org) or write RENOVARÉ, 8 Inverness Drive East, Suite 102, Englewood, CO 80112-5624, USA.

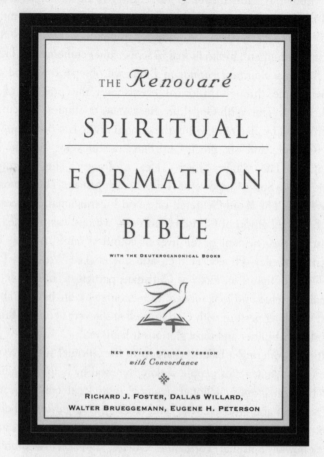